LOOKING FOR A NEW ENGLAND

SIMON MATTHEWS

LOOKING FOR A NEW ENGLAND

ACTION, TIME, VISION

MUSIC, FILM AND TV 1975-1986

Oldcastle Books

First published in 2021 by
Oldcastle Books Ltd,
Harpenden,
Herts, UK
oldcastlebooks.co.uk
@noexitpress
Editor: Jennifer Steele
© Simon Matthews, 2021

A CIP catalogue record for this book is available from the British Library.

ISBN
978-0-85730-411-7 (Print)
978-0-85730-412-4 (Epub)

2 4 6 8 10 9 7 5 3 1

Typeset in 11.75 on 14.6pt Goudy Old Style
by Avocet Typeset, Bideford, Devon, EX39 2BP
Printed by and bound by Nørhaven, Denmark

CONTENTS

1

INTRODUCTION

Most people today know what 'Swinging London' looked like: a visual and aural landscape where the latest clothes, the latest music, the latest cars, the latest design and the latest art were well to the fore and central to whatever was 'happening'. This explosion of the counterculture brought a golden period in which the emerging dominance of UK pop music became bound up with hip contemporary films, both home-grown and international. A massive revolt, in fact, against the austere, shabby world of the 1940s and 1950s and a deliberate embracing of modernism that spawned a 'pop culture' that peaked somewhere between the release of *All You Need is Love* by The Beatles ('67) and the emergence of Ziggy Stardust from his chrysalis five years later. If one had to choose just one example that somehow exemplified it all, you could do a lot worse than home in on the BBC2 series *Colour Me Pop*, which ran from June 1968 to August 1969. Born out of the huge interest in all things pop and youth-orientated in 1967-8, it was a bolt-on accessory to *Late Night Line-Up*, the arts and current affairs programme broadcast from 1964-72.

Late Night Line-Up itself was produced by Rowan Ayers – father of Soft Machine's Kevin – and usually presented by Joan Bakewell. A selection of those featured during its eight-year run reads like an alternative *Sgt. Pepper*-style collage: Peter Sellers, Little Richard, David Frost, the Jimi Hendrix Experience, Tony Hancock, Duke Ellington, Yoko Ono, Willy Brandt, Dave Brubeck, Otto Skorzeny,

Malcolm Muggeridge, Peter Ustinov, Coco the Clown, Michael
Foot, Maurice Chevalier, Ivor Cutler, Sammy Davis Junior, John
Peel, Cecil Beaton, Joseph Losey, Alfred Hitchcock, Harold Pinter,
Bob Hope, the men from U.N.C.L.E. (Robert Vaughn and David
McCallum), playwright NF Simpson and Brigitte Bardot. This
broad-brush approach, the idea that everything contemporary was
part of a unified whole, was replicated in *Colour Me Pop*. Each
week, this showcased artists filmed in a more 'authentic' and less
staged environment than the uber-mainstream *Top of the Pops*, with
no boundaries set about who might appear. The roster of acts
appearing during its run ranged from The Tremeloes to Jethro
Tull, from Bobby Hanna (deemed then by some to be 'the next
Engelbert') to Caravan and from Gene Pitney to Giles, Giles and
Fripp. All were treated as being part of the modern scene and
taken seriously, too: pop now had a space of its own, late at night,
on BBC2.

A harder point to pin down is when and why this type of
approach ended. If 1968-9 was peak 'Swinging London', it was
also the point, arguably, at which the contraction and demise of
that world started. An example of this might be Paul and Barry
Ryan, a duo with fabulous looks - they originally modelled for
Vidal Sassoon - and a modest catalogue of hit singles, who signed
to MGM in August 1967 for an advance of £100,000 (about £3m
today), offset partly against future film appearances. They made
no films and by June 1969 Barry, Paul having retired by this point,
quit MGM for Polydor. Likewise, Eric Burdon, another MGM act,
spent six months in LA in late 1969, fruitlessly searching for a film
role: it would be 13 years before he finally got one, in *Comeback*,
shot in West Germany in 1982. Both the Ryans and Burdon
would have expected, after the huge box-office returns for *A Hard
Day's Night*, *Help!* and *Blow-Up*, that any half-decent UK pop artist
would move automatically into films. Sadly for them, the problem
at MGM in the late '60s was that Kubrick's *2001: A Space Odyssey*
took up so much studio time that suitable projects they might be
considered for simply didn't materialise.

Worse still, a number of UK films that US studios had invested in, on the basis that anything pop/counterculture and London-set would sell, failed to generate decent returns. There were few takers for *The Bliss of Mrs Blossom*, *The Touchables*, *The Magic Christian*, *Leo the Last* (in particular), *Performance* (whatever its later status as a cult hit), or *The Ballad of Tam Lin*. Nor did audiences flock to a home-grown UK production like *Wonderwall*, despite the involvement of Apple. Both Universal and 20th Century-Fox shut down their London offices in 1969 and MGM followed suit a year later. Neither United Artists nor Paramount did much in the UK after 1970 and all of these posted significant losses around this time as the US cinema market buckled under the impact of colour TV and the location of many old movie theatres in decaying downtown sites. With The Beatles (always the driving force in bringing US money to London after their runaway success in 1964) breaking up, the demise of The Rolling Stones Mk 1 with the death of Brian Jones, the shambles at Altamont and the death of Hendrix all occurring 1969–70, Swinging London was ending and anyone hip and fashion-conscious was moving on by the start of the new decade. There were many other indications of this. Record labels closed, notably Immediate and Marmalade, both of which released an embarrassment of riches up until their demise. Others survived but became noticeably mundane – particularly Apple, Dawn and Deram. Local film production companies either went bust or wound down as the UK replicated the diminishing box-office returns of the US. Associated British, Compton, Tigon, Hammer, Hemdale (which relocated, very profitably, to the US), British Lion and Woodfall all faded away, completely or partially, between the early '70s and the mid-'80s. This dismal situation was only very slightly offset by the arrival of George Harrison's HandMade Films from the wreckage of Apple in 1978.

Most startling of all, though, is the list of people who simply disappeared as the tide of optimism receded. In this pre-internet, pre-Twitter era, the roll-call of those who had vanished by the early '70s and whom one would have thought permanent fixtures just a year or so earlier, was lengthy indeed: PP Arnold, Julie Driscoll, Peter Green (and Fleetwood Mac Mk 1), Marsha Hunt, Mary

Hopkin, Paul Jones, Sandie Shaw, Dusty Springfield, Terence Stamp, Anita Pallenberg, Peter Watkins, Mike Sarne, Giorgio Gomelsky, Andrew Loog Oldham, Ronan O'Rahilly, 'Groovy Bob' Fraser... all once well known, all now pushed to the margins at best. There were many, many less stellar others: names which, when remembered in the mid-'70s, seemed to come from a time that suddenly seemed terribly distant.

Nor did any of the other, once vaunted, trappings of the counterculture thrive. Production of *Oz*, *International Times* and *ZigZag* all ceased in 1973-4, though the latter two stuttered on intermittently. Thereafter only *Time Out* survived, with the few scattered additions to the genre, like *Gay News* or *Spare Rib* (both of which launched in 1972), having a narrower, single-issue focus. By 1981, when *City Limits*, in a last hurrah for co-operative communitarianism, emerged from *Time Out*, the big noises in printed pop culture were Nick Logan and Robert Elms, associated with *Smash Hits* ('78) and *The Face* ('80) respectively, both of which dropped the raw anarchic politics of the counterculture and aimed instead at the wider commercial/glossy/popular market. By the mid-'80s the idea of a single overarching movement, complete with its own in-house papers and periodicals, had long gone.

Whilst this is true, and no hindsight was required then or subsequently to appreciate it, knowledge of these changes and how comprehensive they were would have implied a very metropolitan level of awareness at the time. How did people elsewhere see things? The reality was that outside London the idea of a nice tidy cut-off date for 'the end of the '60s' simply didn't apply. In 'the provinces', well into the '70s many young women headed for a big night out in knee-high boots, miniskirts and beehive hair à la Jane Fonda in *Barbarella*; whilst their men maintained the classic hippy garb of greatcoats, tie-dye T-shirts and vast amounts of facial hair. Perhaps the career of Led Zeppelin provides us with some guidance in determining this matter. The perfect distillation of the ingredients that put the UK at the summit of pop culture in 1967-8, they still appeared invincible when their film *The Song Remains the Same* hit the cinema screens in 1976. By 1979, though, and their last ever gigs at Knebworth, there were arguments about how big the audiences were, why there were fewer on the second day (the promoter eventually went bust) and reviews criticising – as was the style at the time – their culture of gratuitous excess. So: for most people, did the 1960s finally end in 1977–8?

The sense of things remaining as they were and providing continuity through a period of decline was also reflected in UK cinema. In 1970, the UK produced 90 feature films and had cinema admissions totalling 193 million. These figures duly plunged: film productions down to 31 by 1980 and a nadir of 29 by 1986 with cinema admissions crashing to 101 million (1980) and 54 million (1984). Once US funding retreated and colour TV became dominant, a general view prevailed in most quarters that cinema was 'finished' and would soon be replaced by video, watched *en famille* in the safety of one's own home, rather than in gloomy, poorly maintained town-centre Odeons, Gaumonts, ABCs and Granadas. As early as 1975, David Puttnam – whose successes by that point included *That'll Be the Day* and *Stardust* – was in despair: '...Nothing good will happen while there are still cinemas that are shit heaps and critics who only like popular films when they are 30 years old....'

Thus, the main British box-office smashes of 1975–86 were respectable US entertainments like *Jaws*, *The Towering Inferno*, *Star Wars*, *Grease*, *Superman* and *E.T.*, whilst in terms of locally produced megahits, the UK clung on to the remains of the increasingly threadbare Bond franchise, notably *The Spy Who Loved Me* and *Moonraker* (the latter actually a co-production with France). Otherwise, The Beatles retained some bankability as Ringo continued with his acting ventures and new albums by him and George still sold heavily in the US long after they were both semi-forgotten artists in the UK. Cinema ransacked the Lennon and McCartney catalogue for *All This and World War II* ('76) and a rather tired adaptation of *Sgt. Pepper's Lonely Hearts Club Band* ('78), whilst *Birth of The Beatles* ('79) plumbed their origins in Hamburg. But, apart from this and 007's annual outing, the British film industry spluttered on with occasional Carry Ons and

Hammers (until 1978–9), a soft-porn slew of Confessions and Adventures (similarly discontinued circa 1978), war films, period dramas and tiny British Film Institute (BFI)-funded experimental productions that played to minuscule audiences. The earlier fashion for films that had bands and a youth angle was continued with *Confessions of a Pop Performer, Never Too Young to Rock* and *Three for All* (all '75), but these were cheap productions that could easily have been made – minus the nudity – in the '50s. Given this inhospitable terrain, leading directors, not surprisingly, sought solace elsewhere.

Ken Russell, arguably the only functioning UK auteur by this point, departed after *Tommy* and *Lisztomania*, making acerbic comments à la Puttnam as he went. In the years that followed, what was left of the film industry in the UK released belated sequels to '60s hits like *Percy's Progress, Alfie Darling, Stand Up Virgin Soldiers* and *Revenge of the Pink Panther*, as well as various concert films, all of which were targeted at an increasingly older audience, like *The Butterfly Ball, To Russia with Elton* and *Give My Regards to Broad Street*. Late ventures into film by Ray Davies (*Return to Waterloo*, '84) and Pete Townshend (*White City*. '85) appeared, but were poorly distributed and barely seen compared with the demand that work from either of these figures would have commanded 15 years earlier. Some survivors of the '60s took a long time dying: as late as 1981 the music of The Pretty Things, in their Electric Banana guise, could be heard in the Vincent Price horror comedy *The Monster Club*.

By the mid-'70s, then, the UK film industry was no longer about the cutting edge, the original, or the avant-garde. Nor was it much about youth. When *The Knack* wowed audiences internationally in 1965, its cast had an average age of 23. A decade later, the remaining bankable UK stars were all decidedly middle-aged: Glenda Jackson, Michael Caine, Oliver Reed, Sean Connery and, greyest of them all, Roger Moore. In terms of emerging new genres, hopes were briefly pinned on pornography (or if not pornography, always difficult to define, nudity and sex) becoming respectable. Perhaps it did: after all, *Emmanuelle* created a long-running franchise. But in the UK the benchmark for this type of work was set instead by stuff like *Confessions of a Window Cleaner* ('74). Backed by Columbia, this made more money for them than *The Odessa File*. (Columbia was also involved with *Emmanuelle*). Perhaps this says it all: the French got tasteful soft-focus erotica, filmed on location with a proper budget, whilst the UK made do with a bawdy seaside postcard-style farce. A few years later, the execrable *Come Play with Me* ('77) had a four-year run at one West End cinema. But none of this translated into a viable rescue mission for UK film production. Films like this ultimately couldn't compete with the hardcore material that quickly took over; nor, if one were looking for anything that explored sexuality seriously, could they rival European productions like *You Are Not Alone* (Denmark, '78), *Taxi zum Klo* (West Germany, '81) or *Équateur* (France, '83).

As British film production declined, the remaining 'quality' pictures being made were often elegant period dramas. Fussy films with good attention to detail and reliable thespian performances such as *A Bridge Too Far* ('77), *Chariots of Fire* ('81), *Gandhi* ('82) and *Greystoke: Legend of Tarzan* ('84), all of which did well and by doing so reinforced a heavily nostalgic view of the UK. There were also a few US co-productions, like *Clash of the Titans* ('81) and a growing number of US films with some sort of limited UK connection: *Logan's Run* ('76), *Midnight Express* ('78), *10* ('79) and *Amadeus* ('84). These reflected the new reality as the best bits of the UK film industry increasingly turned into a service facility for Hollywood. Perhaps we should also add to this *Saturday Night Fever* ('77). Written by Nik Cohn, possibly the greatest UK pop writer of his time, it was based, not on Scorsese-type delinquents, but on the Soho mods he had mixed with some years earlier.

Television suffered too, despite being the alleged cause of films' collapse. The period between 1975 and 1986 saw a huge reduction in the amount of contemporary drama being broadcast into the nation's living rooms. Until the mid-'70s, up to 200 scripts per year were commissioned by the three UK channels, many of these being feature film-length productions. Cut heavily from 1979, much of this was completely gone by 1985. The airtime freed up was duly allocated to less demanding fare. Game shows mushroomed; comedy too. These post-1979 broadcasting changes closely reflected the views of Mrs Thatcher, as put to Peter Hall (Director of the National Theatre and given to much radical experimentation): '...Why do you need public money? Andrew Lloyd Webber doesn't....'

But, even if we accept *Colour Me Pop* as an apogee, its demise in 1969 initially seemed of little significance. Through 1970–71 it was replaced in the same slot by *Disco 2*, the formula and approach of which were broadly similar. When this, too, was ditched, it wasn't really clear why; BBC 2 finally settled on *The Old Grey Whistle Test* as its sole 'flagship' rock music programme. This certainly was different. Unlike its predecessors, it was very serious stuff indeed, focused mainly on acts that produced albums and who gigged to a great extent on the university circuit.

The main presenter, from 1972, was Bob Harris, part DJ and part community activist – he was one of the founders of *Time Out* magazine – whose understated, unspectacular, non-judgemental persona was as typical of this period as the purely fictional Howard Kirk in Malcolm Bradbury's brilliant satirical novel *The History Man* ('75, TV adaptation '81). Under Harris's stewardship a carefully circumscribed version of rock was broadcast, targeted at highly educated types in their mid-to-late twenties. Neither flash nor outrageous, this wasn't pop, though occasional aberrations did creep through: The New York Dolls (November '73) and Dr. Feelgood (March '75) being notable. Between *The Old Grey Whistle Test* and the increasingly tawdry *Top of the Pops*, there were whole spectrums of music that were hardly being heard, other than occasional air play on John Peel's nightly radio show.

Nor was this solely down to the BBC taking a view on what young people should listen to. The draining away of youthful excitement was also seen when Ronan O'Rahilly relaunched Radio Caroline in 1974. The new version had nothing in common with its earlier incarnation or his venture into films with *Girl on a Motorcycle* ('68 – Marianne Faithful), or, for that matter, his promotion of The MC5 at the Phun City Festival ('70). Instead, the last remaining UK pirate station churned out album-oriented

FM progressive rock – a piece of the US Midwest floating a few miles off the UK coast, no less – propagating the embarrassing 'Loving Awareness' concept.

Within the music industry itself the only attempt at starting a significant new label by one of the majors was the Decca subsidiary UK Records. Delegated to scabrous hustler Jonathan King, this duly scored some early successes with 10cc and The Kursaal Flyers, but failed to develop further. A stronger indication of what would, eventually, become the new mainstream came in 1973, when Richard Branson, a record shop owner who emerged from the late '60s student scene, launched Virgin. Its first release, Mike Oldfield's *Tubular Bells*, was the ultimate hippy anthem, lauded by John Peel. More importantly, it sold: no 1 in both the UK and US, with a five-year chart run, helped enormously by its being used as part of the soundtrack for *The Exorcist*, the top box-office film of 1974. An example, whatever the changes, that the counterculture could still be of profitable use to the mainstream. Other Virgin successes were the West German outfits Tangerine Dream, Kraftwerk and Can. Branson also dipped a toe into the emerging dub reggae scene before memorably snapping up The Sex Pistols in 1977. But, in general terms, so staid had UK music become by the mid-'70s that rising figures in it like Dave Robinson, Jake Riviera, Ted Carroll and Roger Armstrong – band managers and, like Branson, record shop owners – were also tentatively setting up their own independent labels, following the trail blazed by John Peel with Dandelion. Relative to their output, they may not have had many hits, but Stiff (Robinson and Riviera) and Chiswick (Carroll and Armstrong) released an array of influential and highly regarded material during their existence.

The story of live music during this period was equally patchy. There were few large-scale festivals after 1972 and almost none were filmed for commercial release. The Isle of Wight hosting Hendrix and Dylan became a distant memory, whilst the Hyde Park concerts stopped in 1971, spluttered on in 1974-6, and then ceased completely. Glastonbury (a tiny version, then, of its present self) was dormant, eventually being relaunched in 1981 for an audience of new-age travellers, punks and middle-aged hippies. It would be joined, in 1982, by WOMAD, launched at nearby Shepton Mallet. Another new arrival on the block was Rock Against Racism, a spirited fightback against the antics of the far right led by a few survivors of the earlier counterculture. Sporadically successful in 1976–9, it eventually morphed into the more orthodox Labour Party-supporting Red Wedge.

Even in terms of live music venues, nothing was sacred. The Roundhouse, launching pad of so many careers, had a last hurrah in July 1976 when it staged The Flamin' Groovies supported by The Ramones, a very significant event in the emergence of the UK punk scene. It closed in 1983, and remained shut for more than 20 years. Other notable casualties were the Lyceum and the Rainbow, both gone by 1981, followed a few years later by much of the London pub-rock circuit. Then, as education funding cuts followed, many of the colleges, universities and polytechnics – always the more lucrative end of live work – booked fewer bands and this contracted too.

And what of the music itself? Instead of being the single cultural entity shown in *Colour Me Pop*, by the mid-'70s it had split into three very different strands.

Firstly, amounting to about 30 per cent of what was on offer, came ongoing success by established '60s acts – the Stones, the Who, Pink Floyd, the Faces, Rod Stewart when he went solo and innumerable UK acts trekking annually across the US – as well as newcomers who could trace their lineage back to the '60s, but had become successful after that decade: Ace, Gilbert O'Sullivan, Alvin Stardust, Gary Glitter (both Stardust and Glitter were actually coffee-bar rockers, Shane Fenton and Paul Raven, from the late '50s and early '60s), Mud and The Sweet.

Secondly, and accounting for maybe as much as 50 per cent of what was heard, seen and sold: safe, officially approved pop – The Bee Gees, Olivia Newton-John, Cliff, the Lloyd Webber-Rice stuff and a huge amount of MOR tat. Included within this grouping would also be those who worked the network of cavernous working men's clubs. Financially attractive but artistically dead, these included even the mighty Walker Brothers, who bowed out in a cabaret tour of the North and Midlands in 1978, playing weekly engagements alongside comedians and magicians.

The 20 per cent that remained was a diverse mix of anybody trying to make a new sound, those who were resolutely uncommercial but somehow kept going, the remains of the old counterculture and the start of the new. In this segment could be found Hawkwind, David Bowie, Roxy Music (all of whom sold), as well as emerging acts from the London music scene like Brinsley Schwarz and Kilburn and The High Roads (who didn't) and, eventually, the multitude of punk and new-wave groups.

The differences among these three groupings extended even to where one bought their releases. For the first two, most of their sales took place in Woolworths, WH Smith or the gramophone and electrical goods sections of department stores. For the third and smaller group, a great deal was sold instead by small independent record shops, venues that functioned as a vital gathering point for the youth of the day and places where many of the bands hung out and where much of the music of the future had its genesis.

But even within the final third the movers and shakers of youth culture were split into a variety of discrete compartments. There were the rock and roll revivalists, seen in the documentary *Born Too Late* ('78); second-generation mods and enthusiasts for electronic dance music featured in *Steppin' Out* ('79); a coterie of bands, mainly out of art school, and much taken with the flash US politico-rock of The MC5 and the decadence of The New York Dolls, for whom, at least some of the time, lip service was paid to notions of 'street' credibility; devotees of northern soul, where dancing to forgotten black American music in decrepit ballrooms and forgotten cinemas meant being part of a sect where one-upmanship and the cult of the obscure reigned; admirers of Branson's German acts and their dreamy, trippy synthesiser heavy instrumentals; a tiny number of enthusiasts for the new dub reggae and the London-centric fans of 'pub-rock' (no film, but eventually compiled on the bestselling LP *Hope and Anchor Front Row Festival*, which reached No 28 in the UK charts in March 1978).

In cinema, the body of work that survived mirrored how pop and rock had splintered into separate compartments. But, despite the new atmosphere of conformity, interesting films and TV shows *were* still made that reflected the new counterculture. Among them were several showing a jaded disillusion with the music business such as *Slade in Flame* ('75), *Rock Follies* ('76), *Breaking Glass* ('80) and *Pink Floyd: The Wall* ('82). Documentarist Wolfgang Büld arrived from Munich to chronicle the changing mores in *Punk in London* ('77), *Bored Teenagers* ('79) and *British Rock* ('80). The leading UK bands of the time got exposure in *Rude Boy* and *DOA* (both '80), warts-and-all studies of The Clash and The Sex Pistols respectively. The black experience in Britain was explored in *Black Britannica* ('78, predictably withdrawn from circulation), *Babylon* ('80) and *Burning an Illusion* ('81); whilst an increasing and sympathetic audience for gay issues and the emerging gay scene (whatever the legislation of the day allowed) brought *The Naked Civil Servant* ('75), *Sebastiane* ('76), *The Alternative Miss World* ('80) and *My Beautiful Laundrette* ('85). A range of films also appeared showing, one way or another, the general vicissitudes faced by the youth of the day, notably *Jubilee* ('78), *Scum* ('79), *Gregory's Girl* ('81), *Oi for England*, *Scrubbers* and *Made in Britain* (all '82). Somewhere amongst this jumble, there was a place too for *The Great Rock N' Roll Swindle* ('80), Malcolm McLaren's deliberate part-fabrication/ part-pastiche about the rise and demise of The Sex Pistols with himself playing the part of a knowing, predatory '50s-style show-business manager.

Against the odds the non-mainstream also managed to produce some box-office hits: *The Rocky Horror Picture Show* ('75), *The Man Who Fell to Earth* ('76), *The Long Good Friday* ('79), *Quadrophenia* ('79) and *This Is Spinal Tap* ('84) all appeared at this time, and one area where it certainly held sway was comedy. The rising tide of '70s and '80s faux sophistication and consumerism was subjected to ruthless satirical barbs in BBC TV's *Abigail's Party* ('77), whilst the later works of the *Monty Python* team, notably *Jabberwocky* ('77) and *Life of Brian* ('79), were big commercial hits as well as making some points about wider social and cultural issues. Peter Cook and Dudley Moore, survivors again from earlier times, re-emerged as 'Derek and Clive', translating very effectively to records and live shows, but less so to film. In fact, one of the lasting features of the period was the appearance of so many new UK and US comics (a number of whom were great admirers of Cook), who gradually moved into spin-off films, many of them benefits for a good cause such as *The Secret Policeman's Ball* ('79). Finally, in this most ideological of times, the politics of the period were commented on via a range of dystopias in films like *Memoirs of a Survivor* ('81), *Britannia Hospital* ('82), *1984* ('84), *Brazil* ('85), *Letter to Brezhnev* ('85 – in which Merseyside is shown as being no better than a pre-glasnost Soviet Union) and *Defence of the Realm* ('86). But none of these, not even the few that were commercially successful, enjoyed anything like the success of *Who Dares Wins* ('82), in which UK and US special forces prevent dangerous political activists ('a militant group attached to CND') wrecking the security of the civilised world. Similarly, and to keep things in perspective, none of the bands and singers that emerged in the UK post-1975 could match Phil Collins in global sales. With a smooth, accessible persona, he emerged from the London stage version of *Oliver* in 1966 and then proceeded via the late psychedelic group Flaming Youth and their concept LP *Ark 2* ('69) to Genesis ('71) and, eventually, a solo career that produced six No 1 albums in both the UK and US between 1980 and 1986.

The abundance of impressive US and European films during this period, and the lack of comparable UK work, ultimately came down to one thing: a shortage of money. Mechanisms had been in place in the UK since 1949 to help fund quality films. These were set up by Harold Wilson, then President of the Board of Trade, when he established the Eady Levy. Funded from cinema ticket sales, this was distributed by the British Film Fund Agency to any film that was 85 per cent shot in the UK or Commonwealth and which had no more than three non-UK people in its cast and crew. In the days of high cinema admissions (basically the '50s and much of the '60s until TV became truly universal), this raised significant sums. Many films, including a large number on contemporary themes, were made in the UK as a result. In fact, the Levy was so successful that when London became a fashionable swinging location, from 1965 onwards, US directors and studios deliberately filmed there so that they could tap into this funding, as well as avail themselves of much lower production costs. Later, the UK hosted a number of European giallo thrillers for much the same reason. But once ticket sales began seriously declining post-1970, and with cinemas closing in large numbers, the Eady Levy had less money to distribute and the prospect of it being used to fund imaginative, contemporary UK films faded away.

The industry was aware of this and in 1975 Wilson, now Prime Minister, came to the rescue again, setting up a working party to advise on 'the requirements of a viable and prosperous British film industry over the next decade'. It reported in January 1976, recommending the establishment of a British Film Authority that would bring together the National Film Finance Corporation (NFFC) (also set up in 1949) and the British Film Fund Agency (BFFA), as well as the promotional and educational activities of the Department of Education and Science and the Department of Trade. Wilson specifically wanted future Eady Levy payments barred from 'high earning' (that is, US) films and the money from this diverted into UK ventures. The use of the UK as a cheap production base was also to be discouraged. Wilson and his civil servants were aware of the practice of US studios, when filming in the UK with Eady Levy money, of charging interest on the loans they made (to themselves) to provide the main funding for their films: thus, few such projects made a profit on paper and little or nothing was ever reinvested by the US studios back into the UK film industry. Despite resigning as Prime Minister in April 1976, Wilson continued with this project, being appointed Chair of the Interim Action Committee (IAC) on the Film Industry by his successor James Callaghan. Between 1978 and 1981, this produced five reports, with copious recommendations, none of which, after the election of the Thatcher government in 1979, was enacted. In the harsh new landscape, no new nationalised industries were going to be set up and Margaret Thatcher was not going to take advice from Harold Wilson. Wilson left Parliament in 1983, the IAC was abolished and the Eady Levy, the NFFC and the BFFA had all gone by 1985 without replacement.

This was a major blow and completed the process that had started roughly 15 years earlier: that of the avant-garde being pushed away from the foreground to a position where it was dismissed, deprived of funds and marginalised, whilst the safe, the commercial and the conventional returned to reign supreme. In short, it was a reversal of the priorities of the previous 40 years. By 1985 what would have once been made into a feature film was now lucky to be a TV play, and what would once have been a TV play might now be no more than a fringe theatre production.

Beyond the English Channel, however, there was still funding for the production of quality films and significant budgets were available for material as diverse and entertaining as *Nosferatu, the Vampyre* ('79, with the gnarled gargoyle-like features of Klaus Kinski and brilliant music from Popol Vuh), *Fitzcarraldo* ('82, Kinski again, though originally intended as a starring vehicle for Mick Jagger) and *Mad Max Beyond Thunderdome* ('85, the ultimate, finely detailed, dystopia). Nor was this merely a question of money. Ireland, The Netherlands and France produced *Light Years Away* ('81), *De Lift* ('83) and *Subway* ('85) respectively, with plots that made imaginative use of everyday surroundings. Animation features, a particularly expensive genre, were also prominent elsewhere. *Fritz the Cat* and *Heavy Traffic* (both '72) did well in the US, whilst in Europe *Tarzoon: Shame of the Jungle* ('75) was scored by the Belgian electro-pop genius Marc Moulin and Paul Fishman (who would later have, as a member of Re-Flex, the ultimate '80s pop hit *The Politics of Dancing*) and *Harmagedon: Genma taisen* ('83, but based on a '67 Japanese sci-fi comic) had a Keith Emerson soundtrack.

It was a shame that the UK, despite the success of *Yellow Submarine* ('68), provided nothing in this field. The career of '60s wunderkind David Hemmings illustrates as well as anything how difficult it became during this period to function creatively in the UK. Departing circa 1972, around the time that his own box-office standing at home ebbed away, Hemmings migrated to

Italy for *Deep Red* ('75), which had the type of high production values commonly seen in his earlier hits. The producers wanted Pink Floyd for the soundtrack, but had to settle instead for local Italian prog-rockers Goblin. Hemmings and Goblin were twinned again in *The Heroin Busters* ('77), one of a number of films that cashed in on the earlier success of *The French Connection*. After this came the biggest budget West German film to date: *Just a Gigolo* ('78) with Bowie and Dietrich, which, though ridiculed in some quarters, wasn't all bad. Hemmings then headed to the Antipodes for *Harlequin* ('80, Australia), originally due to co-star Bowie and Orson Welles, neither of whom turned out to be available; *Strange Behaviour* ('81, New Zealand), as producer only, which featured The Birthday Party on the soundtrack, and *Turkey Shoot* ('82, Australia), producing again, starring Olivia Hussey, another '60s lost soul, and set in a dystopian concentration camp run by someone called Thatcher. Hemmings' work remained interesting, but was barely seen in the UK. Perhaps it was fitting that he wound up in Australia. By 1985, with a fully funded Film Corporation, that country was producing international hits like *Crocodile Dundee* and was turning out, pro rata, five times the number of films that the UK could manage.

Jane Birkin and Serge Gainsbourg, like Hemmings iconic figures just a few years earlier, also thrived in Europe. Birkin, who, after *Wonderwall* ('68) starred in eighteen films in six years, appeared in a further 23 from 1975–86. (In the same period Glenda Jackson made only 14.) For the diminishing band of regular UK cinema-goers, though, she was most likely noticed in stuff like *Death on the Nile* and *Evil Under the Sun*: well-upholstered adaptations of '30s Agatha Christie thrillers. Few would have seen her in either *Je t'aime, moi non plus* ('76) or *Egon Schiele: Excess and Punishment* ('81). The former, a masterpiece that eclipsed in its exploration of sexual boundaries anything on offer in the fleapits of Soho, was set in a deliberately desolate, almost existential location with Joe Dallesandro as co-star – part of the Warhol diaspora then settling across Europe. The latter, another failed

Bowie project, explored the decadent career of one of Europe's great pre-1914 artists.

Gainsbourg, in film, was less prolific, restricting himself through this period to soundtracks (around a dozen), the most noteworthy of which were *The French Woman* ('77), a political thriller about call girls with Murray Head and Klaus Kinski, and *French Fried Vacation* ('78), an early satire about Club Med-style holidays. Being best known for the ultimate late-night smooching record (*Je t'aime...* a No 1 hit despite, or because of, being banned) and having scored Just Jaeckin's *Goodbye Emmanuelle*, he tried his own hand at a steamy tropical erotic thriller, writing, directing and doing the music for *Equateur* ('83), adapted from a Georges Simenon novel. Both Birkin and Gainsbourg also had parallel careers as recording artists, turning out a series of sophisticated pop/rock albums. Most of these were made in London, but, like their films, few got a UK release. This was despite their regular backing musicians having credits that stretched from Georgie Fame, PJ Proby and Mark Wirtz, through Al Stewart, John McLaughlin, Blue Mink, Elton John and CCS to Lou Reed, David Bowie, Tangerine Dream and, eventually, Culture Club. Gainsbourg's *Rock Around the Bunker* ('75, No 4 in France) and *Aux Armes etc* ('79, No 1 in France) were particularly noteworthy. The former was a show business musical send-up of the Third Reich à la *The Producers*, whilst the latter, cut in Jamaica, contained – notoriously – a reggae version of the French national anthem.

To be present and actively interested in material of this type between 1975 and 1986 meant, in the eyes of many other people, belonging to a sect: being part of a derided urban tribe with its own dress code sourced from tiny fashion kiosks, charity shops or even home-made designs. Looking back on the period now, one is conscious that understanding it is all about following the narrow threads that link the acclaimed UK pop culture of the '60s with its wayward grandchildren of the late twentieth and early twenty-first centuries. Each thread inevitably represented a few individuals, or at best a small number of people who shaped the future, often prophets without honour in their own land.

Many of these were British, some European and more than a few expatriate Americans. Most of the latter quit the US when the flower-power and protest era faded into the torpor and reaction of Nixon and Reagan: among others, Paul Theroux (whose novel *The Family Arsenal*, set in Deptford, brilliantly captures the London of the mid-to-late '70s), Chrissie Hynde, Paul Morrissey and Miles Copeland III. For these the UK was cheap, cheerful and more accepting.

The greatest single continuum, of course, was David Bowie, who can, indeed, be seen in a June '68 edition of *Colour Me Pop*, doing a mime to The Strawbs. An all-round entertainer, an epithet he would have appreciated as an early admirer of Tommy Steele and Anthony Newley, he was also the last UK pop star to come anywhere near having a successful film career, cruising from the critical acclaim and success of *The Man Who Fell to Earth* via a batch of TV and film ventures that reflect his Berlin period to an obligatory war film, a vampire thriller (*The Hunger*, '83, actually a giallo about ten years late) and the final car crash of *Absolute Beginners* ('86), a stultifying would-be epic that failed to do anything for the UK film industry and which brings this period to a close.

Tracing the many personal histories that link Carnaby Street, *Blow-Up* and *Yellow Submarine* with Austin Powers, Cool Britannia, Brit Pop and the Young British Artists involves travelling through a submerged hinterland behind the façade of '70s and '80s conformity, past many failed projects, whilst, as many did at the time, looking for a new England.

2

THE LONG TAIL OF THE '60s

Slotting the latest group or singer into a feature film where they trailed their latest single, sang the title theme, hung around in the background or even – on rare occasions – produced an entire score was normal business through the '60s and continued to be so for some time into the next decade.

Nothing was as typical of this approach as *Slade in Flame*, one of the biggest box-office hits of 1975 in the UK. The group had been together since 1966 as mod-pop group The 'N Betweens and, after hooking up with Chas Chandler when he parted company from Hendrix, as skinhead hard rockers Ambrose Slade. Chandler landed them a deal with Polydor and, with the hippy thing mainly played out and many established acts avoiding the 45s market (and the constant gigging that promoting your latest release required), the group cashed in on the huge appetite for an uncomplicated guitar band. They rose to the challenge, and, with six No 1 singles and two No 1 chart albums between 1971 and 1973, comparisons with The Beatles were duly made, as was also the case then with Marc Bolan and T. Rex. As with Epstein and his charges, Chandler wanted a film project to cement their success and duly settled on the story of a group (Flame) climbing to fame, being abused by the record industry and then falling apart.

The style of previous rock/pop films is avoided, and what we get instead is a hefty dose of downbeat '70s social realism with Slade playing the group as an amalgamation of various contemporaries they had known within the 'beat' scene in the West Midlands. The film is set circa 1967, but doesn't really look at all like the period it portrays. A deal was struck with Goodtimes Enterprises to produce. Run by Sanford Lieberson and David Puttnam, their previous work included *Performance*, *Glastonbury Fayre*, *The Pied Piper*, *That'll Be the Day*, *The Final Programme*, *Mahler* and *Stardust*, a hugely impressive CV. Adept at mixing rock and film, they brought in Andrew Birkin (brother of Jane) to write the script and Richard Loncraine, then 28, to direct. Prior to this, Loncraine's only credits were a feature for the Children's Film Foundation and a half-hour documentary about Radio One. He was perhaps better known as the designer of the 'kinetic sculptures' used in the film *Sunday Bloody Sunday*, in which he also appeared as Murray Head's partner. By way of preparation, both Birkin and Loncraine went on tour with Slade for six weeks to see what life in a group was like. The film is really a companion piece to *That'll Be the Day* and *Stardust* and the trio effectively form a triptych that acts as a correction to the optimism of the '60s. The supporting cast is excellent: Tom Conti (in his first starring role), Alan Lake (Mr Diana Dors, in his best film role) and Johnny Shannon (previously in *Performance*). Lake, who plays the vocalist ousted from the band early on, actually had a singing career of his own at one point, releasing a fine cover of Nilsson's *Good Times* in 1970. The soundtrack LP came out three months before the film, but, though selling well, failed to replicate the runaway success of earlier Slade releases, reaching No 6 UK and No 93 US. Spin-off hit singles from it included *Far Far Away* (No 2 UK) and *How Does It Feel?* (No 15 UK), both of which flopped in the US.

Reflecting the tone of the film, the world premiere was held in Newcastle upon Tyne, the home town of Chandler and his assistant (and ex-Animal) John Steel, making this very much a defiantly un-London event. Audiences in the UK liked the end result and it did well, but fared less so elsewhere. It turned out to be almost the last Goodtimes production, as the climate in the UK film industry worsened; and though Slade tried to break the US market afterwards, they failed and their UK popularity diminished quite quickly. With punk and new wave quickly ascendant, they became a semi-forgotten act, flickering back into life in 1981 and 1983–4 before finally calling it a day in 1992 – after 28 years. The film had an uncertain reception amongst critics at the time (for years it wasn't even in *Halliwell's Film Guide*), but is highly regarded today, conveying the seediness of the music scene with some accuracy and being comparable, in style and tone, to UK TV series of the time like *The Sweeney* and *The Professionals*.

There was also – as was the case in those days – a book of the film. Written by John Pidgeon, a very significant film and music journalist, and editor of *Let It Rock*, a UK magazine that briefly challenged *Rolling Stone*; it sold 250,000 copies. Most of them would have been bought, one imagines, by the adolescents who lapped up Slade's singles: they were not seen as a 'cool' act in many quarters. Like Slade, Pidgeon was a great survivor, with a career that stretched over 30 years and concluded with him producing much of the ground-breaking UK comedy of the '90s and early '00s – *Little Britain* and Steve Coogan to name but two.

Whilst audiences were flocking to *Slade in Flame*, the final instalment of Michelangelo Antonioni's three-film deal with MGM appeared. Providing an interesting example of how London's lustre faded, *The Passenger* completed a contract that had begun with *Blow-Up*, a huge commercial hit full of pop actors, locations and music, moved on to *Zabriskie Point*, which transferred the vibe to the US but kept some UK music (Pink Floyd) and finally wound up with a film that has not much music at all and a quietly evolving plot. As with his previous efforts, it centred on loss of identity, uncertainty about who the central character is, what motivates him or even where he is. Never a quick or prolific worker, the five-year gap between *The Passenger* and *Zabriskie Point* was explained by Antonioni accepting a commission in 1972 to do a feature-length documentary about Chairman Mao.

But... it does have a cast at the top of their game: Jack Nicholson (*Easy Rider, Five Easy Pieces* many others), Maria Schneider (*Last Tango in Paris*), Steven Berkoff and Jenny Runacre (*The Final Programme*). This was a rare major role for Berkoff who, at this point, was rapidly emerging as a bête noire in UK theatre with *East*, his play in verse about the East End of London which deployed a vast amount of swearing and violence. In the film Nicholson assumes the identity of an arms dealer, loses his own identity (a classic hippy trope, synonymous with 'dropping out') and ends up being killed by gangsters. A dreamy piece with absolutely brilliant visuals filmed across Spain, Germany, Algeria and London, the screenplay was by Mark Peploe, who previously did Jacques Demy's film *The Pied Piper* with Donovan and the little music there was came via an uncredited Ivan Vandor.

The Passenger was not a box-office success but was critically liked. In truth, by 1975, the year *Jaws* swept all before it, fare of this type – the 'European' art movie – played to smaller, more select audiences. It is interesting to compare the careers of the main actors. Nicholson would remain an enormously significant US star for the next couple of decades, but Schneider's career stuttered. Tired of being seen purely as a sex symbol, from here she went to *Caligula*, but walked out of that in 1976 and never reached – though working continuously – the heights that had been predicted for her after *Last Tango in Paris*. Berkoff would become one of the most industrious and interesting, not to mention provocative, figures in UK theatre and film, whilst Runacre, like Berkoff part of the new counterculture that was emerging in the UK, subsequently featured in several Derek Jarman productions.

Antonioni may have been slow in working through his obligations, but compared to Lindsay Anderson and his Travis trilogy, he was actually quite timely in completing his contract. *Britannia Hospital*, the final instalment in Anderson's work, didn't appear until 1982, trailing in many years after *If....* ('69) and *O Lucky Man!* ('73). It uses chaotic and sinister goings-on at a hospital as a metaphor for the UK as a country in serious decline. Given the success of Anderson's preceding films, expectations were high. Production began in 1976-7 with 20th Century-Fox, who then withdrew and were replaced by EMI. In addition to this, screenplay writer David Sherwin found himself entangled with a new version of *Robin Hood* – starring Jon Voight, Bob Dylan and Muhammad

Ali – and Anderson's film eventually took so long to complete that during its troubled history he took time out to shoot a remake of *Look Back in Anger* ('80), which was barely released, and even did an acting turn himself in *Chariots of Fire* ('81).

Malcolm McDowell reprises his role as Travis alongside a huge and generally reliable UK supporting cast. The plot has much would-be political satire augmented by slapstick-style comedy. But whilst *If....* and *O Lucky Man!* could claim to be Swiftian, their overall feel remained broadly optimistic. This has no optimism. And, of course, like many films that take too long to reach the screen, it was overtaken by events. A great deal of it concerns paralysing and irritating strikes instigated by bureaucratic shop stewards and idiotic reactionary managers. Had it appeared in 1978-9, this imagery would have been spot on. By 1982, though, it was increasingly a thing of the past and some of the country instead was in a patriotic frenzy celebrating victory in the war with Argentina over the Falkland Islands. Thus, despite some virtues, the end result is messy and actually not that funny. (*I'm All Right Jack*, the Boulting brothers' 1959 industrial relations farce is much better.) Nor was this an original idea by either Anderson or Sherwin. Back in 1969 the Peter Nichols play *The National Health* was a big hit at the National Theatre with a cast led by Jim Dale and music by Marc Wilkinson (who, coincidentally, had done the music for *If....*). A film version followed in 1973 with Dale joined by Lynn Redgrave and Bob Hoskins. Thus, using the NHS as a metaphor for the UK was not new.

A rare failure for Davina Belling and Clive Parsons, the film flopped at the UK box office. After it did so, Anderson moved on to film Wham! on their tour of China (*Wham! in China: Foreign Skies*, '86). The money must have been good because this was quite a change from his usual output. *Britannia Hospital* has less of a score than either *If....* or *O Lucky Man!* The music it does have is by Alan Price, whose contribution was done whilst preparing a musical version of *Andy Capp*, with Tom Courtenay, and writing the main title theme for *The Plague Dogs*, the animated film version of Richard Adams's follow-up novel to *Watership Down*.

Prior to the appearance of *Tommy* in 1975, The Who, one of the giant acts of pop and rock produced by the UK in the '60s, had never appeared in a feature or contributed any of their music to one either – a strange omission given the involvement in cinema of many of their contemporaries. Stranger, too, given that their managers, Kit Lambert and Chris Stamp, had both worked in the film industry on kitchen-sink dramas like *The L-Shaped Room* and had originally come across The Who when searching for a young anarchic group about whom they could make a documentary. In the years that followed they turned down the chance to appear in *Blow-Up*, announced that the group would star in their own 'black comedy' film in 1967 (it was never made) and made it into *The Rolling Stones Rock and Roll Circus*, in late 1968, only for the finished production to be shelved.

Eventually, after years of touring and recording, a debut film project for the band gelled around their 1969 concept album. Starting with a proposal for a TV adaptation and moving through a stage where a *Yellow Submarine*-type cartoon was envisaged, a film version was formally announced in *Billboard* in December 1970 as one of two Who projects, the other being *Lifehouse*, which spluttered to a halt and only finally appeared as a play on BBC Radio 3 in 1999. Universal was set to produce at this stage and had previously done eclectic stuff like *Work is a Four Letter Word*, *Three into Two Won't Go* and *Two-Lane Blacktop*, but declined to fund the script proposed by Lambert. After a two-year hiatus Ken Russell, probably then the most bankable UK director, came on board, with his treatment being approved in August 1973.

Following various ballet, opera and stage versions, *Tommy* ('75) proved to be a very full-on, big-screen production and no expense was spared by producer Robert Stigwood (who had his first massive movie hit in 1973 with the film of *Jesus Christ Superstar*) in assembling an all-star cast for the project. Roger Daltrey stars as the main character, with Ann-Margret, Oliver Reed and Elton John in support. The Elton John part had in fact originally been intended for David Essex, who appeared in the stage adaptation, and Russell's film has a distinctly 'rock-opera' tone throughout.

Essex had starred in *Godspell* and Paul Nicholas, seen in a smaller role, was noted then as far as most people were concerned for having played the lead in both *Hair* and *Jesus Christ Superstar* on the London stage a few years earlier. Ann-Margret was clearly present to ensure that the film had appeal in the US, where she had won accolades for *Carnal Knowledge*; but she also had a parallel singing career, notably alongside Lee Hazlewood on the 1969 album *The Cowboy and The Lady*. Elsewhere, Jack Nicholson, by this point the biggest new star in the world, agreed to appear in a small part purely because he wanted to work with Russell. Other members of the massive supporting cast were Robert Powell, Tina Turner, Eric Clapton and Arthur Brown, as well as Townshend, Entwistle and Moon from The Who.

What emerged was a huge box-office success, the ninth biggest film of the year in the US (where it was rare for any UK film to do well) and the twelfth biggest in its home country. The plot, which Russell adapted himself, broadly follows the narrative taken by Townshend on his album... there are changes, but not such that you'd be outraged at any liberties being taken. In fact, one way of looking at the finished product is that the story, with the action taking place in the '40s and '50s, demonstrates how much the generation that grew up post-1945 were affected by living in a world where every adult had experienced or served in the Second World War, where many children played on bomb sites and where many town centres still had damaged buildings and abandoned land. This wasn't just the long tail of the '60s... it was the long overhang of the war, which, psychologically, a great many people in the UK were still dealing with, one way or another, 30 years after it had finished. Releasing the film in 1975 meant, though, given the plot starts circa 1943, that the Daltrey character would have to be at least 30, a bit old for 'a deaf, dumb and blind kid', whilst the central theme of the film, that love and compassion will conquer even the greatest alienation, is defiantly late '60s counterculture.

Filmed in and around Portsmouth, a part of the UK that had not apparently changed for some time, with *That'll Be the Day* being shot on nearby Isle of Wight a couple of years previously, the film works well visually because the *outré* style matches the fantasy of the plot. In fact, art director John Clark had previously done *Performance*, another film with a rich attention to detail. The very last really big commercial hit to emerge from the golden period of '60s UK music, the film soundtrack LP also sold heavily, reaching No 2 US and No 21 UK.

It also launched Daltrey on a substantial acting career, with Russell retaining him for *Lisztomania*, a study of Franz Liszt and a continuation of the biographical films he directed between 1962 and 1974, where he reimagined the lives of Elgar, Bartók, Debussy, Prokofiev, Tchaikovsky and Mahler. An accomplished mid-nineteenth-century pianist and singer song-writer, as we'd now say, Liszt toured Europe during that period and was hugely popular with audiences of young women. Russell portrays him as a bombastic, flashy rock star, with Roger Daltrey in the title role and Sara Kestelman (from *Zardoz*), Paul Nicholas and Ringo Starr in support.

David Puttnam produced and the end result was not deemed a success, representing in some ways a car crash of the excessive late '60s high design/high-art type of film. In fact, the production design, by Philip Harrison, who also did the equally visual *How I Won the War* and *The Final Programme*, was rather good. Part of the problem was that Russell concentrated a great deal on the relationship between Liszt and Wagner, solely it would seem on the basis that Liszt's daughter (Cosima) eventually married Wagner in 1870 and subsequently – from then until the early 1900s – steered the Bayreuth Festival, which celebrated and promoted Wagner's work, in the direction of right-wing German nationalism and its belief in Aryan supremacy. The connection that Liszt himself had with this is not clear. (Liszt died in 1886, Wagner in 1883.) But Russell careers off into territory to do with Hitler and the Nazis and the film ends with Daltrey piloting some kind of spaceship. As to why *Lisztomania* failed, in an era when excess (and prog-rock music) remained popular, we may consider that this came down to Liszt being a much lesser known composer than, say, Mozart or Tchaikovsky. Certainly, for US and UK audiences he was a bit obscure and the Nazi analogies were dubious and in poor taste. The film's failure led to Russell abandoning the idea of doing an updated *Hamlet* with Elton John and David Bowie.

The supporting cast in *Lisztomania* includes Rick Wakeman as the god Thor. Wakeman also scored the soundtrack, on synthesiser, with Daltrey and Nicholas singing throughout. Other musicians employed included Jack Bruce and drummer Dave Mattacks, but the resulting album did nothing in the UK and, reaching no higher than No 145, only scraped the US charts. This was far worse than the sales enjoyed by *Tommy* and significantly below any of Wakeman's solo efforts at the time. Viewed today, one may take a kinder approach than audiences did when the film appeared and feel that although Russell certainly over-reached himself with the political analogies, this remains an entertaining film.

By the mid-'70s The Who had disentangled themselves from Stamp and Lambert and, as well as being the longest running and most reliable survivors of the great '60s UK acts, had diversified into film and TV in quite a big way by purchasing Shepperton Studios and establishing their own production company, Who Films. Given the rising interest throughout the '70s in rock music and its recent past, a documentary about them was almost inevitable.

Back in 1971, Jeff Stein, who at that point had no previous experience of working in any branch of show business, produced a book of photographs of the band touring the US. By 1975 he had put together a compilation of archive footage of them playing live, including material from a concert at the London Coliseum ('69), as well as stuff sneaked in from the then embargoed *The Rolling Stones Rock and Roll Circus* ('68). This was unusual, difficult even, by the standards of the time and impressed Pete Townshend. The group decided they wanted a documentary made and Stein was hired to direct, with Tony Klinger producing. Klinger was a shrewd choice – by the late '70s he was possibly the only UK-based music-oriented filmmaker whose work the cinema-going public might have had a chance of actually seeing in a commercial setting and his prior credits ranged from *The Festival Game* ('70), *Extremes*

('71) and *Deep Purple Rises over Japan* ('75) to *The Butterfly Ball* ('77 – with images by pop artist Alan Aldridge). Stein duly assembled concert footage of The Who from 1967 onwards, spliced in new material (filmed 1977-8, by Anthony Richmond, cameraman on *The Man Who Fell to Earth*) and what emerged was a very decent account of the group's history with some reviews regarding it as being as exhilarating as watching a gig by the band in their prime.

Although shadows were cast when Keith Moon died in September 1978, after the film was complete but prior to its release, the group elected to continue. The film was very popular, got good reviews and accelerated a trend (started by The Jam) towards a full-blown late '70s mod revival. Its soundtrack LP also sold well: No 26 UK/No 8 US. Stein subsequently moved to the US, where he did much TV comedy work and directed a large number of music videos.

The Kids Are Alright was released simultaneously with a film adaptation of *Quadrophenia*. Like Ken Russell's *Tommy* (this too had gestated for some time before reaching the screen. After the band rejected, in July 1972, a proposal by then co-manager Stamp to film a Nik Cohn script, *Rock is Dead – Long Live Rock*, Townshend wrote *Jimmy*, the story of a '60s mod and his vicissitudes. Quickly recorded as the 1973 concept album *Quadrophenia* (No 2 UK and No 2 US), raising funds for a film version, given the sales of the album and the prior success of *Tommy*, was relatively straightforward. Indeed, all the stops were pulled out to ensure this was a big hit. Produced by Roy Baird, who also did *That'll Be the Day*, *The Final Programme*, *Stardust* and, coincidentally, a great deal of work with Ken Russell, it was directed – in the absence of Russell, at that point in LA working on his late psychedelic masterpiece *Altered States* – by Franc Roddam, best known at the time for *Dummy* ('77), a controversial TV play, about a child prostitute in Bradford, that attracted a 14m audience when screened. The script was co-written by Dave Humphries, who had worked on *Flame*, and Martin Stellman, the latter previously a member of The Principal Edwards Magic Theatre, a late '60s act much favoured by John Peel.

When work on it started in early 1978 John Lydon sought the leading role, only to fail the audition. Surely, even at the time it would have occurred to him that – being so associated with the snarling punk culture – he couldn't realistically play a '60s mod? Instead, Phil Daniels stars and this part, with others, briefly made him a box-office figure in what was left of the UK film industry. Those taking supporting roles include Leslie Ash (who had previously been in the execrable *Rosie Dixon – Night Nurse* and became, quite some time later, mega-famous via *Men Behaving Badly*), Phil Davis, a reliable figure in UK TV and films with many appearances in Mike Leigh's productions, Mark Wingett, who like Davis did much TV, Sting, Ray Winstone and Toyah Willcox.

Quadrophenia does a better job than *That'll Be the Day* or *Flame* at providing a reasonable facsimile of the recent past (it is set in 1964), but it is still not overly convincing. A retro greatest hits-style soundtrack duly appeared à la *That'll Be the Day* and sold well: No 23 UK and No 46 US. Together with *The Kids Are Alright*, this helped to accelerate a 'mod' revival in the UK, which lasted, roughly, until 1982 and took place alongside a parallel 2-Tone/Ska revival. At around this time Daniels got a recording deal with RCA as Phil Daniels and The Cross, his group including Peter-Hugo Daly, the young actor from *Breaking Glass* and *The History Man*, on keyboards. None of their releases sold particularly well, but Daniels has maintained his musical interests ever since: singing on *Parklife*, a huge hit for Blur in 1994, and performing Bowie numbers like 'Five Years' on stage in 2016-2017 in *This House*, a drama about the 1974–9 Labour government. The number of cast members here who both acted and made records is in fact very striking. As well as Daniels, Phil Davis was signed to Rocket, Sting achieved global success via both The Police and his solo career, Toyah Willcox had eight hit singles and six chart albums between 1981 to 1986 and even Ray Winstone eventually got in on the act in 1982 as part of the fictional group The Looters, with two of The Sex Pistols and Paul Simonon.

Much of the music in the film was 'curated' (as we would say now) by Jeff Dexter, who also choreographed the nightclub dance scenes. Dexter had first come to attention circa 1962 at the Lyceum Ballroom on the Strand as the ultimate mod – small, neat and incredibly precise in his dress and movements. After a spell as a hippy DJ at the Middle Earth club and managing the US group America, he returned to the fold here. The film of *Quadrophenia* was a box-office hit, though not massively so. Now minus Keith Moon, The Who broke up in 1983, only reforming (after a couple of lucrative reunions) in 1996 and not releasing another studio album until 2006.

A year after *Quadrophenia*, Daltrey starred in the third and final Who Films production. An adaptation of his autobiography by John McVicar, a celebrated UK gangland figure in the '60s who had once been dubbed Public Enemy No 1 by Scotland Yard, it was directed by Tom Clegg, who had done *The Sweeney* TV series and, like that, was a good example of a well-made UK crime melodrama. Adam Faith and Cheryl Campbell (from the TV series *Pennies from Heaven*) co-starred. Set, like *Quadrophenia*, in the previous decade it has reasonable but occasionally uncertain period detail. The end result is quite entertaining and it fits neatly into a small genre of films and TV productions made at that time about either wrongful convictions or the criminal justice system being inherently corrupt: *Law and Order, Scum, A Sense of Freedom, Scrubbers.*

Daltrey also did the soundtrack with Billy Nicholls and Russ Ballard. Most of the material ended up on his album *McVicar,* which made No 22 in the US with a single from the film, *Without Your Love,* reaching No 20. But, all in all, both the film and the music were less successful in the UK. Although he remained busy, Daltrey's subsequent acting career faltered with the thrillers *Murder: Ultimate Grounds for Divorce* ('84 with Toyah Willcox and Leslie Ash) and *Cold Justice* ('91, with Dennis Waterman) failing to replicate the success he had enjoyed, and seemed set for, in the mid-'70s.

The most prolific UK band in terms of film credits remained Pink Floyd, who also continued to function through this period as one of the surviving giants from the preceding decade. Like The

Who and *Tommy*, their own project – *Pink Floyd: The Wall* – took a while to reach the screen. A long cherished autobiographical work by Roger Waters, who wrote the screenplay and composed the music, this was about a young rock star whose dad (like Waters' in real life) is killed in the war and who ends up being completely alienated by the music industry. Realistically, looking at the timescales this requires the action to have been set no later than the late '60s or early '70s, thus making the plot seem a bit dated when it finally reached the screen in 1982.

Its origins can be traced back to *Dark Side of the Moon* which, with a 17-year chart run and sales in excess of 45 million, made Pink Floyd the biggest band in the world from 1973 onwards. Once the touring to promote this behemoth was complete, the group was barely functioning and slowly dissolving instead into a collection of individuals working on solo albums, one of which, from Waters, emerged as something that they could coalesce around. Originally written as a follow-up to *Animals* ('77), it also met the requirements for a film (their thirteenth) that was planned to tie in with the release of the album. Thus, the first incarnation of *The Wall* appeared in November 1979, as a 26-track double LP with every song written (or co-written) by Waters. It hit No 1 everywhere bar the UK (where it peaked at No 3) and yielded *Another Brick in the Wall*, a huge hit that put the Floyd back in the UK singles charts for the first time in 12 years. But hopes of EMI following through with a film were dashed when they pulled out, claiming they couldn't 'understand' the project.

Instead, MGM stepped up to the plate, bringing in Alan Parker as director. The connection here was *Fame*, the phenomenally successful '80s musical that MGM produced and Parker directed, though whether MGM ever saw *The Wall* as a similar film must be doubtful. Like *Tommy*, its plot originates in the war, and dramatically is put over in the format of a rock opera. But, unlike *Tommy*, which is flashy and entertaining, *The Wall* is terribly serious, with political overtones. To ensure a fully contemporary feel Bob Geldof was cast as Pink, the main character, and by virtue of this achieved at a stroke a bigger film career than either John Lydon or Joe Strummer. Bob Hoskins and Nell Campbell also appear, Hoskins as Pink's predatory manager. Though there are effective set pieces, the tone varies throughout from indulgent navel-gazing to bombastic self-pity and it is clear that the portrayal of Pink as rock-star-who-can't-handle-success-and-goes-mad appears to be heavily based on Waters' view of original Pink Floyd member Syd Barrett. There is an anti-establishment undertow, but it seems trite and chimes, one assumes inadvertently, with '70s TV shows like *Yes, Minister* and *The Fall and Rise of Reginald Perrin* rather than high drama. What are effective are Gerald Scarfe's animation sequences. The UK's most acerbic political cartoonist, Scarfe was married to Jane Asher and had done *Shine On You Crazy Diamond* ('75), an earlier promo-film for the Floyd and a kind of dummy run for this.

Despite critical misgivings, MGM (and Waters) got their hit and the film was a big rock and music industry event. It subsequently became, with its mangled anti-authority/anti-war message, a franchise that Waters was still touring with and promoting 30 years later. It clearly had, and has, immense appeal, but also shows why *I Hate Pink Floyd* T-shirts (as worn by J Lydon) were once so popular.

The continuance of a '60s cinematic style into the '70s and '80s was not solely the preserve of Antonioni, Anderson, The Who and Pink Floyd. A number of other releases, of which *The Squeeze* was typical, retained the feel of an earlier era. Given that it is rated by its adherents as being as good as Don Siegel's *Dirty Harry*, this is a somewhat forgotten film with none of the cachet of either *Get Carter* or *The Long Good Friday*. The success of the former in the US led, in fact, to Hollywood money being – very briefly – available for hard-boiled UK cop thrillers, with even Siegel himself in town for the 1974 Caine drama *The Black Windmill*.

Very much part of what one might call the 'cardboard box' period of London crime films – because the action invariably includes car chases along streets littered with abandoned and wrecked vehicles and cardboard boxes, the typical debris of light industrial manufacturing – *The Squeeze* was filmed in various dowdy London locations in mid-to-late 1976. The landscape visually is the same as that portrayed in the popular TV series *The Sweeney* and *The Professionals*: a mixture of warehouses, dingy factories, drab houses and businesses operating out of semi-occupied terraces. Stanley O'Toole produced for Warner Brothers, his other credits at this time including *The Seven-Per-Cent Solution* ('76) (about a drugged-up Sherlock Holmes) and *Nijinsky*. Michael Apted, who had previously done *The Triple Echo* and *Stardust*, directed from a screenplay by Leon Griffiths, who went on to do *Minder* with Dennis Waterman and George Cole, based on the novel *Whose Little Girl are You?* from prolific crime writer Bill James.

Richard Harris was sought for the lead, but opted instead to do *Orca: The Killer Whale* with Charlotte Rampling. Still, *The Squeeze* deploys a very strong cast – Stacy Keach stars, supported by David Hemmings, Edward Fox and Stephen Boyd. Carol White is here, too, once again in distress in south London, as is Freddie Starr. This was Starr's first serious film role since playing a teenage delinquent in *Violent Playground* ('58). Once rated the best rock and roll singer to emerge from Liverpool, he moved instead into the lucrative desolation of cabaret and all-round entertainment. On the evidence here, he could and should have done more straight acting.

The soundtrack was done by David Hentschel, producer of Genesis, Alan Price and Renaissance and at one point the very first signing to Ring O'Records – the label set up by Ringo Starr. Assisted by John Gilbert, who had produced the 1968 Family LP *Music in a Doll's House*, the score incorporated material from Warner Brothers acts Liverpool Express and The Doobie Brothers. All in all, *The Squeeze* is a very solid UK film and one wonders why it disappeared so quickly.

Choosing the best of Pete Walker's oeuvre, one might opt for *Home Before Midnight* ('79), a late addition to the age of consent moral panic films that had started a decade earlier with *All the Right Noises* and *Twinky*. Walker began his career as a strip-club comedian – similar, one imagines, to the character played by Anthony Newley in *The Small World of Sammy Lee* – moving into

making soft-core films before upgrading to cheap second features
like *Cool it Carol* and *Four Dimensions of Greta*. Michael Armstrong,
like Walker familiar with the lower end of the UK film industry,
and previously director of *The Haunted House of Horror*, assisted
with the script.

Prior to launching out on *Home Before Midnight*, Walker had
been asked by Malcolm McLaren in late 1977 to do a Sex Pistols
documentary tentatively called *A Star is Dead*, but the deal collapsed
when the band broke up. This, then, is the film he did rather than
spend time on what became *The Great Rock N' Roll Swindle*. Most
of his films had a pop or music angle. James Aubrey, whose career
ranged from *Lord of the Flies* to *The Hunger* (and he was also in *The
Great Rock N' Roll Swindle*) stars as a 28–year-old rock lyricist – for
the fictional band Bad Accident... which with Throbbing Gristle
and *Spinal Tap* is a name so resonant of its time... having an affair
with a girl who turns out to be only 14. Mark Burns (*The Stud,
The Bitch*) co-stars alongside Richard Todd and Chris Jagger. The
soundtrack was by jazz guitarist Ray Russell and Jigsaw, the latter
contributing ten songs, which finally got a belated release thirty-
four years after the film was made.

But however efficient Walker was at turning out product
like *Home Before Midnight*, soon there would be no space in the
shrinking UK film industry for even modest independent features
of this type. Today the film is hard to track down, with no listing
in *Halliwell's* and very nearly impossible to find to watch despite
being the best of Walker's output. After this he did *The Comeback*,
with US crooner Jack Jones and Pamela Stephenson, about a singer
reviving his career. This too also has a slightly dated feel and even
has The Pretty Things, via their alter ego Electric Banana, on the
soundtrack.

The sharp decline in the number of feature films in production
in the UK after 1970 led to self-appointed saviour Lew Grade
bullishly announcing in 1974 '... I intend to produce more feature
films than any studio in the world. I am only 68 and just beginning.
By the time I am 70, British films will rule the world....' True to his
word, he funded 16 major productions between 1975 and 1982,

kicking off with *The Return of the Pink Panther* ('75), which certainly did pretty well but set the tone: commercially safe, competently made films targeted at a family audience.

Grade's bombast, however, did not mean that his films would actually be shot in the UK or even have UK actors. *Green Ice* was typical. A reasonable thriller, most of it was done on location in Mexico, with a cast headed by Ryan O'Neal, Omar Sharif and Anne Archer. The film was originally started in '1979 by Anthony Simmons (who also co-wrote the script) as his follow-up to *Black Joy*, but he left and was replaced as director by Ernest Day, previously cameraman on *Made* and *The Song Remains the Same*. With exotic locations, a crime-caper plot (emeralds, left-wing guerrillas, a mysterious woman and so on), a big title theme and a cosmopolitan cast, this is the type of international thriller with a specially scored soundtrack that could have been made circa 1967, but seemed a bit dated ten to fifteen years later. Which is not to say it's a bad film: it's actually quite entertaining. In that respect comparisons could be made with *Flash Gordon*: both are survivals into the '80s of older genres. One thing that does occur to the viewer, though, is that Latin America wasn't exactly a happy place in 1981. Watching the film in the knowledge of what was going on in Nicaragua and El Salvador at the time definitely produces mixed feelings.

The soundtrack was handled by Rolling Stone Bill Wyman and his long-term associate Terry Taylor (formerly of The End, a group Wyman managed and promoted in the '60s). Among those playing on it are Dave Mattacks, of Fairport Convention, on drums and Dave Lawson on keyboards. They cut eighteen pieces of music, two of which have Maria Muldaur on vocals. *Si Si, Je Suis un Rock Star* reached No 15 UK and went out credited to Wyman.

Based on a '30s strip cartoon, *Flash Gordon* was an obvious choice for Dino De Laurentiis, who had some skill in converting popular graphic art into feature films. Both *Danger: Diabolik* ('67) and *Barbarella* ('68) did good business in the period, roughly between *Modesty Blaise* ('66) and *Tiffany Jones* ('73), when productions like this seemed the latest type of modern, hip entertainment. The film rights to *Flash Gordon* were acquired by Laurentiis at this time, but actually getting the film made proved problematic. In the mid-'70s both Federico Fellini and George Lucas came and went and *Performance* director Nic Roeg spent a year toiling on the project before dropping out. Finally, in late 1978, after the success of *Superman* and *Star Wars*, Mike Hodges (noted for *Get Carter*, *Pulp* and *The Terminal Man*, but not for any affinity to pop-culture cartoons) agreed to direct from a script cobbled together by several participants including Michael Allin, who'd done *Enter the Dragon*, and Lorenzo Semple, who'd worked on the '60s *Batman* TV series.

The cast is amazing and essentially a late example of the type of '60s excess seen in films like *Casino Royale* or *The Magic Christian*. Clad in fantastic and highly colourful costumes, the ensemble includes Max von Sydow, Topol, Ornella Muti, Peter Wyngarde, Timothy Dalton, Brian Blessed, Richard O'Brien and John Osborne. The main role was considered for Kurt Russell, who'd just played Elvis in a TV movie, and Arnold Schwarzenegger. Both were disregarded (Schwarzenegger because of his heavily accented English) in favour of Sam J Jones, previously a *Playgirl* centrefold. Melody Anderson, who, like Russell, appeared in the 1979 TV film *Elvis*, co-stars. With a preposterous plot, huge sets, marvellous faux-thespian dialogue and not very good special effects – even by 1980 standards, this is no *2001* – the end result is actually quite beguiling and up to a point rather entertaining.

The original intention, somewhere between their mega-successes *Dark Side of the Moon* and *Animals*, was to have Pink Floyd do the soundtrack. (They were also considered back then for *Dune*, another Laurentiis project.) Instead, once production got under way, Queen were selected at the point when they were one of the biggest bands in the world, having broken through in the UK and US in 1973–4 with a highly commercial sound that astutely mixed together elements of Zeppelin, Bowie and Jagger. Given carte blanche by Laurentiis, their album, with 18 pieces of original music, reached No 10 UK and No 23 US and was massive in Europe. The single, *Flash*, also did well, No 10 UK and even higher placings in Italy, France, Germany and Austria. Nor would this be the only film Queen scored during this period: they contributed a significant amount of material to *Highlander* ('86), much of which was subsequently released on the LP *A Kind of Magic* (No 1 UK and No 46 US).

Flash Gordon had good box-office returns, despite derisive contemporary reviews. There were plans for a sequel set on Mars – but leading man Jones and Laurentiis fell out and it was never made. Hodges later did *Squaring the Circle* ('84) with Tom Stoppard about the Solidarity union in Poland, *Morons from Outer Space* ('85) with many of the UK's new crop of comedians and *A Prayer for the Dying* ('87) about an IRA hitman, as well as several videos for Queen.

Laurentiis's other venture, *Dune*, was an adaptation of a 1965 sci-fi classic by Frank Herbert and eventually arrived in cinemas after 14 years in production with three different directors. Originally optioned back in 1971 by Arthur Jacobs (of *Planet of the Apes* fame), after his death efforts were made, and abandoned, in 1974–6 by Alejandro Jodorowsky to get it on the screen with a Pink Floyd (or Virgin records) soundtrack. Instead Laurentiis, who had given the world *Barbarella*, and would subsequently deliver both *Flash Gordon* and *Conan the Barbarian*, arrived circa 1978 and wanted Ridley Scott to direct. Scott quit the project to do *Blade Runner* and Laurentiis turned to David Lynch, having been impressed with his 1980 hit *The Elephant Man*. Lynch's debut had been *Eraserhead* ('77), one of the great art-house/late-night successes of the time alongside *Pink Flamingos* and *The Rocky Horror Picture Show*. He came on board in 1982, turning down George Lucas and *Return of the Jedi* for a chance to film the unfilmable.

Set 8,000 years in the future, the film of *Dune* is a reasonable enough version of the book and somehow condenses its massive, complex, pan-galactic plot into an okay sci-fi film. But, as had long been predicted, it lost money. Heavily. As with the quirky, claustrophobic *Eraserhead* ('77), and the Victorian gloom of *The Elephant Man*, Lynch went for atmosphere and achieved it with exceptional set design from Tony Masters (whose previous work included *2001: A Space Odyssey*), who created a gothic cathedral look for the film. Similarly, the costumes were remarkable part-retro, part-futurist creations – today we would say steampunk – by Bob Ringwood, who had dressed *Excalibur* ('81) and *The Draughtsman's Contract* ('82). The cast is so big that assigning star billing to any one individual proved impossible and so many different actors and actresses appear that they couldn't all be listed on any of the posters. However, among those on show are Sting, by then box office in the US after the success of The Police, Francesca Annis, Sian Phillips, Virginia Madsen, Jürgen Prochnow, Kyle MacLachlan, Patrick Stewart and Max von Sydow. Sting, in whom filmmakers had detected a certain ethereal other-worldly quality (with his peroxide hair and gaunt cheekbones), previously featured in *Artemis 81*, a three-hour-long BBC science-fiction drama with Hywel Bennett, and later starred in *Bring on the Night* ('85), a Michael Apted documentary about his debut as a solo artist, and *The Bride* ('85), Franc Roddam's adaptation of *Frankenstein* alongside Alexei Sayle, Quentin Crisp, Phil Daniels, Timothy Spall and Ken Campbell.

The soundtrack was by Brian Eno and US band Toto. Originally West Coast session players of some repute, Toto enjoyed commercial hits from 1978 onwards and were very popular across Europe. After emerging from Roxy Music, Eno began his solo career with *Here Come the Warm Jets* (No 26 UK) and had explored film music on several albums from 1977, notably *Music for Films* (a minor hit in '78) and 15 others through to 1986, as well as finding the time to produce Talking Heads, Ultravox, Devo and U2. A few years before *Dune* he had collaborated with David Byrne on *My Life in the Bush of Ghosts* (No 29 UK). A case can thus be made that Eno was the best, most modern, UK film soundtrack composer from the mid-'70s onwards.

With the masses not flocking, *Dune* achieved only a limited release and interested parties typically had to hunt it down at a small circle of art houses. It is now rarely seen, but as time has passed its reputation has recovered somewhat from its original treatment by the media. A sequel was planned, but Lynch filmed the original in such a way as to exclude the possibility of this.

Rather like *Green Ice*, to which it might be compared, *Scandalous*, ('84); too, was a late example of the highly popular 'Swinging Sixties' crime-caper genre that spawned hits like *Kaleidoscope, Gambit, Only When I Larf* and *The Italian Job*. A US–UK co-production, it was co-written by Larry Cohen, who had previously done *Daddy's Gone a-Hunting* ('69, starring Carol White) and the blaxploitation dramas *Black Caesar* and *Hell Up In Harlem* (both '73) and John Byrum whose CV included *Mahogany* ('75 – a big melodrama built around Diana Ross) and the shambolic *Harry and Walter Go to New York* ('76). Cohen was in fact a very efficient writer of good quality, hard-boiled US cop thrillers, such as *Best Seller* ('87), an exceptional piece of work with James Woods and music from Jay Ferguson of Spirit. Rob Cohen, no relation, directed and, coincidentally, had also done *Mahogany* as well as *The Wiz*, both of which were Tamla Motown forays into cinema.

Set in London, *Scandalous* avoids serious violence and anything overtly musical and opts instead for easy, slick, comedy, possibly because Larry Cohen (whose own vision of the film was somewhat darker and was based on his 1976 play *Motive* that had starred Honor Blackman, George Cole and Ian Bannen) was edged to one side as writer. The plot has an investigative journalist, Robert Hays from *Airplane*, falling in with some genteel UK con artists, played by Pamela Stephenson and John Gielgud. Stephenson had arrived in the UK from Australia in the mid-'70s as something of a star down under. Having been top of the bill in the comedy *Private Collection* ('72), she managed a small part in *Stand Up Virgin Soldiers* ('77) before marrying Nick Ball, of the TV series *Hazell*, and making *The Comeback* ('78), after which she divorced Ball and took up with Billy Connolly. Dabbling, like Connolly, in the new 'alternative' comedy scene, she also tried her hand at a recording career, releasing a single on Mercury in 1982. In one scene Gielgud is decked up in leather as a punk (something which by 1984 was clearly passé, but possibly still of relevance to the film's target audience in the US); and to ram home the point that this is London in the '80s – think here the Iranian Embassy siege, *Who Dares Wins* and, possibly, the Falklands – the SAS also makes an appearance. The city is treated as a backdrop, with the bits that are seen being those that would be familiar to tourists. (Another example of a US film shot in London without any real feel for the city would be the 1980 Chevy Chase comedy *Oh! Heavenly Dog*, which had a main title theme by Wings.)

As with '60s films of this type there is an obligatory band, in this case Bow Wow Wow shortly before they broke up. Formed by Malcolm McLaren in 1980 after he had washed his hands of The Sex Pistols, they were known for their Anglo-Burmese singer, Annabella Lwin, who was only 14 years old. The rest of them were ex-members of Adam and The Ants and, as with The Sex Pistols, McLaren's management was calculated to ensure maximum outrage, and therefore publicity, at all times. Their debut release caused issues with EMI as it allegedly promoted home taping, after which they switched to RCA for the album *See Jungle! See Jungle! Go Join Your Gang Yeah, City All Over! Go Ape Crazy!* (No 26 UK), the cover of which became notorious for having a nude picture of Lwin, and, in typical (and deliberate) McLaren style, was banned. They play a couple of numbers in *Scandalous* in footage filmed at the now defunct Rainbow venue in Finsbury Park, but most of the soundtrack was by Dave Grusin with a main title theme by Amanda Homi.

The film that emerges is flawed but reasonably entertaining, and, like the TV series *Dallas*, very consumer-oriented: the clothing, furnishings, hair and sundry other trappings are all prominent in the slightly trashy, high style that was so prevalent in the '80s.

Appearing as late as May 1985, *Steaming* really does feel like an end-of-an-era piece. Based on a play by Nell Dunn (of *Up the Junction* and *Poor Cow* fame), it was originally staged at the Theatre Royal Stratford in 1981 with Carol White. The plot takes place in a nineteenth-century municipal 'warm baths', where local women find solace, company and time for reflection (and the dishing out of home truths and sympathy), whilst relaxing in the Turkish steam room. The surrounding area – beyond the baths – is alluded to and is clearly unfashionable and drab, whilst the building itself is threatened with closure. So: very London, very

'70s. The dialogue in *Steaming* may seem trite and unadventurous now, but it would not have happened at all without the '70s boom in feminist writing. This is about women and their struggles with a male-dominated world and economic marginalisation. As with much of Dunn's material, the characters are a bit hackneyed, but the overall message was popular and the play was a big hit.

A film version followed, which in itself was by no means a certainty in the UK by the mid-'80s. New World produced, having previously put money into ventures like *The Kids Are Alright* and *Christiane F.* With all the action taking place on a couple of sets and a limited cast, it was clearly economical to make and the prospects of turning a profit must have looked good. White wasn't available to star (she'd been sacked from the play for being late and missing performances), so the leading roles, after Julie Christie and Jacqueline Bisset had turned them down, were taken instead by Vanessa Redgrave and Sarah Miles. Diana Dors supports with Patti Love, seen in *The Long Good Friday*, co-starring. Redgrave and Miles had last appeared together in *Blow-Up*, and in another echo of times past this would also turn out to be both the final film directed by Joseph Losey and the last performance in Dors' extraordinary career. With a list of credits that ran from *Dance Hall* ('50) to *West 11* ('63) and *Deep End* ('70, another drama set in a swimming pool), her appearance in Adam Ant's *Prince Charming* video in 1981 led to attempts, ultimately unsuccessful, to star her in a film version of *Dick Turpin* a couple of years later. In *Steaming* she presides as the manager/caretaker of the crumbling establishment. She died in May 1984, at only 52, before the film was released, and this is an adequate swansong after a career that also included releasing an album and several singles in the '60s and writing the sleeve notes for a Lenny Bruce LP.

The soundtrack was by Richard Harvey, formerly of the band Gryphon, but it was not released commercially, even though the film included a main title theme by Stephanie de Sykes.

3

TRASH!

The idea that '60s London was a paradise for the young didn't last very long. *The Knack* and *Blow-Up* both had absurdly youthful casts, but, by the end of the decade, Edna O'Brien's *Zee and Co* ('71) portrayed something very different. Although the similarities remained – fashionable clothes, contemporary music, sexual freedom, central London locales, studios and penthouses – the characters enjoying this were now all middle-aged. Slightly paunchy types, turned on to the delights of 'the permissive society' rather like the swingers portrayed in Alex Comfort's *The Joy of Sex* ('72).

No better example of where this trend eventually led exists than the big box-office films of Joan Collins, several of which were written by her sister Jackie. Set in a tiny cosmopolitan enclave of London W1, they feature men, usually jet-setting playboys, with bigger hair than the women, who come clad in a series of fashionably chic outfits that aim for, and usually miss, opulence. Anyone under 25 in the '70s looked askance at how a once vibrant pop culture had degenerated into this commodified, glossy world. In fact, one thing that united both the 1967 and 1977 generations was that both frowned on traditional glamour, regarding it as 'heavy' (or even 'anal': a description much used in Malcolm Bradbury's *The History Man*) and rejected commercialism as being inauthentic and non-artistic, unless, of course, the glamour in question was in some way subversive, as with the clothing of Vivienne Westwood.

Perhaps placing the Collins sisters in this derided territory is a bit harsh. Both had done some good work. Joan, for instance, had a respectable run of decent film parts from *I Believe in You* ('52) to *Alfie Darling* ('75) and dabbled successfully in the '60s satire boom with *Fool Britannia* ('63), a stage production send-up of the Profumo affair with Peter Sellers and Anthony Newley (her husband), the LP of which reached No 10 in the UK. After discarding Newley in the early '70s, Joan married Ronald Kass, an executive at Apple 1968–9, who, after being moved out of the organisation by Allen Klein, produced the films *Melody* ('71) and *The Optimists of Nine Elms* ('73). Sibling Jackie started out as an actress too, decorating an early British rock and roll exploitation piece, *Rock You Sinners* ('58). A decade on and, inspired by *Valley of the Dolls*, she turned to writing, knocking out the high-trash epic *The World is Full of Married Men* ('68). Set in an advertising agency in 'Swinging London', it – eventually – got made into a film, shooting beginning in 1978 with a cast headed up by Anthony Franciosa and Carroll Baker, both of whom started in big budget US films before doing colourful stuff in Europe and then tat in the UK. Paul Nicholas co-starred. As with *Black Joy* and many other '70s films there was a greatest hits-style soundtrack album, on Ronco, that made No 25 in the UK with tracks by Bonnie Tyler, Gene Chandler, The Three Degrees, Shalamar and A Taste of Honey.

Both the book and the film sold. And it followed into the Odeons and ABCs an earlier screenplay that Collins had knocked out with Dave Humphries, writer of *Slade in Flame*, based on her 1969 follow-up novel *The Stud*. Starring sister Joan and Oliver Tobias (like Nicholas, a mainstay of the London production of *Hair* a decade earlier), this was shot in late 1977 and released in April 1978. Collins plays a predatory nymphomaniac who hangs around a discotheque and has an affair with its manager (Tobias). The discotheque scenes were actually shot at Tramp, a club in the billionaires' playground of Jermyn Street SW1 and owned by Oscar Lerman and Johnny Gold, Lerman being Jackie Collins' husband. Opened in 1969 – Michael Caine and Peter Sellers were founding members – Tramp was the successor to Lerman's earlier venture, the Ad Lib (just off Leicester Square, then, as now, a somewhat seedier location), which had been much frequented by the pop glitterati circa 1965–6. Indeed, the geographical importance and ongoing dominance (in exclusive circles) of Lerman's club seems in some ways not dissimilar to the same qualities that attended 430 King's Road SW10 and its various occupants. If either *The World is Full of Married Men* or *The Stud* had been made in 1969–70 starring David Hemmings and Jane Birkin and with Pink Floyd playing (in Tramp) we'd probably all think them, with some allowance for their melodrama, classics: but what emerged on the screen was ten years too late and aimed squarely at a much older audience. The average age of the cast in *The Stud* was 41 and there was no band in situ (there surely would have been one in 1970 and *Zee and Co* boasted no fewer than three), but the soundtrack was done by John Cameron assisted by Biddu. The album made No 2 in the UK, flying out of the department stores that stocked it and included many contemporary hits. Again, the problem was that this was the youth culture of the '60s appropriated as entertainment for 'grown-ups', rather like seeing your mum and dad dancing to *Top of the Pops*, and, in naffness, a close second (albeit unintentionally) to *Abigail's Party*. Critics likened *The Stud* 'to being buried alive in a coffin stuffed with back numbers of *Men Only...* '. It also showed a world that was nothing like the UK of the time. Not that this mattered, given that it was made for £450k and grossed £6.5m.

The *Stud* was a Brent Walker film, the production company run by George Walker, formerly a gangster who had moved into redeveloping dog tracks as massive mixed-use leisure and shopping parks. Walker had also run a club in the '60s, in his case Dolly's (also in Jermyn Street W1), which was reckoned to be the prototype for Tramp. His own film ventures, though, were essentially dated, and both *The Stud* and *Loophole* ('81) could have been made 15 years earlier. But Walker and his backers calculated, correctly, that audiences would lap up the West End high life from which they were economically excluded, in much the same way that an earlier generation living in a world of rationing and shortages had voyeuristically devoured *Spring in Park Lane* with Anna Neagle.

A sequel, *The Bitch*, shot and released in 1979, was immediately rushed out by Brent Walker as another major starring vehicle for Collins, based, again, on a novel by her sister. With more 'sexy' goings-on, this has the central character battling gangsters in Las Vegas. It was written and directed by Gerry O'Hara, whose earlier credits included *All the Right Noises* ('71). The success of *The Stud* allowed for a bigger budget and the supporting cast now included Kenneth Haigh, Ian Hendry and Chris Jagger. Biddu did the soundtrack again, making a tiny concession to the emergence of new wave via the inclusion of a solitary Blondie track. The genre continued with an original Jackie Collins screenplay, *Yesterday's Hero*, which Elliott Kastner produced. A drama about a UK footballer (for Leicester Forest FC) making a comeback, this starred Ian McShane, Paul Nicholas and Adam Faith. Again, an embarrassing disco soundtrack was crucial and featured throughout the film, which came with a John Motson commentary and Frank McLintock as 'football adviser'. An amazingly insular product, but very of its time, and, like the others, a commercial success.

Mention should also be made of *Hussy* ('80), a melodrama about a prostitute eventually escaping her occupation with the help of the man she really loves. Starring Helen Mirren and produced by Don Boyd (*Scum*, *The Tempest*), this is less risible than the Joan Collins vehicles, though, like them, it is set in a 'glamorous' London locale. Supporting roles in it are played by Jenny Runacre and also Patti Boulaye as a 'cabaret singer'. Like Nicholas and Tobias, Boulaye too had begun her career in the London production of *Hair*, taking over the Marsha Hunt role, before becoming a rather cheesy British disco star. Despite their popularity then, and the affection still shown by the wider public for Ms Collins now, films like this are rarely, if ever, revived.

A similar transition from cutting-edge style to tired glamour attended the Bond franchise post-1970. The most lucrative money-making series created by UK cinema could never be allowed to die, and, in the search for the perfect 007, the producers went determinedly for safe mediocrity. In 1972, with Connery wanting to do grown-up dramas like *The Offence*, and left-field futuristic extravaganzas like *Zardoz*, the most likely choice was between Roger Moore or David Warbeck, and would remain that way for over a decade. Initially, no one was sure or not if Moore would be wanted for a second series of *The Persuaders* (he wasn't – it flopped in the US), so considerable attention was paid, at one point, to Warbeck as a replacement. Fully 14 years younger than Moore, he had classic matinee idol looks, had been in TV from the '60s and in the film *The Legend of Young Robin Hood* ('69), but was best known, by some distance, as the man who abseils through your bedroom window at night and leaves a box of Milk Tray on the dressing table. Yes: he was the Cadbury's Milk Tray Man, looking to upgrade.

But Moore *did* become available and Warbeck's opportunity never came – not that he wouldn't have brought his own baggage to the role. Like George Lazenby, he was from the Antipodes, was a male model and was best known for appearing in a confectionery commercial. Then, to cap it all, Warbeck went off to make *Black Snake/Serpent Noir* ('73), a Russ Meyer slaves-on-a-plantation drama shot in the West Indies that nobody watched for the acting. Or plot. But, in a strange twist, Warbeck was unofficially kept in reserve, with a clause in his contract that wherever he was in the world and, whatever he was doing, he had to be available to take on the Bond role at no notice in case Moore was suddenly incapacitated. Thus, while Moore plodded through seven Bonds in twelve years, Warbeck enjoyed himself in noisy entertaining trash like *The Last Hunter* ('80), *The Hunters of the Golden Cobra* ('82), *The Ark of the Sun God* ('84) and *Treasure Island in Outer Space* ('85), all of which were Italian facsimiles of US hits like *Apocalypse Now*, *Star Wars* and *Raiders of the Lost Ark*, shot quickly and cheaply in places like Turkey and the Philippines with second-string casts, ludicrous plots and inadequate special effects.

Eventually, at 58, Moore handed in his Walther PPK, collected his pension and opened up the field again. In the frame once more, Warbeck now lost out a second time to Timothy Dalton, who might have been in *Sextette*, squiring an octogenarian Mae

West with Alice Cooper and Ringo Starr, and *Flash Gordon*, but could actually *act*, as a string of stage credits for the RSC testified. (Although from the point of view of selling him to US audiences his stint as Mr Rochester in a 1983 BBC TV adaptation of *Jane Eyre* probably meant more.)

What a shame then that audiences couldn't enjoy a Bond linked with Russ Meyer, ludicrous fantasies about chocolate or laughably bad macho adventures. A national icon deliberately trading on the same notions of glamour as the Collins sisters, but sending it up as he did so. To the end, though, Warbeck remained up for it, finishing his career in the late '90s in stuff that went straight to DVD like *Pervirella* (with music by Billy Childish) and *Razor Blade Smile* (nonsense about the Illuminati), spoofing everything to perfection.

The business of actively packaging rock music for a safe middle-aged audience (rather than dismissing it automatically as a teenage fad) can, therefore, be traced back to at least the early '70s. In particular, the TV production *Rock Follies* was very much an example of this trend. Made when rock operas were sweeping all before them, and decked out with elaborately staged musical sequences, this was a six-part Thames TV series broadcast in February and March 1976 that rapidly accrued huge popularity.

In it, three young women scramble about trying to make it in the music industry. Starring Julie Covington, best known at this point for *Godspell* and a solo recording career, Charlotte Cornwell, from *Stardust*, and Rula Lenska, from *Alfie Darling*, it was produced by Andrew Brown and Verity Lambert, both of whom were TV stalwarts, Lambert having previously done *Adam Adamant* and *Take Three Girls*. In *Adamant*, Andrew Brown had kicked off the faux Victoriana trend of the mid-'60s, but *Rock Follies* is very much an in-your-face variant of the latter: the women have troublesome boyfriends, experience situations, argue, have affairs and live in less than desirable circumstances (squats and a commune), much as any struggling musician would have done then. Having joined a band, they deal with the usual predatory hustlers encountered in Tin Pan Alley, tour the provinces and eventually end up in a soft-core sex film. Each programme had them in a variety of costumes – they even do an Andrews Sisters act at one point – which in some ways echo the tendency toward parody and retro seen in *The Rocky Horror Picture Show*.

Musically, *Rock Follies* was a post-Roxy Music project for Andy Mackay, saxophone player in what, between 1972 and 1975, was arguably the most interesting new act to emerge in the UK. Combining high-fashion gloss, retro kitsch and commercial success, the band released five albums and six singles that enjoyed significant chart runs. For *Rock Follies* Mackay put together a group with Ray Russell (guitar, whose huge list of credits went back to Graham Bond and much else besides), Tony Stevens (bass, ex-Savoy Brown Blues Band) and Peter van Hooke (drums), all of whom at that point were the house band for the Lloyd Webber–Rice show *Evita*. By the mid-'70s the crossover between rock operas and 'mainstream' rock was quite pronounced indeed. What is on offer in *Rock Follies* is safe rock for people who watched evening TV rather than got their music in pubs and clubs. Whatever the intentions of Brown and Lambert when making this, middle-aged audiences lapped it up as they accepted and even sought out the trappings of the counterculture, a trend similarly displayed in the films of Joan Collins, where the nightclubs and discos were mainly populated by 40+ swingers and mercilessly satirised in *Abigail's Party*. The series produced an album, released by Island, which sold massively, reaching No 1 and indicating how 'grown up' rock/pop had become by the mid-'70s. It may be frank and adult – but it's no threat to the established order.

Rula Lenska – in echoes of David Warbeck – went on to make *Queen Kong* (with Robin Askwith), an absurd and cheaply made cash-in with the remake of *King Kong* that hit the screens in 1976. In some ways this was somewhat more entertaining and was scored by the band Pepper. A second series of *Rock Follies* ran in 1977 and Mackay did the soundtrack for that too, which reached No 13 in the UK. But by then the centre of gravity in the UK's music industry had shifted back to teenagers and further extensions of the genre were not considered.

For the best rendition, though, of how the external facets of '60s culture (faux trendy fashion, longer hair, a free and easy attitude to drinking, smoking, dancing and sex and selected acquisition of pop music) were adopted by adults in the '70s, *Abigail's Party* remains the outstanding example. Something of a peak for TV drama, it was a BBC *Play for Today*, adapted from a small-scale theatre production by Mike Leigh. As an example of the variety, quality and depth of what was then available to the public, the week prior to its broadcast viewers could have watched in the same slot Michael Darlow's *Come the Revolution*, whilst a week later a Jewish-Catholic romance, *Oy Vay Maria*, was offered, directed by Richard Loncraine (of *Slade in Flame*). Leigh's career is worthy of mention. Defiantly a child of the '60s, he was at Camberwell School of Art, before taking minor acting parts in *West 11* ('63) and *Two Left Feet* ('64). His big break came at only 22, directing the original stage production of *Little Malcolm and his Struggle Against the Eunuchs*, a late kitchen-sink/northern drama about student revolutionaries which Apple later optioned for a film. Moving into film, Leigh had a minor success with *Bleak Moments* ('71) which is the absolute opposite of *Abigail's Party*, all Cassavetes, Pinter and Beckett: a slow, difficult portrait of hesitant and isolated young middle-class people. What he shows us in *Abigail* is a brash satire à la Brecht of crude lower middle-class aspirationalism done in much the same way that Speight had skewered the white working class 14 years earlier in *'Till Death Us Do Part*.

This is the new England, emerging, as predicted by JG Ballard, from the suburbs – a society devoid of any real intellectual curiosity or political radicalism and driven by nasty, nativist behaviour. *Abigail's Party* is in fact a very accurate portrayal of typical mid-'70s London overspill housing developments. Reckoned to be set near Romford, or possibly Croydon (one of the cast plays a former Crystal Palace footballer), in one of the rapidly multiplying cul-de-sacs on the outskirts of the metropolis, the action takes place entirely within a modern and characterless living room where everything is remorselessly accurate down to the tasteful evening wear of the main character and the cheap three-piece business suits of the men, all flapping lapels and broad flares. As a fashion statement this, of course, was the complete opposite of what Westwood and her acolytes were putting into the marketplace at around the same time.

Alison Steadman, Leigh's then wife, stars as Beverly, the manipulative and tyrannical central character, and the plot focuses on an alcohol-sodden evening during which local teenagers, led by Abigail, who is never seen, hold an 'unsuitable' party down the road against which the adults attempt to assert themselves. Exactly what their party consists of is difficult to ascertain – a muffled extract of *All Around the World* by The Jam can be just about heard – but we can assume it to be the opposite of the 'sexy' '70s disco music and easy listening (Demis Roussos, Donna Summer, Tom Jones) being played throughout Beverly's gathering.

Leigh later became a mainstream director with variable commercial, though great artistic, success. His first real box-office hit came with *Vera Drake* (2004) at the age of 61. *Abigail's Party* still retains its power today. The original has been repeated on TV several times and stage adaptations are still appearing 40 years after its inception.

4
TRANSGRESSION

By the late 1960s, the UK film industry was sufficiently confident, and sufficiently flush with US money, to release several features that tackled previously taboo themes like homosexuality, bisexuality, lesbianism and transvestitism. *The Killing of Sister George* ('68), *Entertaining Mr Sloane* ('70), *Sunday Bloody Sunday* ('71), *Girl Stroke Boy* ('71) and *I Want What I Want* ('72) were all properly funded and distributed films with decent production values and recognisable star players. Of these, *Sunday Bloody Sunday* won a clutch of international awards and was nominated in four categories, ultimately unsuccessfully, for Academy Awards. Given this, it is perhaps no coincidence that Bowie's breakthrough in early 1972, with much use of androgynous imagery, came towards the end of this period.

Within a few years, though, such openness and tolerance had all but vanished. Instead suburban attitudes, philistinism and bigotry were much more openly displayed, and traditional 'gay' stereotypes prevailed and thrived even. By the mid-'70s, a period when Larry Grayson and John Inman attracted huge audiences on TV, serious gay and lesbian cinema had been forced underground. Some of this was wrapped up in the general decline of the industry, but some was also due to the continual stream of police raids and obscenity trials that targeted bookshops, publishers and theatres, a backdrop that warned off many funders and distributors.

Thus, although Derek Jarman's *Sebastiane* was a critical success, there were only tiny audiences for *Nighthawks* ('78), John Maybury's *The Court of Miracles* ('82, with Siouxsie Sioux) and *Framed Youth: The Revenge of the TV Perverts* ('83, with Jimmy Somerville and Soft Cell). *More Lives Than One* ('84, with music by Tom Robinson) remained the solitary attempt by TV to portray bisexuality. The extent to which the UK avoided LGBT themes in the '80s can be seen by Bowie's 1983 brace *The Hunger* and *Merry Christmas, Mr. Lawrence*, which were respectively an MGM production partly filmed in New York and a Japanese co-production filmed in New Zealand. Even Ireland, not noted then for its liberality, produced *Lamb* ('85, music by Van Morrison) about a Catholic priest and his relationship with an underage boy. As the '80s progressed, the arrival of AIDS and the misreporting of its origins and prevalence complicated matters further and the deserved art-house success of *My Beautiful Laundrette* ('85) remained very much the exception in a country where values would not significantly change for another decade.

Whilst this was depressing and indicative of the times, through this period avenues were found and pursued that enabled some transgressive drama to exist. There were even some commercial hits, none greater than *The Rocky Horror Picture Show*. Devised by Richard O'Brien, a New Zealand actor best known then for playing parts in *Hair*, 1970–71, and *Jesus Christ Superstar*, 1971-2, this was part parody of '40s and '50s horror and science fiction films, part musical pastiche of '50s rock and roll and part a hippy/personal liberation comedy-drama about 'squares' losing their inhibitions. It first saw the light of day in a theatre on the King's Road in June 1973, with Michael White, who had done *Oh! Calcutta!*, producing. The cast, led by O'Brien and Tim Curry (like O'Brien, from *Hair*), with Julie Covington (from *Godspell*), had played in several of the rock operas then in vogue on the London stage and the public response was sufficient to catch the attention of Jonathan King, who immediately produced and released an original cast album on UK, his record label. Both King (20 per cent) and White (80 per cent) funded the venture, which tapped into the same '70s wave of nostalgia for retro rock and roll that propelled *That'll Be the Day*.

A film version became possible once 20th Century-Fox agreed to produce, which they did after the US stage adaptation in San Francisco was a hit in 1974. Shot quickly in the UK between October and December 1974 at Hammer Studios, the screen adaptation amalgamated the UK cast led by Curry and O'Brien with Susan Sarandon and Meat Loaf from the US production. Sarandon was familiar to audiences from her co-starring role in *The Front Page* ('74), whilst Meat Loaf at that point was another former participant in *Hair*, having appeared in the US version of that show.

Visually the film has gleaming interiors, rather like an art deco Astaire–Rogers musical, something very on trend at the time, and is bright, clean and decadent, in the manner of an outré fashion show. It didn't gross well when released, but remained viewable on the late-night circuit and in selected independent cinemas for years, gradually becoming a popular 'cult classic'. It was particularly favoured by student union and college film societies. Both B J Wilson (Procol Harum) and Phil Mckenzie (Manfred Mann Chapter III and formerly a member of the house orchestra for the rock opera *Catch My Soul*) played on the soundtrack which eventually became a hit in the US, reaching No 49 with a chart run over 58 weeks in 1978–9. Earlier musicals like *South Pacific* and *West Side Story* had enjoyed stupendous levels of success and the sales for *Rocky Horror* were much lower than those, but by any other standards it was a consistent bestseller. One wonders, though, if in the last resort *South Pacific* and *West Side Story* didn't have slightly better tunes, as, oddly – given the anthemic nature of most of the material – neither the show nor its film adaptation produced any hit singles.

Today it is regularly voted the second most popular film released in 1975, behind *Jaws*, and the stage show has been running constantly, somewhere in the world, since 1973. It is now the longest running musical franchise of all time. O'Brien was either very prescient or perhaps just lucky in seeing this in 1972, just before the retro craze really got off the ground with *American Graffiti* and a slew of other parody horror films: *Vampira* (David Niven), *Son of Dracula* (a late Apple production with a cast of '60s rock musicians), *Young Frankenstein* (Mel Brooks) and *Phantom of the Paradise* (Brian De Palma) (to which we might add, although they are not strictly parodies, Paul Morrissey's *Flesh for Frankenstein* and *Blood for Dracula*).

An interest in transvestism by the wider public that went beyond the counterculture and devotees of glam rock was also at play here. After all, the '70s were the heyday of Danny La Rue, voted entertainer of the decade and at one point the highest paid performer in UK showbusiness. Another factor in its success might have been that within rock and pop itself there had always been a trend towards dressing as horror characters: Screaming Lord Sutch being a key exponent. A few years later both The Tubes and The Damned drew on this tradition of extravagant theatricality. Trying to decide in such circumstances on where the dividing line between cult success and mainstream success lies can be a difficult process.

But, however one views it, *Rocky Horror* was definitely the launching pad for Tim Curry, who made it big in the US where he recorded three LPs for A&M and starred in films such as *Times Square* ('80) and *Legend* ('85). Richard O'Brien, co-star Nell Campbell and various other members of the cast subsequently turned up in *Jubilee* ('78). O'Brien later wrote and starred, with Campbell, in a sequel, *Shock Treatment* ('81), which predicts the growth and popularity of reality TV shows. It flopped, but has its devotees and has recently been revived.

Nine years after homosexual acts between consenting adults were decriminalised and five years after *Boy Stroke Girl* dealt with same-sex relationships as knockabout comedy, *Sebastiane* appeared as the first UK feature to deal openly with homosexual desire and the first significant film from Derek Jarman. Previously set designer on the Ken Russell films *The Devils* and *Savage Messiah*, Jarman shares the directing and writing credits on *Sebastiane* with Paul Humfress, who, after scripting the highly rated gothic thriller *Schalcken the Painter* ('79), worked primarily in Australia. *Sebastiane* was a brilliant debut for them both. Cheaply made with an unknown cast, only one of whom (Richard Warwick, previously seen in *If....* and *The Breaking of Bumbo*) might have been recognised by the wider public, sharp eyes would have spotted in one sequence various members of the London cast of *The Rocky Horror Picture Show* in cameos alongside Jordan from the Westwood/McLaren King's Road clothes shop *Sex* and wider members of Jarman's social circle, including Andrew Logan and artist Duggie Fields, at one point Syd Barrett's flatmate.

An imaginatively made account of the life and death of the third-century Catholic martyr and saint (who had become by the nineteenth century a figure of interest to the gay community), Jarman and Humfress's budget was so low that much of the nudity on display was purely to save on hiring costumes, but their pronounced eye and ear for authenticity produced an entire screenplay in Latin. Partly filmed on location in Sardinia, it was highly praised on release and thought – wrongly – to represent a moment of hope for the UK film industry. Not a major commercial success, and restricted to the art house, community cinema and student union circuit, it did well enough to secure the reputation of Jarman, if not Humfress, for a wider audience.

A soundtrack of modern electronic music, which works very well given the historical context, was by Brian Eno who, like Jarman, came out of the '60s art school milieu and had previously been an innovative keyboardist in Roxy Music. Jarman later shot several music videos for The Sex Pistols, Throbbing Gristle and The Smiths, but, given the restrictions of funding in the UK and attitude of the wider establishment, did not become a great auteur along European lines, remaining instead someone who produced consistently interesting work on a small scale. One wonders what he might have done with a decent budget.

As a film, *Sebastiane* came and went without causing an uproar, which was strange given the impact other not dissimilar productions had at the same time. It was released within a few weeks of Mary Whitehouse launching a prosecution of *Gay News* on the grounds that it had published a poem, written from the viewpoint of a Roman centurion, implying that Jesus was gay. In and out of the courts for the next six years, the case produced a Gay News Fighting Fund to which the Monty Python team, embroiled themselves in a dispute about *Life of Brian*, made a hefty contribution. While all this rumbled on there was also *The Romans in Britain* ('80), a Howard Brenton play at the National Theatre with Roman Britain portrayed as an allegory of contemporary state repression in UK and Ireland. This had a (simulated) homosexual rape scene and Mary Whitehouse prosecuted again, but this time failed.

For a follow-up, Jarman went for something equally provocative. Despite the prevailing circumstances in the UK in 1977 (when unemployment stood at 1.7 million and 111 people were killed in sectarian violence in Northern Ireland), the country celebrated the 25th anniversary of the accession of Elizabeth II with some gusto at a variety of official and unofficial events. There was a BBC TV series (*Jubilee*) which broadcast 13 plays portraying life, with barely a black face in sight, in the UK from 1952 onwards, one episode of which included appearances by Phil Daniels and retro pop band Slik.

Simple patriotism was not the only thing on offer, however. Between April and October 1977, Jarman worked on his second feature, also called *Jubilee*. This began as a cine essay about his muse Jordan (aka Pamela Rooke) and her provocative dress sense, earlier footage of which can be seen in *Dressing for Pleasure* ('77), John Samson's brilliant documentary about rubber and latex fetishists. After a few weeks' work, and with his central character now singing sporadically with Adam and The Ants, the focus of Jarman's film became punk itself. The budget remained modest and much of the footage was actually shot in Jarman's own warehouse flat by the Thames and the (then) down-at-heel areas of Bermondsey, Deptford and Rotherhithe. The plot has Jenny Runacre (*The Final Programme, The Passenger*) as Queen Elizabeth I, visiting the UK in 1977 after the current monarch has been killed in a mugging and being appalled by what she sees. Supporting parts were played by what was virtually Jarman's own repertory company at that point: Nell Campbell and Richard O'Brien (both ex-*Rocky Horror Show*), Toyah Willcox, Jordan, Wayne County,

Adam Ant (who was paid £40 for appearing), The Slits, Siouxsie and The Banshees and Duggie Fields.

What emerges, as is always the case with Jarman, is highly inventive and an accurate portrait of a capital city then in extensive physical decay. There is much arch, declaimed dialogue, and the mixing of this with violence and a generally sexualised atmosphere is reminiscent of Steven Berkoff's *East*. Both are, in fact, in a line of descent from Kubrick's *A Clockwork Orange*. On release it was disliked by Vivenne Westwood – for reasons that aren't clear – and the *NME* came out against it too, but it was one of a small number of works that dared to take a stance against the official 'line' of the Silver Jubilee. Others included the Jim Allen TV play *The Spongers* (January '78, where a single mum with a disabled child is ground down by 'the state' against the backdrop of the Jubilee and its robust patriotism) and Michael Moorcock's 1978 novel *Gloriana*, an extended *Gormenghast*-type fantasy featuring Queen Elizabeth I, in which her Palace has abandoned chambers, hallways, passages, balconies, stairways, and caverns in the style of *Jabberwocky*.

Quite an array of talent was assembled for the soundtrack – Brian Eno, Wil Malone, Mark Perry and Miles Copeland III taking the lead – with other material by Chelsea, Wayne County and The Electric Chairs, Siouxsie and The Banshees and The Maneaters, the last a short-lived Toyah Willcox venture. It was shown at Cannes. Despite its content and attitude, Jarman remained unchallenged by those who would be censorious and continued in his adopted role as a gay cultural terrorist. His next venture would be an anything-goes adaptation of *The Tempest* (September '79), again with Toyah Willcox.

One way or another, quite a lot of the activity that later crystallised into the UK punk scene ended up being connected with Jarman, and a case can be made that his living and working space at Butler's Wharf, Shad Thames, was as central to how the movement developed as the McLaren-Westwood boutique at 430 King's Road SW10. Jarman shared his accommodation with Andrew Logan and the property itself was within an abandoned block of warehouses... huge silent buildings jammed up against the river that were licensed from 1971 to a motley collection of small businesses, artists, writers, musicians and performers, of whom Logan (an architect) and Jarman were but two. Logan, like Jarman, was at the epicentre of an extensive social circle that included the artists Duggie Fields and Luciana Martinez de la Rosa, Janet Street-Porter, presenter from 1975 to 1979 of *The London Weekend Show*, and actresses Nell Campbell and Jenny Runacre. If one assumes two to three degrees of separation, between them these would link up just about everyone in the '60s and '70s counterculture. It was also to be at Logan's studio, a venue that hosted many legendary parties, that Malcolm McLaren and Vivienne Westwood chose in early 1976 to introduce The Sex Pistols to the wider world.

Logan never practised as an architect, preferring sculpture, jewellery design and mixed media. From 1972 he became well known for the Alternative Miss World competition, mainly for the entertainment of the burgeoning gay community. Over the years it grew in popularity, with both male and female contestants and cross-dressers, and by 1978 the event was being held in a circus tent on Clapham Common and compèred – his role was actually Guest of Honour – by Divine. Inevitably the star, Divine burst onto the UK scene a year earlier in the London stage production of *Women Behind Bars* (a brilliant parody of '50s US women in jail movies) alongside glamour model and porn star Fiona Richmond. For a few he was already well known: he ate dog-shit in John Waters' *Pink Flamingos* ('72), which, like *El Topo*, *Performance* and *The Rocky Horror Picture Show*, was a seemingly permanent booking on the all-night cinema circuit. Due to *Women Behind Bars*, Divine met Logan, fashion designer Zandra Rhodes and photographer Robyn Beeche.

The 1978 Alternative Miss World was filmed by director Richard Gayor and premiered at the Odeon in London's Leicester Square, something of a slap in the face to the Whitehouse-Thatcher crowd, and was even screened at the Cannes Film Festival, with Divine attending both events. It is actually rather good, with a robust sense of humour being required to enjoy it fully. A limited release followed in the UK and US. In 1981 Divine diversified into music – as a kind of heavily overweight version of Warhol drag artiste Wayne County – and in 1984 had a big hit with *You Think You're a Man* (No 10 UK).

Neither Jarman nor Logan could ever be described as being mainstream. And the mainstream then still avoided for the most part anything that presented an awkward, controversial or contrary view of sexuality. An exception to this conformism was Nic Roeg, whose film *Bad Timing*, his follow-up to *The Man Who Fell to Earth*, was a study of destructive relationships that included, in one scene, a possible descent into necrophilia. It was very different to *Flash Gordon*, which Roeg had been lined up for, and was mainly filmed in Vienna with Art Garfunkel and Theresa Russell starring. For Garfunkel it was his first leading role since *Carnal Knowledge* ('71), another cinematic exploration of sexuality, whilst for Russell it was a massive breakthrough part as an out-of-control and wayward young woman involved in a doomed affair whilst drinking heavily. In many ways the film echoes the plot of *The Third Man*, based as it is on a love triangle that descends into a criminal enquiry. Casting the part of the Austrian police inspector, who unravels how messy the tryst between Garfunkel and Russell has been, proved unexpectedly difficult. Both Albert Finney and Malcolm McDowell declined, Finney to appear in the psychological thrillers *Looker* and *Wolfen*, McDowell choosing instead to fulfil his commitments to *Cat People* (with Nastassja Kinski and a title theme from David Bowie) and *Britannia Hospital*. At the last moment Harvey Keitel, who was in the UK making *Eagle's Wing*, *Death Watch* and *Saturn 3*, became available and played the part expertly, accent notwithstanding. Supporting roles are taken by Denholm Elliott, as Russell's much older husband, and Dana Gillespie. Gillespie – who also had a lengthy singing career – provides another Bowie connection: briefly his girlfriend in the '60s, the two put out a promo-LP in 1971 seeking interest from record companies, and, on the strength of this, both were subsequently signed by RCA, Bowie ascending to stardom.

Jeremy Thomas produced and Rank provided the finance, but

famously regarded the finished product as decadent ('... a sick film
for sick people... ') and only gave it a limited distribution. *Bad
Timing* wasn't really the type of material they were looking for.
With a reputation for middle-brow family entertainment, their
other films at this point were remakes of old chestnuts like *The
39 Steps*, *The Lady Vanishes* and *The Riddle of the Sands*. Predictably,
then, the film was no *Third Man* and failed at the box office,
despite critical plaudits for fine ensemble playing and the script by
Yale Udoff. In its way, with its milieu of casual sex and multiple
references to Freud, Klimt, Billie Holiday and Theda Bara, this is a
very '70s entity. Russell subsequently married Roeg and decamped
with him to the US where they made *Eureka* and *Insignificance*,
their migration being a sad loss to the UK film industry. Richard
Hartley oversaw the soundtrack, which includes material by Tom
Waits, Billy Kinsley and Zoot Money. Kinsley (The Merseybeats)
and Money (The Big Roll Band) were both '60s survivors, but
the inclusion of Waits, whose material explored seedy themes
and peripheral locations, was interesting. His contribution, *An
Invitation to the Blues*, was culled from his 1976 album *Small Change*
and its inclusion in the score was part of his slow and steady rise to
commercial success in the UK.

Bad Timing lost money and neither *Sebastiane* nor *Jubilee* attracted
anything other than niche audiences. With this, and the decline
in the UK film industry generally, interest in transgressive dramas
waned, until, marooned in the mid-'80s, *My Beautiful Laundrette*
appeared as a modest beacon of hope. A big career breakthrough
for Hanif Kureishi, who just prior to this had four plays staged
in London but was not yet widely known, this was the essence
of early Channel 4 drama. Tackling class, race and sexuality, the
action takes place in London, specifically Battersea and Stockwell,
at the point that its decline stopped and its expansion and renewal
began. Producers Tim Bevan and Sarah Radclyffe commissioned
an original script from Kureishi, who duly provided a plot centred
on a gay relationship between a charismatic working-class thug
and a young Pakistani laundrette owner.

Stephen Frears directed, confirming his reputation as one of the most interesting UK auteurs of the period. Modestly budgeted and made originally for TV, Daniel Day-Lewis stars, supported by Saeed Jaffrey and Roshan Seth with Shirley Anne Field and Ram John Holder in small roles. Gary Oldman might have been in it too, but he rejected the script, stating that 'people in London don't speak like that'. He might have been right, up to a point, and he was clearly closer actually to being working class than, say, either Joe Strummer or Malcolm McLaren, but he clearly didn't 'get' the dialogue written by Kureishi for both his Asian characters and the complex individual portrayed by Day-Lewis. In fact, the characters played by Jaffrey and Seth both emerge as sharp business people with decidedly Tebbit/Thatcher tendencies. Given their support for those establishment figures, they are puzzled why they are discriminated against by the local white population. An early and relatively successful portrait of the country that was emerging by the mid-'80s, it was shown in cinemas and much liked, possibly an indication of relief that new social mores were now widely accepted, and eventually won an Oscar for best original screenplay. *Sammy and Rosie Get Laid* was made by the same team (Kureishi, Frears, Bevan and Radcliffe) in 1987 and is somewhat similar.

The soundtrack was by Stanley Myers and included a synth/dance title theme performed by Rita Wolf, who also appears in the film. This was subsequently issued on Stiff Records and Wolf was later one of the bhangra act Saffron with Nazia Hassan and Meera Syal. For his part, Kureishi continued to explore race in a London setting, most notably with *The Buddha of Suburbia* (book '90, TV series '93) filmed in and around Bromley and featuring a late David Bowie score.

5

BOWIE

The centrality of David Bowie in UK music throughout the '70s and '80s was unique. Not so well recorded is his parallel acting career, the roots of which stretched back to his days as a '60s mod. Not that many of the early efforts made by him to break through in film and TV came to fruition. Between 1967 and 1971 he failed many times, prior to his ascent to UK pop stardom, to land major film roles, not being wanted at all in *The Touchables, Oh! What a Lovely War, The Haunted House of Horror, Sunday Bloody Sunday* and *Dulcima*, and only being given a minute uncredited part in *The Virgin Soldiers*. Worse still, in 1968 he auditioned for three roles in the London stage production of *Hair*, and didn't get hired for any of them. If an aspiring mime artist and singer-songwriter couldn't make the grade there, when so many others could, what precisely was he lacking? But, ever the trouper, he persevered, saying in 1972 (when declining – a sound decision – to take part in Apple's shambolic *Son of Dracula*) '... I feel like an actor when I'm on stage rather than a rock artist. I very rarely have felt like a rock artist. I don't think that's much of a vocation, being a rock and roller....' Down the years he made many similar comments, with the result that fans and critics alike, despite his record in auditions, had long awaited his emergence as a major force in acting.

After a decade of trying he finally landed a starring part in *The Man Who Fell to Earth*, as Thomas Jerome Newton, an unknown and inscrutable genius who turns out to be an ambassador from an alien civilisation. It was his big break and came in one of the last films to be produced by British Lion and Michael Deeley, previously noted for *The Knack* and *The Italian Job*. Even better, it was a Nic Roeg project that got off the ground after the critical success of the supernatural thriller *Don't Look Now*, which, unusually for a mainly art-house film, recouped its costs and made a decent profit. Filmed entirely in the US and based on a 1963 Walter Tevis sci-fi novel inspired by the life of Nikola Tesla – the prototype 'thin white duke' and a figure rediscovered by the emerging environmentalist counterculture of the late '60s – this is a study of alienation, the failure of relationships and alcoholism. For Roeg and Deeley it also helped, when securing funding, that Tevis had written *The Hustler* ('59), subsequently a huge screen success for Paul Newman. Adapted by Paul Mayersberg, who did the 1972 script for Hermann Hesse's *Siddhartha*, another hippy tome of the time, the finished product can be read as a parable about the failure of the US 'dream', a topic of some resonance post-Watergate. With so much of the plot focused on the isolation and loneliness of the main character, Bowie, an austere, detached and rather unclubbable figure, was well cast in the leading role. In fact, he was offered the part shortly after Roeg saw him in a BBC Omnibus documentary, *Cracked Actor*, in early 1975. Prior to this and whilst touring the US a year earlier, Bowie was announced as co-star with Elizabeth Taylor in *The Blue Bird*, a stodgy US–USSR détente-era collaboration. Luckily his antennae twitched and he pulled out – when made without him, it was a turkey. *The Man Who Fell to Earth* is far superior.

Tevis's plot is about a human-like population on a distant planet who, suffering from some sort of unspecified ecological catastrophe, send an emissary (Bowie/Newton) to Earth to seek out a supply of fresh water. As shot by Anthony Richmond, whose prior credits included both *Don't Look Now* and *Stardust*, the landscapes are magnificent, the city centres and urban locations gleaming and the overall modernity of what is on offer remains undated, even now. The main supporting parts went to Rip Torn, previously seen in the big sci-fi hits *Westworld* and *The Omega*

Man, and Candy Clark, lately of the box-office smash *American Graffiti*.

There was an expectation that Bowie, who had broken through in both the US and the UK in 1972, would do the soundtrack for release on RCA, helped by Paul Buckmaster. One of many eminent UK arrangers and composers to emerge from the '60s, Buckmaster had previously worked with Bowie on his 1969 breakthrough hit *Space Oddity*, later adding Arrival, Elton John, Nilsson and Carly Simon to his credits before helping to score the Third Ear Band's *Music from Macbeth*. Between them, Bowie and Buckmaster composed various disparate bits of music by playing along to a videotape of the film in Bowie's house in LA, only for their efforts to be deemed unusable by RCA who opted instead to reissue *Space Oddity* in late 1975 as a 'tie-in' (of sorts) with the film. It reached no 1 in the UK, but hardly scraped the US charts. With Roeg finding himself without a soundtrack shortly before the film's planned premiere in March 1976, he turned to John Phillips, one-time leader of The Mamas and The Papas. Phillip's third wife Genevieve Waite, previously the star of *Joanna*, had introduced the two back in 1970 when Roeg was in the US promoting, fruitlessly it would transpire, *Performance*. Phillips was an interesting choice, having done the music for Robert Altman's weird 1970 comedy *Brewster McCloud* and even, with Waite, writing a sci-fi stage musical, *Man on the Moon*, about an astronaut leading a mission of interplanetary dignitaries to prevent the destruction of the universe by a bomb that has been placed on the Moon by an evil scientist. (At one point this was slated to star Elvis. Without him it lasted two days on Broadway in 1975, closing after crushing reviews that focused on its incompetent production by Andy Warhol.) Assisted by ex-Rolling Stone Mick Taylor and session players BJ Cole and Henry Spinetti, Phillips came up with a dozen or so tracks. A further six were provided by Stomu Yamashta, who had worked on the thriller *Phase IV*, another '70s production about the human race being doomed following an unknown cosmic event. *The Man Who Fell to Earth* opened on time, but, given the rushed and confused way the music was assembled, no official soundtrack LP for the film was forthcoming for decades afterwards.

The fifth biggest grossing film of the year, despite mixed reviews that commented on its surface flashiness, *The Man Who Fell to Earth* did well in the UK and Europe. Though some deemed it too obscure and too long, all commentators acknowledged its visual brilliance. There was even a 1987 remake for US TV. Given the stuttering nature of the UK film industry in the mid-'70s, Deeley stayed in the US where he produced the popular hits *Convoy* and *The Deer Hunter* and later reached the pinnacle of his career with *Blade Runner*. Bowie and RCA used stills from the film to promote his albums *Station to Station* (No 5 UK and No 3 US) and *Low* (No 2 UK and No 11 US), which greatly expanded his appeal in the US.

After this, there were expectations that Bowie would quickly move on to a high-quality follow-up. Instead he left Los Angeles in the spring of 1976 for Switzerland and by August that year was living in Berlin with Iggy Pop. Here he finished work on Pop's album *The Idiot* (No 30 UK, April '77) and, in collaboration with Brian Eno whose film score/soundtrack montages he admired, started work on *Low*. After this came *Heroes* (No 3 UK and No 35 US, October '77) and an offer to score Skolimowski's adaptation of *The Shout* ('78), which he declined. Nor did Bowie proceed with *Wally*, which was announced in *The New York Times* in 1978 as a Clive Donner-directed biographical study of Egon Schiele, co-starring Charlotte Rampling and with music by Brian Eno.

Named after Walburga Neuzil, the muse of Austrian artist Egon Schiele, a protégé of Gustav Klimt, who flourished circa 1911-15, this was something Bowie very much wanted to do whilst in Germany producing his classic trio of albums. In fact, his gesture with his hands on the cover *Heroes* was taken directly from a Schiele self-portrait. But there were weaknesses early on. The involvement of Clive Donner was a curious choice for a period drama about troilism, decadence and the grotesque, as whilst he had come to prominence with *The Caretaker* ('63, a faithful adaptation of Pinter's grim, depressing but accurate play), for most filmgoers he remained best known for the cheerful caper *Here We Go Round the Mulberry Bush* ('67). The project finally collapsed when Rampling got involved in marriage and motherhood with Jean-Michel Jarre and Bowie opted instead for *Just a Gigolo*.

But like many films that go through several permutations prior to actually being made it was reworked and emerged a couple of years later as *Egon Schiele: Exzess und Bestrafung*. Jane Birkin replaced Rampling as Wally and Mathieu Carrière took the Bowie role as Schiele. Carrière had many credits in '70s films with erotic plots, notably *Malpertuis* ('72), *If Don Juan Were a Woman* ('73), *Charlotte* ('74, which had a Mike Oldfield score) and *Bilitis* ('77). The story focuses on Schiele's relationship with Wally, the teenage model he lives with and paints and the 1912 obscenity trial that ensues. A French–German production shot in Austria and Yugoslavia, it was directed by Herbert Vesely and is very elegant with a great deal of emphasis on nudity, possibly not that much of an advantage as it gives an impression that Schiele only painted naked women. A decent European art film, it bears up well today. Throughout the development process Brian Eno remained in situ and produced a great soundtrack, only for the film not to get a UK release and the opportunity of releasing an album of his material to be passed over by the producers. In fact, *Egon Schiele: Exzess und Bestrafung* remained relatively obscure for many years with no listing in the *Time Out Film Guide* and no US release until 1996. Despite this, given what followed with *Schöner Gigolo, armer Gigolo* (*Just a Gigolo*), it might have been better for Bowie to have remained with it.

This, on paper at least, looked a good idea. After the success of *The Damned* ('69), *Cabaret* ('72) and *The Night Porter* ('74), Nazi-themed dramas had a certain vogue. At one point there was even a 'Nazi chic' sub-genre, some of which rubbed off on teenagers wanting to cause outrage in the '70s: *The Damned* was chosen as the name of the first UK punk group to get a recording contract, whilst Tony James, bass guitarist of Generation X, spelt out what motivated those using such murderous imagery by saying '... the great thing about Nazism is that your parents hate it!'

The script for *Just a Gigolo* was co-written by Ennio de Concini, whose previous work included *Hitler: The Last 10 Days* ('73) and *Salon Kitty* ('75), the latter being possibly the ultimate 'Nazi chic' work. The film had the largest budget up until then of any West German film and was the final credit in the long career of Rolf Thiele, although most of his other productions had been pot-boiler sex comedies. It was directed by David Hemmings, whom everyone remembered from *Blow-Up*, and whose early work had won the Silver Bear at the Berlin Film Festival. Hemmings also co-starred. A drama set in Berlin in the aftermath of Germany's defeat and humiliation in World War I it shows the subsequent rise of the Nazis and features, as was then typical in expensive European pictures, a large international cast led by Bowie and Sydne Rome (a US actress in many Italian, French and German ventures) supported by Kim Novak, Maria Schell, Curd Jürgens and Erika Pluhar.

Up to a point it is quite well made. The production design is good: as in *Salon Kitty* and Ken Russell's *Mahler* ('74), there are highly stylised Nazi-era costumes, the ones for *Mahler* being done by Vivienne Westwood, and gleaming art deco sets. The plot takes us through the German journey of the inter-war years: defeat, recession and the ascent of political extremism, with Bowie as a young Prussian officer reduced to working as a gigolo in a brothel run by Marlene Dietrich, then 76 years old, in what would be her last part.

The soundtrack, on Ariola, was assembled by Gunter Fischer, an East German composer given carte blanche by the GDR politburo to work frequently in the west. For its part, East Germany, for ideological reasons, celebrated the sexual decadence of '20s and '30s Germany as being (largely) anti-Nazi, with the subsequent persecution of homosexuals by the Third Reich making that community automatically comrades of other oppressed groups. (In an odd detail, one of many in the film for which a working knowledge of central European history is helpful, both Thiele and Fischer were Sudeten Germans, part of a minority unwillingly embraced by the Third Reich and later expelled from their homeland by Communism.) The music itself is a real hotchpotch, with material by Manhattan Transfer, The Village People, The Pasadena Roof Orchestra (a UK act that pastiched '20s music), the Gunther Fischer Orchestra, Marlene Dietrich, singing *Just a Gigolo*, not actually written until 1928, a decade after the film starts, but with lyrics pointing up the drama in the plot, and Bowie himself chanting – it has no words – *The Revolutionary Song*, which is actually rather good, but was only issued as a single in Japan. The film includes some big Busby Berkeley-style numbers à la *The Producers*, which worked in *Cabaret* (on a smaller scale), but don't gel here. Certainly, the interpolation of disco acts like Manhattan Transfer and Village People was a mistake, but underscores how endemic that genre was in the '70s: the Lew Grade-produced *Escape to Athena* ('79), a WWII prison camp drama, similarly boasts Heatwave performing the main title theme.

The film wobbles between comedy and tragedy. A thin Bowie acts with a deadpan south London accent throughout, projecting a vacant, empty persona that shows no development since *The Man Who Fell to Earth*. (Certainly, he had other things on his mind whilst making the film, notably overseeing with Brian Eno the recording sessions in Berlin for the debut Devo album, *Q. Are We Not Men? A. We Are Devo!* (No 12 UK and No 78 US). Audiences were uncertain and it failed at the box office. Originally 2 hours and 27 minutes – most parties regarded this as too long – it was reduced to 1 hour 45 minutes in the UK and 1 hour 38 minutes in the US, but however Hemmings cut it, it didn't work commercially or artistically and remained an oddity, at best. In the aftermath Hemmings and Bowie were slated to go to Australia to make a political thriller, *Harlequin*, with Orson Welles. But this didn't happen either. A great 'what if', *Harlequin* eventually appeared with Robert Powell replacing Bowie and Broderick Crawford taking over from Welles.

Bowie's next notable screen appearance came in *Christiane F.*, where he appeared in a lengthy concert sequence performing music drawn mainly from his Berlin trilogy, which for rock archivists is akin to Picasso's 'Blue Period'. His interest in Berlin, then a dangerous frontier and a transit point between east and west, lasted for three years and the material included in the film contains nine tracks released as a soundtrack LP on RCA. These were taken from *Low*, *Station to Station*, *The Lodger*, *Heroes* and *Stage* and were mainly co-written with Brian Eno, also a Berlin resident at this point.

Adapted from her 1979 book, *Christiane F.* is a semi-autobiographical dramatised account of Christiane Felscherinow's time as a 14-year-old pilled-up heroin addict and prostitute in the seedy surroundings of the Berlin Bahnhof Zoo. Co-produced by Maran Film, who some years earlier had done *Deep End*, it was directed by Uli Edel, whose later works included *Last Exit to Brooklyn* and the Madonna vanity project *Body of Evidence*. Extremely well made and with an abundance of background detail, the leading role (Christiane F.) is played by Natja Brunckhorst and the cast contains many teenage actors making their debut including Jens Kuphal, later a significant German music producer for the likes of Nena and Hildegard Knef.

For some, politically, this was an emblematic and accurate account of life in the west – the grim descent-into-squalor plot about heroin-addicted kids being just the type of material that was highlighted by the GDR and Soviet Union, who regarded West Berlin as an outpost of decadent capitalism in an ocean of socialist purity. In real life, at the time the film was made, Felscherinow's boyfriend was Alexander Hacke of the synthesiser band Einstürzende Neubauten, pioneers of industrial music who performed in a network of music clubs in one half of the city. Felscherinow, who became for a few years something of a style icon for German girls, also tried her hand at recording with Hacke producing and both of them appear in the 1984 film *Decoder*.

Returning to a starring role and in his fourth German-themed film in a row, Bowie played the title role in *Baal*, a BBC adaptation of an early Brecht play, shot in late 1981. About a dishevelled artistic genius who lives beyond the confines of bourgeois society, this had been written in Munich in 1918 (during the ructions caused by the flaring into life of the Soviet Republic of Bavaria and the counter-coups that followed) and was first staged in Leipzig in 1923. The central character – Baal – is an outsider whose character serves as a prototype for the 'outsider' figures later found in the writing of Sartre, Camus and Colin Wilson. Not surprisingly, a character of this kind had great resonance with the 1968 generation and *Baal* was duly filmed as early as 1969 by Volker Schlöndorff with Rainer Werner Fassbinder and Margarethe von Trotta in the lead roles and the character of Baal played by Fassbinder as a loose-living student activist. The music for this production came from Klaus Doldinger, who led psychedelic fusion band The Motherhood, and the film itself was done in the style of a rock opera.

A UK version finally appeared when the BFI funded *The Life Story of Baal* ('78). Directed by Edward Bennett this starred Neil Johnston, Patti Love (also seen in *The Long Good Friday* and *Steaming*) and Jeff Rawle, but played to predictably limited audiences. A more substantial adaptation finally arrived when the BBC commissioned Alan Clarke to direct from a script by John Willett. Willett was a long-standing Brecht scholar (he'd even met the man himself in the '40s) and was also the author of *Art in a City*, a pioneering study of Liverpool and how its '60s scene coalesced. The original choice for the main role was Steven Berkoff (who would have been wonderful) based on his edgy, demented stage performance in *East*. But Berkoff was committed to his new play *Decadence* and after that opted to play a Bond villain in *Octopussy*. Instead Bowie, at the pinnacle of his UK recording success with *Scary Monsters (and Super Creeps)* (No 1 UK and No 12 US), took the lead looking like a scarecrow with rotten teeth. Still interested in German material at this point, and not long after his stint in *Christiane F.*, he had enjoyed a one-off chart hit in March 1980 with Brecht's *Alabama Song* (No 23 UK). An effective period drama, with a setting that is 'bleak, austere and radical', it reflects the prevailing conditions when Brecht wrote the work: a time of violence, hunger, shabbiness and disorder.

Baal was a popular and much-liked film that should really have been a prestige cinema release. There was no soundtrack as such, but Bowie released an EP of Brecht songs on RCA which peaked at No 29 in the UK. The accompanying music was from Dominic

Muldowney, who also did a 1981 LP – with Robyn Archer – in which she sang the works of Brecht. In a curious example of synchronicity, when Berkoff's *Decadence* appeared as a film in 1994 (with Berkoff and Joan Collins in the main roles), the main title theme would be written by Bowie.

Leaving his German period behind, Bowie moved on to *The Hunger*, an MGM UK–US production and the debut feature by Tony Scott, whose brother Ridley enjoyed enormous success with *Alien* and *Blade Runner*. Tony Scott had directed advertising commercials through the '60s and '70s, including some very elegant stuff for Chanel Nº5, and *The Hunger* stars Catherine Deneuve (who had actually been the face of Chanel Nº5 in 1979, albeit not in Scott's particular commercial) and Susan Sarandon, well known to UK audiences via *The Rocky Horror Picture Show* alongside Bowie, reprising here his style of acting from *The Man Who Fell to Earth*.

Scott had originally wanted to adapt Anne Rice's *Interview with the Vampire* ('76), a part religious, part sexual, part Gothic work, with the protagonist as an elegant, tragic figure. (A film version of this finally emerged in 1994, directed by Neil Jordan and starring Tom Cruise and Brad Pitt.) Instead, MGM gave him a 1981 Whitley Strieber novel. Like Scott, Strieber had started in advertising and his debut, *Wolfen* ('78, a supernatural urban thriller), had been made with Albert Finney and Michael Wadleigh directing; quite a change for Wadleigh, who had previously done the sprawling concert movie *Woodstock* ('70). Produced by Richard Shepherd, whose other credits included the Audrey Hepburn classic *Breakfast at Tiffany's* ('61), *The Hunger* is a very stylish contemporary vampire thriller. It's a shame that Strieber didn't explore this type of material more fully, rather than delve into his later alien abduction stuff like *Communion*.

When the film was shot in 1982, Bowie was looking to 'break' the US market in a big way. He did *Putting Out the Fire* (No 26 UK), the main theme for the remake of *Cat People* with Malcolm McDowell and Nastassja Kinski at the same time that he was working on *The Hunger* and the film's supporting cast is

strong and carefully chosen, with Cliff de Young, ex-lead singer
of US '60s group Clear Light, co-starring. The PR for its release
clearly assumed a significant degree of inside knowledge from its
intended cognoscenti (not to say elitist) audience proclaiming '...
The Hunger is a mood, a look, an ambience created by Tony Scott. It
is the lighting of Stephen Goldblatt. It is the production design of
Brian Morris. It is the clothes created by Milena Canonero ....' To
unpack this: Goldblatt had a background in advertising like Scott
and had shot Breaking Glass, Morris did design work on That'll Be
the Day, Stardust and Flame and Canonero did the costumes for A
Clockwork Orange. So, visually, this is a feast. The Hunger was very
successful on the art-house and independent circuit, but less so
elsewhere and in truth is only remarkable as an example of the
UK and US finally making (in 1983) the type of polished thriller
that had been common in Europe ten years earlier.

The soundtrack was done by Howard Blake, who started out
with easy listening LPs in the '60s, moved into film with All the Way
Up (The Scaffold) and proceeded to Flash Gordon with Queen. He
was assisted by Dave Lawson (formerly keyboardist in The Web and
Greenslade). On screen Bauhaus made a memorable appearance
performing Bela Lugosi's Dead, the sequence for this being shot at
Heaven, the most on-trend music venue in London in the early '80s.
After recording this proto goth/punk single in Wellingborough in
early 1979, Bauhaus were successful in the UK in 1981–3, enjoying
their only hit with a cover of Bowie's Ziggy Stardust (No 15 UK).
We also get to hear Iggy Pop's and David Bowie's rendering of Fun
Time. The Hunger also had an original score by Michel Rubini, who
had worked on all of Sonny and Cher's '60s hits, and Denny Jaeger,
but a UK release was not forthcoming.

Next, in his seventh role in as many years, Bowie appeared in
Merry Christmas, Mr. Lawrence. Set in the Far East after the British
defeat at Singapore he plays a British officer mutually attracted
to a Japanese guard, played by musician Ryuichi Sakamoto. The
POW drama was a particularly English sub-genre of post-1945
cinema, yielding a string of immense domestic successes from The
Wooden Horse ('50) and Albert RN ('53) to The Colditz Story ('55,

TV series '72) and perennial favourite *The Great Escape* ('63). But *Merry Christmas, Mr. Lawrence* is no *Colditz*, and certainly not even a *Bridge on the River Kwai*.

The homoerotic theme runs through the film, not that this should particularly surprise us, given that it is directed by Nagisa Oshima, whose *In the Realm of the Senses* ('76) was banned virtually everywhere due to unsimulated sex scenes. A staple of the late-night and alternative cinema circuit for years – the only ones who could show it, being private clubs – it ensured that Oshima enjoyed a reputation as a daring auteur. Ian Dury's collaborator, Chaz Jankel, even wrote a song, *Ai No Corrida*, based on the title in Japanese, which was a hit in 1981 for Quincy Jones (No 14 UK and No 28 US). The prospect of Oshima filming in the west came when Jeremy Thomas, whose previous projects included *Bad Timing*, put up the money to produce an adaptation of a Laurens van der Post novel (based, partly, on his own wartime experiences) set in the Far East in the '40s.

Bowie was cast after Oshima saw him in the Broadway production of *The Elephant Man*. For someone who was keen on an acting career, it is a sign of what was available that Bowie, in accepting this, had still not yet managed to star in a contemporary UK film set in the UK. Perhaps he wasn't overly concerned. After all, for some years his desire had been to move beyond UK confines and seek international stardom. The supporting cast, led by Tom Conti, are fine, but some considered Bowie's performance a bit wooden. Other commentators also pointed out that the source material – from Laurens van der Post, not universally regarded as a reliable narrator – had been considered by his contemporaries, particularly those also subject to Japanese imprisonment, to be a rather romanticised version of events.

As well as making his acting debut Sakamoto did the soundtrack, which was released on Virgin in the UK. One track, *Forbidden Colours* (the title derived from a Japanese homoerotic work by Yukio Mishima), is sung by David Sylvian and reached No 16 in the UK charts. Sylvian was originally in the band Japan, who were close followers of Bowie (and close geographically too: they

were from Beckenham, while he was, famously, from Bromley).
Signed up by German label Hansa in 1977 they initially seemed
a bit of an anachronism at the time and enjoyed most of their
success in Japan itself. If punk hadn't happened groups like Japan,
with their elegant visual sense (derived from Bowie circa 1974 and
Roxy Music a couple of years earlier) and fragile music would have
come to the fore earlier in the UK.

Once he had been signed by EMI in 1982, with a massive
advance of $17.5m, Bowie speedily left the UK and the droll,
deadpan deliveries of *Scary Monsters* and set about the serious
business of really cracking the US market, where previously
his levels of success had been moderate to good but never truly
outstanding. On film he would soon be heard doing the main
title theme for John Schlesinger's *The Falcon and The Snowman* (the
excellent *This is Not America*, No 14 UK). For the main business
at hand, however, he engaged Nile Rodgers as his musical director
and recorded *Let's Dance*, which went on to be his biggest selling
release to date, reaching No 1 in most territories. It yielded three
hit singles too, the title track plus *China Girl* and *Modern Love*.
Unsurprisingly, a concert film, *Ricochet*, quickly appeared, which
showed his progress around the world promoting the album.

Not that it was actually much of a film, as such. Written by
Martin Stellman, who did *Quadrophenia* and *Babylon*, it is much
more of a greatest-hits show, and follows Bowie and his entourage
across Thailand, Singapore and Hong Kong as he determinedly
goes for the world market. Gerry Troyna directed. A BBC figure
who did a lot of travel and railway documentaries, Troyna was a
low-key choice, as if having someone a bit more prominent might
have resulted in their trying to impose their own style on the film.
Bowie at 37 certainly looks his best... but without the slightest
hint of his usual transgression. No cross-dressing or playing about
with occult/hippy themes and certainly no dallying with Third
Reich imagery. Instead he resembles an immaculately turned-out
pre-Beatle singer from, say, the Joe Meek era.

The concentration throughout on a single performer means
that *Ricochet* is really a collectable for the hardcore fans, and

despite a cinema release is rarely mentioned in reference works. It is also a reminder – given the huge success of the album and tour – that Bowie's acting ventures amounted to relatively little compared with his recording career. The US market also got *Serious Moonlight*, a concert video of his appearance in Vancouver on the same global tour. This sold heavily (reaching No 10 in the US video charts) and was directed by David Mallet, a long-standing exponent in that field. Significantly, both *Ricochet* and *Serious Moonlight* show Bowie performing much material from his classic 1969–81 period. In the UK both appeared at virtually the same time as a cinema release for *Ziggy Stardust and the Spiders from Mars*, a belated concert documentary shot ten years earlier.

This led some to conclude that despite the phenomenal success enjoyed by *Let's Dance* and a couple of subsequent albums, Bowie's star was waning as the '80s progressed. Their views may have been confirmed with *Absolute Beginners*, in which he was billed third, after two teenage leads. Truly the great UK cinema disaster of its time, *Absolute Beginners* was £1m over budget before shooting even started and arguably the most over-promoted UK film since *London Town*, the doomed 1946 attempt by Rank at selling the city to the post-war world and, like this, a musical. The gap between the intention and the end result is so broad, and the type of film that it might have been if a degree of common sense had been applied is so different to what emerged, that a starting point for any discussion must be the source material: the 1959 Colin MacInnes novel that followed the adventures of its various characters in Soho and beyond over a three-month period.

One of a trio of works, the others being *City of Spades* and *Mr Love and Justice*, it was successful enough to run to four editions by 1980, and originally had an iconic cover photo shot in Southam Street W10 (a location much loved by filmmakers) by Roger Mayne, husband of playwright Ann Jellicoe, who was the author of *The Knack*. A full-time writer, MacInnes did scripts for the BBC, hung out in Soho during the '50s, greatly admired Tommy Steele and the other coffee-bar rockers and ended up in the late '60s as a cheerleader for race activist Michael X. He was an outsider who chronicled the emerging youth and ethnic cultures of London, the closest the UK had to a 'beat' writer.

Paul Weller read him and in October 1981 nicked the title of his book for The Jam's hit single *Absolute Beginners* (No 4 UK), at which point MacInnes, who had died in 1976, was rediscovered. Or, to be accurate, slightly more than that. He became something of a cult, wrapped up with notions of cool exemplified by *The Face* magazine and its main writer – and guru – Robert Elms. With more emphasis now being placed on the history of the UK's pop culture than had been the case in the past a film version was quickly mooted. Selling the idea can't have been too difficult. With MacInnes being regularly proclaimed and re-evaluated in the music press (individual papers and magazines of which then had a readership of up to 500,000 each), Weller and The Jam scoring their hit and a new generation buying up reprints of his books, an audience clearly existed. Goldcrest and Virgin agreed to put up the money, with Stephen Woolley producing. Between them they had funded or produced all the major UK successes of the '80s. Julien Temple was brought in to direct, presumably on the basis of *The Great Rock N' Roll Swindle*, which Virgin had distributed and helped to finance.

Alarm bells should have rung early on. Despite being a relatively successful author during his lifetime, none of MacInnes's works had been filmed or adapted for TV. Nor did he write anything *for* film or TV: his output at the BBC consisted of 1,500 radio scripts. His books featured a lot of very arch, highly stylised slang (which was not how most people spoke in the '50s, even in Soho) and trying to get a workable screenplay together took the efforts of five different writers including Don MacPherson (*The Bawdy Adventures of Tom Jones*), Christopher Wicking (*Scream and Scream Again*), Terry Johnson (*Insignificance*), Michael Hamlyn and Richard Burridge. Along the way, the decision was taken to do the story as an out-and-out musical – somewhat in the style of *Expresso Bongo* ('59) – and a huge ensemble cast of actors, singers, dancers and musicians was put together led by Patsy Kensit, an 18-year-old singing actress, who was offered the part after being seen by Stephen Woolley performing in her band Eighth Wonder. (They had a No 1 in Italy in 1985, after filming was complete.) Her co-star, Eddie O'Connell, had no prior credits and was cast in the central role of the young photographer on a scooter, recording and commenting on the action. Bowie, James Fox, Mandy Rice-Davies (yes, the girl with the neat turn of phrase from the Profumo scandal), Ray Davies, Steven Berkoff and Lionel Blair all have supporting roles, but there are so many guest stars and cameos that watching the film is rather like sitting through the 1967 version of *Casino Royale* and constantly spotting well-known faces in tiny roles, some uncredited: in this case Sade, Edward Tudor-Pole, Robbie Coltrane, Jess Conrad, Ronald Fraser, Irene Handl, Peter-Hugo Daly, Johnny Shannon, Zoot Money, Sandie Shaw and Eric Sykes to name a modest selection.

Berkoff (playing a Mosley-type figure) and Lionel Blair (as an effete '50s pop promoter) are actually rather good. The problems start elsewhere. Kensit is neither as slatternly nor as vulnerable as suggested in the book. A young Diana Dors would have been perfect and, if not, the 1986 equivalents – wherever they were – of Carol White or Gillian Hills might have been better. Eddie O'Connell is much too young for his part. He looks about 17 whilst the photographers who emerged in the late '50s (Bailey, Donovan *et al.*) were all by this point in their mid-20s, had done military service and looked more considerable figures even if they weren't that much older. Bowie, playing a senior advertising executive with megalomaniac tendencies, looks about 30 and constantly on the verge of shooting a rock video. The reality in 1959 would have been that someone of that type, or anyone like it (say, a modernist architect about to brutalise the city with concrete towers), would have been older (about 50) and a heavyweight intellectual. The book is set amidst race riots but here they are choreographed like the fight scenes in *West Side Story*, which both minimises their impact at the time and plays down the urban disturbances that had occurred in the UK only a few years earlier. In summary, the film apes *Expresso Bongo*, which because it was a satire of a flimsy self-regarding world (rather like a UK version of *The Girl*

Can't Help It, '56) was actually better. With so many major fault lines the fact that the clothes and décor are not always accurate is a relatively minor point.

Nor is the music much like 1959. In keeping with the reverential approach to recent pop culture in *The Face*, much of the pre-publicity for the film talked about it having a 'jazz' soundtrack. Gil Evans, whose career stretched back to legendary collaborations with Charlie Parker and Miles Davis, was duly appointed to do the score. But Evans – by 1986 – was no longer recording in the style of 30 years earlier. (Post-1967 he led various ensembles that were closer to jazz-rock and at one point had planned to build a band around Jimi Hendrix.) He provides nine pieces of music here, which are a reasonable attempt at recreating the era, but somehow sound not quite of it. Instead the big winners musically were Bowie, who had a hit with the title song (No 2 UK and No 53 US) and Weller's post-Jam band The Style Council, who reached No 14 in the UK with *Have You Ever Had It Blue?* Sade appears in the film as a Billie Holiday-type figure singing *Killer Blow*, which, other than inclusion on the soundtrack album, went unreleased, an astonishing omission given her popularity at the time. Arguably the best and most surprising track on the official soundtrack, which came out on Virgin and was produced by Clive Langer, comes from Jerry Dammers, formerly of The Specials, whose *Riot City* is an eight-minute long jazz instrumental that sounds much more at home with the mood of the original book. In another striking omission, not all of the music included in the film made it to the soundtrack album; some by Smiley Culture and Tenpole Tudor were only on the CD and one, from Elvis Costello, was missing completely. Another oddity was the use of period music to recreate the mood of the time, hence we hear stuff by Wee Willie Harris, The Scorpions, Bertice Reading and Preston Epps (all accurate) alongside The Paragons, none of whose records was released in the UK. Laurel Aitken's *Landlord and Tenant*, a 1969 reggae single, is also included – and jars, being over a decade out of date. Were there no calypso tracks they could have found?

As to what might have been done instead, well: in the early '80s there had also been a rediscovery of the classic British social realism films of 20 years earlier: *Saturday Night and Sunday Morning*, *A Kind of Loving*, *Billy Liar* and so on. One wonders why, if MacInnes was rated so highly, his book wasn't filmed in this style – in black and white, in as many authentic locations as possible, with a carefully honed script and some of the British jazz from the period in question: Don Rendell, Tony Kinsey and others. Instead, the path chosen confirmed that the British don't do musicals. Not that the film was bereft of admirers. The scale and ambition of *Absolute Beginners* was liked, particularly by Martin Scorsese. But in box-office terms it was a major flop, which, with *Revolution* and *The Mission* also posting huge losses, caused Goldcrest to go bust and Virgin to hold back from film production for a couple of years.

Not that Bowie was particularly damaged by this spectacular implosion. In the mid-'80s his standing remained high in Germany and here he elected to do *Labyrinth* in 1986. Pitched somewhere between *Legend* and *The Company of Wolves*, this was developed by UK fantasy illustrator Brian Froud and US puppeteer Jim Henson from 1983 onwards. Henson's big commercial breakthrough had come with *The Muppet Show*, which ITV screened from 1976 onwards after Henson moved his entire production team to the UK because he couldn't get adequate backing for his various projects in the US. When his films *The Dark Crystal* ('82) and *The Muppets Take Manhattan* ('84) did well commercially, George Lucas agreed to produce his next feature. Terry Jones from the *Monty Python* team provided a script and had form in this area, having published a couple of much-liked children's books, *Fairy Tales* ('81) and *The Saga of Erik the Viking* ('83). Apparently, the original intention was to do *Labyrinth* as an adult-level entertainment (albeit one with an adolescent as the central character, rather like both *Time Bandits* and *The Company of Wolves*) with the action taking place in Victorian England.

Given the accumulated box-office receipts by the mid-'80s of *Star Wars*, *The Muppets* and *Python* could it fail? Unfortunately, yes. To begin with, films mixing live action, puppetry and special effects are always awkward and difficult to get right, and this was no exception. The script had problems too. After around 25 rewrites the end product was no longer similar to what Jones had started out with and had become instead a kind of semi-comedy. Then, the plot was switched to the US. As the production took shape, non-partisan observers noted so much of a resemblance to Maurice Sendak's '60s children's work *Where the Wild Things Are*, that Sendak ended up – after he had threatened legal action – being acknowledged in the credits. Casting the main roles also proved to be tricky. Sting, Mick Jagger, Prince and Michael Jackson all turned down the lead part of the goblin king before Bowie accepted it, and Helena Bonham Carter, 20, and just noticed after a supporting role in *A Room with a View*, was considered for the female lead before the role went instead to Jennifer Connelly, 16. Christopher Malcolm, who was in the original stage version of *The Rocky Horror Picture Show* in 1973, heads the limited number of supporting (non-puppet) roles. By way of contrast, Henson's great success, *The Muppets*, was satirical and targeted as much at adults as children. This, by comparison, is aimed at adolescent girls and rather than playing as a cyberpunk drama, as Jones originally intended, ended up being a traditional fairy-tale musical for children. It was released to mixed reviews and failed to perform at the box office, though as with many interesting failures it has its devotees today.

Bowie took the part because he sensed an opportunity to be in something that would be both a big-selling film and album in the US. He was wrong. The soundtrack album, made by him with a huge array of session players, was released on EMI but climbed no higher than No 38 UK and No 68 US. A single from it, *Underground*, reached No 21 in the UK. Not that any conclusions were drawn from this at the time. Bowie's reputation was still so stratospheric then that it wasn't yet apparent that he had passed a creative peak. The verdict on his career in later years was that between 1969 and 1981 he reigned supreme artistically, and commercially never surpassed *Let's Dance* ('83), his massive breakthrough in the US market. It was sad in some ways to see him, though competent, so thoroughly emasculated by *Labyrinth*. The role itself, and the setting of a children's film, was a bit of a regression for him back to the type of stuff he had done in his Anthony Newley period. Even his appearance is peculiar, sporting a huge amount of mullet-style hair. In truth, his acting career, which showed so much potential at the time of *The Man Who Fell to Earth*, was, by 1986, amounting to much less than expected. In the years that followed he would carry on appearing in film and TV projects, but managed just one more starring role in *The Linguini Incident* ('91), with his last major performance of any type being *Everybody Loves Sunshine* ('99) about gangs in Manchester (with a soundtrack to match) and essentially a vehicle for rapper Goldie.

6

DYSTOPIAS (I HAVE SEEN THE FUTURE: AND IT DOESN'T WORK)

The big trope in all historical and dramatic accounts of the '70s is the background landscape of power cuts, rubbish in the streets, political chaos, rioting strikers and general tattiness. Despite these circumstances being ascribed almost uniquely to the UK they were in fact common across the developed world throughout much of that decade, particularly after the 1973 oil price increase, which, following *The Limits to Growth*, a 1972 report from environmentalist group Club of Rome, seemed to justify gloomy expectations about the future. Factor into this as well the physical surroundings of London, where because of post-war planning policies, the population dropped by 25 per cent between 1939 and 1986 (which meant 2,000,000 fewer people in the city) and one can see how optimism draining away at the end of the '60s wasn't just about bands breaking up and US film producers going elsewhere.

Catastrophism had been a sub-genre of English literature since the '40s, producing works like *The Day of the Triffids* ('51, filmed '63) and *The Death of Grass* ('56, filmed '70). By the '70s, drawing inspiration from contemporary events, the same approach led to the TV series *Survivors* (April '75) about a virus that quickly wipes out most of the population, and *1990* ('77), which portrays the UK of the near future as a deeply repressive bureaucracy. The Anthony Burgess novel *1985* ('78) should also be noted. Here the country is run by unpleasant bullying trade unions, Burgess's vision having hardened considerably since *A Clockwork Orange*

('62). A wider (and somewhat more serious) socio-political view was shown in *Destiny*, a 1978 BBC *Play for Today* directed by Mike Newell from a 1977 West End stage hit about the impact of the collapse of Empire and the rise of the National Front. *Plenty* ('78) was a David Hare play about the crisis within the UK ruling class in post-war Britain; it was subsequently made into an all-star film ('85) with Tracey Ullman and Sting. Around the same time Hare wrote and directed *Wetherby* ('85), which, like *Plenty*, concentrated on a sense of national failure and wrong turnings being taken. A very entertaining study of changing social mores came from *The History Man* (BBC TV, '81) starring Anthony Sher and adapted from a Malcolm Bradbury satirical novel ('75) about the rise of an amoral, self-serving and superficially hip middle-class university lecturer.

Theatre was particularly receptive to works that explored the political, cultural and social direction of society. Given that by the mid-'70s many novels and short stories which would once have been made into films were now being made for TV, it was not surprising, in a similar downgrading, that material which once would have made it as far as a TV production ended up instead on the stage. Thus, notable examples of this type were *Line 'Em* ('80) with Zoot Money and Phil Daniels, a drama about a bitter industrial dispute directed by Christopher Morahan, *Way Upstream* ('81), an Alan Ayckbourn allegory about the state of the UK at the time, and *May Days* ('83), a David Hare play charting the journey of the UK political left since 1945, with Anthony Sher.

Dystopias were of course by no means just a UK fixation. Peter Watkins, once doom-merchant in chief with *The War Game* ('65), went to Denmark for *Evening Land* ('77) and considerably more mainstream equivalents from elsewhere included the Italian–German *Contamination* ('80), which owed not a little to *Alien*, the post-apocalyptic *Le Dernier Combat* ('83) from France and the Australian *Dead End Drive-In* ('86).

In terms of British productions, one of the earliest with a decent budget to emerge was *The Quatermass Conclusion*. Originally a typical early '70s drama involving societal breakdown, this is mixed up with stuff about stone circles, ley lines and UFOs and as such is the only film realisation of the philosophy of John Michell. A key '60s counterculture figure, Michell seemed to be almost everywhere at one point: allowing his home in Notting Hill Gate to be a meeting point for both Michael X and his activists and the London Free School, writing for the *International Times*, writing one of the great hippy texts of the period (*The View Over Atlantis*, '69) and eventually helping to organise the Glastonbury Fayre festival in 1971.

What we have in *The Quatermass Conclusion* though is not a happy, communitarian vision of the future. Like Michell's writing it's a bleak anti-humanist fable reflecting the right-wing points of view taking hold during the '70s and, as with the opinions of those partial to such tales, doesn't withstand very much factual analysis. The script, by Nigel Kneale, dated back to 1972 and forms the final chapter in his *Quatermass* series, arguably the best British science fiction of its time. Kneale had also done first-rate film adaptations of the kitchen-sink plays *Look Back in Anger* ('59) and *The Entertainer* ('60), as well as rather more curious works like *The Year of the Sex Olympics* ('68) and *Kinvig* ('81), the latter a UFO comedy. Originally due to be made and screened in 1973, it was delayed when the BBC protested about its budget. Eventually picked up by Thames TV it was finally filmed in early 1979 and shown that October in three parts. It ended up costing £1.2m – a huge amount then for a TV production. Possibly the best known and most watched of the dystopia dramas then popular, it was released as a film in the US and Europe.

Piers Haggard directed and John Mills stars alongside Simon MacCorkindale. The plot faithfully reflects Michell's predictions: civilisation has broken down – cue usual shots of rubbish-strewn city streets, derelict buildings and so on – and the remains of the population are gathering at stone circles near a few surviving hippy communes. From here, UFOs abduct them away. None of this is badly done at all, it's just that by 1979 notions of large-scale hippy communes were more than a tad dated.

The film has music by Nick Rowley and Marc Wilkinson.

Rowley briefly played keyboards with The Fabulous Poodles, who lived in a squat in Deptford and had done the arrangements for the only album released by therapist RD Laing: *Life Before Death* (Charisma, '78, and – bizarrely – produced by '60s hit makers Alan Blaikley and Ken Howard). Wilkinson's career included previous work on *If....*, *Family Life* and *The Triple Echo*. The first of these had been a Memorial Films production (they also did *Privilege* and *O Lucky Man!*) and in the early '80s Memorial also backed *Memoirs of a Survivor*. Based on a '74 Doris Lessing feminist science fiction novel about the UK in 'the near future', this was directed by David Gladwell, a film editor who formerly worked with Lindsay Anderson and had made many industrial documentaries. The book itself was written against the backdrop of power cuts, the three-day week, bomb attacks in UK cities and a consideration – by some – that an environmental collapse of an unspecified type was imminent. The setting is a wreckage-strewn and semi-derelict London, after a 'breakdown' of society, possibly caused by a nuclear war. The viewer today may look at this and consider, given that Lessing's UK of the near future resembles the street scenes in *Jubilee*, is this really science fiction? In the circumstances it was hardly surprising that although pigeon-holed as sci-fi, the critics didn't really know what to make of it and what we see is very much a mixture of *Concrete Island*, *1984* and *Alice in Wonderland*. Perhaps there is too much imagination on show here with a plot that trippily has a parallel narrative with flashbacks to and from an idyllic nineteenth-century house.

Julie Christie stars in what was her first role solely filmed in the UK since *The Go-Between* a decade earlier, and her first entirely UK film since *Far from the Madding Crowd*. The supporting cast is led by Leonie Mellinger playing a character clearly based on Jenny Diski, Lessing's lodger for a number of years, who eventually emerged as a writer in her own right and a sharp observer of the cultural mores of the '60s and '70s. Mellinger was a name to conjure with at this time, appearing in a BBC TV adaptation of *Sons and Lovers* the same year, as well as several quality films including a trio for Ken McMullen: *Ghost Dance* ('83; music by David Cunningham of The Flying Lizards assisted by Michael Giles and Jamie Muir, both ex-King Crimson), *Zina* ('85) and *Partition* ('87). Christopher Guard, an actor-singer, co-stars.

Memoirs of a Survivor has an electronic soundtrack, which remains unreleased, by Mike Thorne who produced Wire and Soft Cell and had also been the man behind the compilation LP *The Roxy London WC2*. Lessing's marginality was not restricted to her fiction. She was a political outcast too (within the Communist Party) and her next book, *The Good Terrorist* ('85), was set in the London of squats and communes. Representing the polar opposite of her world view, *Who Dares Wins* appeared only six months after *Memoirs of a Survivor*, but crucially premiered in the aftermath of the UK's victory in a war with Argentina over the status of the Falkland Islands. Based on a script by George Markstein (*Robbery*, *The Odessa File*) from a book by James Follett (who did a great deal of high-quality radio drama in the '70s and was a former MOD employee), it actually drew its inspiration from the May 1980 Iranian Embassy siege, the conclusion of which – the storming of the building by the SAS – had been broadcast live on TV. The heroics of the SAS were immediately considered worthy of a film by Euan Lloyd who had several big hits with noisy entertainments like *The Wild Geese* ('78) and *The Sea Wolves* ('80). Because of these Lloyd quickly landed distribution deals with Rank (UK) and MGM/United Artists (US).

The plot very much reflects the world view of rather paranoid right-wing types: the Campaign for Nuclear Disarmament (CND) has been infiltrated by a radical left group (The People's Lobby) who plan terrorist acts but are foiled by a joint UK–US operation. Ian Sharp, fresh from the cheap commercial populism of *The Music Machine*, directs and it stars Lewis Collins, whose career stretched back to Merseybeat as one of The Mojos (not something widely known in the '80s) before a switch to acting brought him a big hit with the TV series *The Professionals* ('77). The rest of the cast are led by Judy Davis (*My Brilliant Career*) and the ever-reliable Richard Widmark and Edward Woodward. The producers were so sure of the validity of their 'message' that the film was shown pre-release to President Reagan, who warmly endorsed it. Lloyd, believing this to be the start of a new genre, planned three follow-up dramas on similar themes and signed Collins to appear in them (presumably roaming around the UK sorting out troublemakers), but replaced him in *Wild Geese II* and never made the other two. Instead Collins made do with thick-ear stuff like *Code Name: Wild Geese* ('84) and *Commando Leopard* ('85). Off the back of *Who Dares Wins* he also auditioned for Bond. With Roger Moore now labouring through the part at 55, Cubby Broccoli was looking for young blood and Collins must have thought his chances of landing the role pretty good. But after being considered (as was David Warbeck, again), the producers stayed with Moore. Perhaps he used the wrong knife for eating fish.

One way of looking at *Who Dares Wins* might be that it was one of several attempts across the political spectrum to portray 'threat to democracy' issues in the early '80s. Two others, also dating from 1982, include Chris Mullin's novel *A Very British Coup* (filmed for TV in '88), in which a democratically elected left-wing UK government is overthrown by the establishment working hand in glove with the US, and Peter Flannery's play *Our Friends in the North* (filmed for TV in '96), which has the political establishment inflicting corruption on ordinary people and periodically sacrificing one of its own to cover this up. *Who Dares Wins*, of course, is firmly on the political right and offers a simple, nicely unsophisticated right-wing message for the times: any views other than the official views on the Cold War and nuclear weapons are dangerous pseudo-communist propaganda that must be rooted out. Like all Lloyd's successes, it was well made and despite bad reviews raining down did good business at the box office in both the UK and the US. And yet... neither Collins nor Lloyd progressed much further. By the mid-'80s Lloyd had retired from film production and Collins had returned to a diminishing array of TV parts.

The soundtrack was done by Roy Budd assisted by Marc Donahue, formerly of French folk-psych outfit Tangerine. Donahue also appears in the film as one of various hirsute band members entertaining the CND revolutionaries in a squat

somewhere, the others being Gerry Conway (previously in Cat
Stevens' backing band), Dave Pegg and Jerry Donahue (both ex-
Fairport Convention). The same team had scored Lloyd's earlier
hit *The Wild Geese*, which even boasted a main title theme by Joan
Armatrading: indicating, possibly, that the producer was straining
to create something elegiac.

Inevitably, as the '80s progressed the opportunity arose – and
was taken – to film *1984*, the dystopia from which all others
sprang. A world in which the future looks like 1948 imagined
in a distant parallel universe, the book had been published in
1949, with author George Orwell having to be dissuaded from
calling it *1948*. The adaptation that appeared in the year it was
set was the fifth for film or TV and reached the screen as a grim
drama, faithfully reflecting the downbeat nature of its material.
Produced and financed by Virgin films, it was written and
directed by Michael Radford after he had completed the WWII
drama *Another Time, Another Place* and boasts a big UK cast led by
Richard Burton and John Hurt, supported by Suzanna Hamilton
(*Brimstone and Treacle*, *Wetherby*) and Cyril Cusack. Critics thought
both Burton and Hurt 'monotonous', though what else they
could have done with their roles is hard to imagine given that the
material remorselessly points that way. Both Burton and Cusack
had previously worked together in the equally glum *The Spy Who
Came in from the Cold* ('65), the tone of which (futility, betrayal,
grubby compromise) is replicated here. An excellent adaptation of
the book, this has good sets, décor and performances.

For some years Orwell's classic had attracted the attention of
singers and groups as a source from which ideas and images could
be culled. In 1974 Bowie released *Diamond Dogs* (No 1 UK and No
5 US), a state-of-the-nation concept album with songs like *1984*
and *Big Brother*, having previously tried – circa 1972 – to stage
a rock opera of the work. There was even talk, then, of a film
version of the same with Wayne County and Terence Stamp, no
less. But nothing emerged. Later, in 1977, The Jam referenced the
book on their LP *This is the Modern World* (No 22 UK) and in
1981 Rick Wakeman rolled out a concept album, *1984*, assisted by

the likes of Tim Rice, Chaka Khan and Steve Harley. It charted, reaching No 24 in the UK, confirming that material inspired by or adapted from Orwell's work was hot and marketable. For the film Bowie was approached to do the soundtrack, but declined due to his US and global commitments. Instead an original score was commissioned from Dominic Muldowney, who'd worked with John Cage and Bowie (on *Baal*), but ended up being heavily supplemented – at the insistence of Virgin – by electronic disco music from The Eurythmics. This was subsequently released as the LP *1984 (For the Love of Big Brother)*, reaching No 23 in the UK with a spin-off single *Sexcrime (1984)* peaking at No 4.

It was Burton's final performance, at only 58, and he went out in style. The film itself is in some ways an interesting example of that typically British product: the elegantly mounted period drama or literary adaptation. It got its costs back in the UK and Europe, but wasn't a success in the US.

Radford shot *1984* in many of the same places mentioned in the original book, which illustrates perfectly how little some parts of London had changed since the '40s. It shared many of its locations, including the recently decommissioned Battersea Power Station, with *Brazil*, so much so that the latter film was nicknamed *1984½*. A brilliantly conceived dystopian fantasy directed by Terry Gilliam, *Brazil* portrays an alternative future in which society is dominated by a massive bureaucracy. Based on a script co-written by Tom Stoppard, who was on something of a roll at this point, like much of his work, notably *Jumpers* ('72) and *Travesties* ('74) in particular, it explores absurdist situations in which the characters confront the nature of power, social control and historical forces. Stoppard had moved into feature films with *Despair* ('78, a crazy Fassbinder drama set in the Weimar Republic) and *The Human Factor* ('79, from Graham Greene and set in Africa), but *Brazil* is his best script and as Kafkaesque as anything by the great man himself. (Like Kafka, Stoppard was Czech, having fled the country as a child.) The film was produced by Arnon Milchan, who had previously been involved with *Black Joy* and whose other mid-'80s credits included *King of Comedy*, *Once Upon a Time in America* and

Legend. Jonathan Pryce, Robert De Niro and Michael Palin star, with Pryce playing a harmless simpleton who stumbles through the plot before being eliminated by the forces of the state.

As with the film version of Orwell's *1984*, great attention was paid by Gilliam to ensuring that the end result had a fully realised and richly detailed appearance. This was entrusted to John Beard, Keith Pain and Norman Garwood, all of whom had worked with Gilliam and the Python team previously, and who, collectively, were responsible for what we would call today the cyberpunk visuals. Garwood, in particular, had prior credits in TV where he had recreated the look of the '40s and the totalitarian era generally in *London Belongs to Me* ('77) and *Red Monarch* ('83).

The music is by Michael Kamen, once of The New York Rock and Roll Ensemble, a rock-classic fusion band rather like The Nice (but with a gentler, less bombastic sound) who signed to Atlantic in 1967. His prior film work ranged from *Zachariah* ('71) through *The Next Man* ('76, a Sean Connery thriller set in the Middle East) to *Polyester* ('81, Divine). He also produced Tim Curry's various forays into the music world and worked with Pink Floyd on the film soundtrack of *The Wall* ('82). Ray Cooper assisted him. Another long-standing Gilliam/Python collaborator, Cooper's film work included Apple's indigestible *Son of Dracula* ('74), *Tommy* ('75) and *Scrubbers* ('83).

To evoke the period and match the film's general mood, the song *Brazil* was selected and versions from both Geoff Muldaur and Kate Bush were used in the film. Muldaur had originally recorded it with his then wife Maria on his 1968 album *Pottery Pie*. However, Bush's contemporary cut serves as the main theme. The song itself, a bossa nova, dated back to 1939 and first charted with Xavier Cugat in 1943. With lyrics that suggested a mixture of the exotic, grim and hopeless, it was a good choice. Gilliam's bleak vision proved a difficult sell to distributors, particularly in the US. A straight to video release was mooted, but it eventually reached cinema screens (as did *Blade Runner* after similar tribulations) with a happy/happier ending tacked on rather than the original downbeat conclusion. It lost money, as did most of Milchan's

The formidable Jordan, aka Pamela Rooke, outside 430 Kings Road SW10

David Bowie begins his journey in *The Man Who Fell To Earth* (1976)

ONCE UPON A TIME IN BRIXTON
Norman Beaton confronts Trevor Thomas in *Black Joy* (1977)

SOMEWHERE IN LONDON, 1978 **A typical scene from *Jubilee***

DELIBERATELY OBSCENE AND HUGELY AMUSING
Peter Cook and Dudley Moore as Derek and Clive (1979 – Derek and Clive)

THE SCIENCE FICTION THEATRE OF LIVERPOOL PRESENTS
THE SPECTACULAR STAGE VERSION OF DOUGLAS ADAMS'

THE HITCHHIKER'S GUIDE TO THE GALAXY

STEAM-RADIO BROADCAST MARCH A.D. 1978 (EARTH)

Don't Panic!

I.C.A. THEATRE, THE MALL
TUES. MAY 1 – SAT. MAY 19
TUESDAY-SUNDAY: 8·00
SATS. MAY 5 & 19) MATINEE 2·30
SUN. MAY 6 }
TICKETS £1·50

FEATURING UNIQUE AIRBORNE AUDITORIUM!
AIRSKATES BY ROLAIR SYSTEMS (UK) LTD
AIR BY MOTIVAIR.

DEMAND THE IMPOSSIBLE

The programme for Ken Campbell's stage adaptation of
The Hitchhiker's Guide to the Galaxy (1979)

SHELL SHOCK ROCK

THE FILM OF ROCK MUSIC IN NR. IRELAND.
FEATURING:—
* THE UNDERTONES
* STIFF LITTLE FINGERS
* THE OUTCASTS
* RUDI
* PROTEX & MANY OTHERS

AND LIVE

RUDI
THE OUTCASTS

AT THE U.C.C. DOWNTOWN CAMPUS.
ON SAT. 30th. JUNE, FROM 10.00-2.00

TYPICAL OF MANY OF THE DIY PUNK FILMS
Shellshock Rock (1979) features many of Ireland's finest acts of that time

MICHAEL WHITE presents

THE CLASH

RUDE BOY X

Produced and Directed by
JACK HAZAN
DAVID MINGAY

Michael White made a lot of money producing Monty Python and Rocky Horror;
sadly The Clash in their sole film outing failed to replicate this – *Rude Boy* (1980)

Michael Moorcock's novel of the album of the film
of *The Great 'N' Roll Swindle* (1980)

Time Bandits (1981), the first of a remarkable trilogy of films from Terry Gilliam

IN HER NATURAL HABITAT
Joan Collins models the 70s idea of eroticism and glamour from *The Bitch* (1979)

productions around this time, but critically was regarded as a significant cultural success. It's almost a great film and after this one felt that Gilliam could do almost anything. His next project, *The Adventures of Baron Munchausen* ('88), also lost a huge amount, but, like *Brazil*, was another superbly realised vision.

Almost as brilliant was *Max Headroom: 20 Minutes into the Future*. Set in a *Blade Runner*-type world where corporations rule the Earth, this was originally a UK TV film produced by Terry Ellis, long the force behind Chrysalis records. Like many ventures at this time it had a lengthy genesis. In 1981 Channel 4 were looking for programmes they could commission and asked Chrysalis to come up with some ideas: what emerged was a concept for a music-video series, based on a treatment worked up – mainly – by Peter Wagg, a rock video producer, and George Stone, an advertising copywriter and science fiction writer. This envisaged the series being presented by the character Max Headroom, for whom an elaborate and detailed backstory was devised by Stone assisted by Rocky Morton and Annabel Jankel, who, like Wagg, were directors of music videos. It turns out that Headroom is an artificial man-made replacement for Edison Carter, a campaigning TV reporter dedicated to exposing corruption and greed. During the course of various misadventures Carter collides accidentally with a sign labelled 'Max. Headroom 2.3m' and is then sedated and replaced by his employers with a computerised version of himself (Headroom), which they use to disguise his disappearance. But the replacement keeps stuttering 'max headroom' and eventually turns out to be quite a success with its own show on a pirate TV station. Finally, Headroom (and Carter, whose body comes back to life) defeats his corrupt employer and triumphs. Chrysalis and Channel 4 were so fascinated by the intricacies of the plot that they decided to make a standalone film in addition to the series. Once the funding was in place – it eventually came from HBO, which bought both the film and the series for its cable network in the US – Morton and Jankel, who had done promos for Elvis Costello and Tom Tom Club (a Talking Heads offshoot), were assigned to direct.

The task of turning Stone's ideas into a manageable screenplay fell to Steve Roberts, who in 1980 had written and directed *Sir Henry at Rawlinson End*, another odd feature film, adapted from an equally odd Vivian Stanshall album (and study of English eccentricity) much loved by John Peel. Further work in polishing the end product came from none other than Colin Wilson: circa 1956 he was the prototype Angry Young Man and subsequently a writer much taken with the occult, as well as being the author of several highly rated late '60s science fiction novels. In fact, sci-fi is the genre where *Max Headroom: 20 Minutes into the Future* most properly belongs. It plays around with the Philip K Dick notion that we can't really be certain about what is human (and what isn't), is set in a near-future with a still vaguely recognisable landscape, à la Michael Moorcock and JG Ballard, and effectively gives us an early example of cyberpunk.

Both the film and the series premiered in April 1985, with Carter/Headroom played by Matt Frewer, a tall, angular Canadian actor. Virgin distributed and the weekly shows lasted through to December 1986 featuring various top musical acts of the time. It was hugely popular in the US where another series was commissioned in 1987. *Robocop* ('87), a massive US hit and a franchise that ran for 30 years across film, TV, animation, video games and comic books, is similar with its premise of an individual fighting corruption inside a faceless 'corporation' and being replaced by a robot. The migration of *Headroom* across the Atlantic, where it was exploited much more efficiently, thus provides yet another example of a missed opportunity in the '80s for what was left of the UK film industry. And typically, despite the US success, many of those involved found the immediate rewards rather limited. Jankel and Morton eventually did a remake of the '40s thriller *DOA* ('88) and followed that up, five years later, with *Super Mario Brothers* ('93), a film version of a video game with Bob Hoskins and Dennis Hopper. Frewer played many smallish supporting roles before landing a big starring part in *Honey, I Shrunk the Kids* ('89). George Stone fared worst of all – his name was missed off the credits and he struggled to work for years afterwards, with many disbelieving his assertions that he was the man who created Max Headroom.

The title theme, a fine piece of symphonic synthesiser pop, was by Midge Ure and Chris Cross, still at this point members of Ultravox, and was produced by Rik Walton, whose credits included work with Ian Dury, Tenpole Tudor, This Heat and The Gang of Four. An interesting by-product was *Paranoimia*, featuring Headroom (Frewer) and The Art of Noise, which charted at No 12 UK and No 34 US in May '86.

But of all the grim, futurist works so beloved of film and TV producers in the '70s and '80s, *Edge of Darkness* ('85) was surely the bleakest, the weirdest and in some ways the trippiest. It must be a candidate for being possibly the ultimate '80s dystopian thriller: a genre where the action is usually shown as either being accidental (a meteor strike, an epidemic), or caused by a helpless, incompetent government (a breakdown of law and order, a sudden collapse of society) with some variations on these even having a benign 'back to the land' message. The plot in *Edge of Darkness* reflects the hard politics prevailing in the UK by the mid-'80s: the government is deliberately executing a plan that will inflict damage on part or even all of the country. But unlike *The Quatermass Conclusion*, with which this makes an interesting comparison, this isn't based on unverifiable assumptions about UFOs and alien abductions being 'covered up' by the state. Instead, it was written at the peak of the Cold War and in the expectation (accurate as it turned out) that a massive strike would be provoked with the National Union of Mineworkers, at the conclusion of which much traditional industry would be destroyed, with the government being clearly complicit in this. It also appeared at a time when TV networks were backing away from thought-provoking drama: *Play for Today* ended in August '84, and the new emphasis was mainly on entertainments... game shows, comedies and soaps that explored – at best – emotional rather than openly political agendas.

The script came from Troy Kennedy Martin, a very highly regarded BBC writer who moved from the pioneering series *Z*

Cars in 1962 to big screen credits like *The Italian Job* ('69), *Kelly's Heroes* ('70), as well as the much less well known *The Jerusalem File* ('72). The last, a drama about attempted peace initiatives in the Arab-Israeli conflict, how they are undermined and people who are not always who they seem to be, has some similarities to his plot in *Edge of Darkness* about a policeman investigating the murder of his daughter, who ends up enmeshed in the murky depths of government cover-ups and nuclear espionage. In fact, Martin was heavily influenced by the politics of the time, particularly the aura of secrecy surrounding the nuclear industry. Considering it unlikely that his script would be produced, he wrote it anyway so that in a worst-case scenario it would survive as a document of what might have been made, had the circumstances been better. He also had time for the views of environmentalist guru James Lovelock and the Gaia hypothesis: namely that all elements of life on Earth are interrelated and if recklessly interfered with by Man, nature will take its revenge.

The soundtrack has original music composed by Eric Clapton and Michael Kamen and also features songs by New Model Army and Tom Waits, the latter a long-standing John Peel favourite who was just beginning to crack the UK market at this time. Much of the material has a quasi-mystical feel, in keeping with the script, which explored pagan notions about the spiritual world and the need to defend long-standing civilised values. Little of it was

Martin Campbell directed, having made his reputation on TV series like *The Professionals* ('77), and the cast was led by stage actor Bob Peck as the police officer and Joe Don Baker, usually seen in westerns, as a CIA officer. Joanne Whalley, who had been in the bands Cindy and The Saffrons and The Slowguns between 1979 and 1983, plays Peck's daughter. Broadcast in six episodes on BBC TV in late 1985, it won immense praise for the enormous power of its script, acting and the thought-provoking nature of its plot. It is still rated one of the best TV dramas broadcast and swept the board at the 1986 BAFTA awards. Campbell subsequently moved on to make the Bond reboot *Casino Royale* (2006) and in 2010 even did a remake of *Edge of Darkness* with Mel Gibson.

released: BBC Records and Tapes issuing instead a limited edition on vinyl of the six Clapton/Kamen tracks.

A softer approach to *Memoirs of a Survivor*, *Brazil* and *Edge of Darkness* was taken by *When the Wind Blows* ('86). The first UK animation feature since *Yellow Submarine* ('68) and only the second since *Animal Farm* ('54), this was based on the Raymond Briggs graphic novel of the same name. By the mid-'80s Briggs was massively popular, particularly following the publication of *The Snowman* ('78), and had worked in cartoons and illustration since a spell in art school back in the '50s. Because of the turn that UK politics took in 1979 he found himself drawing overtly political material that chimes with the views of those who opposed Thatcher and Reagan.

And, as many maintained then, there was much to be concerned about with both these individuals. Specifically, the increased threat of nuclear war, due, it was considered, to the deployment by Reagan of cruise missiles in the UK, and the complete destruction of all life in the country should a conflict start with the Soviet Union. In the early '80s membership of CND increased at a phenomenal rate, Duncan Campbell published his gloomy study of the British secret state in *War Plan UK: The Truth about Civil Defence in Britain* ('82) and matters were only inflamed by the appearance of *Protect and Survive* ('80), the laughably inadequate official guidance prepared for issuing to households in the event that a nuclear attack was imminent. The plot in Briggs' book shows how a simple, trusting elderly working-class couple die an agonising death after a nuclear war with the Soviet Union has started – despite following government advice. The film is a huge critique of the complacent UK position, which left people in ignorance of the actual consequences of such a catastrophe.

Produced by John Coates, who worked on *Yellow Submarine* as production supervisor, it was directed by Jimmy Murakami, who produced an animation feature of Nilsson's *The Point* in 1971 before directing the film of *The Snowman* ('82). Coates had also done *Heavy Metal*, a 1981 animation feature set to music by Devo, Blue Oyster Cult, Cheap Trick, Nazareth, Black Sabbath and others. The big screen version of *When the Wind Blows* followed adaptations for stage and radio and featured main characters voiced, all the more effectively, by the quintessentially understated English thespians John Mills and Peggy Ashcroft.

There was probably no one better to do the soundtrack than Roger Waters, one-time Chair of Cambridge Young CND (in the late '50s), whose writing and recording of anti-war pieces stretched back to Pink Floyd and *Corporal Clegg* ('68). He released a solo album, *The Pros and Cons of Hitch Hiking*, in 1984, but compared to the Floyd it sold poorly (No 13 UK and No 31 US). A film was planned of this but nothing emerged, and *When the Wind Blows* became, in effect, his debut film score as a solo artist, his departure from the band having been confirmed a year earlier. Hugh Cornwell, Genesis, Squeeze and Paul Hardcastle (whose anti-Vietnam single *19* hit No 1 in the UK and Europe in '85) were also involved. David Bowie was on hand, too, for the main title theme, *When the Wind Blows*. The fifth release from him used in a major film or TV production, it was the least successful, reaching only No 44 in the UK and not troubling the US charts at all.

The tone of the film was in fact very much an exception: throughout the '70s and '80s the UK tended to avoid cosy entertainment-based versions of catastrophic events, preferring instead the grim documentary style of TV shows like *Threads* ('84), where a nuclear war breaks out and Sheffield is incinerated. Extremely realistic (its credits list many eminent scientific advisers), like Watkins' earlier film *The War Game* ('65) this stresses what a nuclear war, and life for those surviving it, would actually be like. Written by Barry Hines (best known for *Kes*, '69), *Threads*, like *When the Wind Blows*, was made at a time when there was much concern in the public domain about nuclear apocalypse and both films serve as fictionalised composites of *War Plan UK* and *Protect and Survive*. Mick Jackson directed and, staying in Sheffield, later did *A Very British Coup* ('88, from the '82 Chris Mullin novel), in which a left-wing UK government is eased out of power by the machinations of the secret state.

But, whatever the quality of *Threads, Edge of Darkness* and

Memoirs of a Survivor, as far as most people were concerned the best, most successful and stupendously well-done dystopias were surely the gleaming visions of Ridley Scott revealed in *Alien* ('79) and *Blade Runner* ('82). Scott had worked in TV in the '60s before concentrating on commercials and *Alien* itself was shot in the UK in 1978-9 with a cast that included Ian Holm and John Hurt. *Blade Runner* was filmed in the US with a US cast after Scott had abandoned the idea of doing *Dune*, though UK producer Michael Deeley raised funds for it from Hong Kong. Both were huge and lasting international successes and eclipsed anything the UK produced; and 40-odd years later neither has dated. As with *Max Headroom: 20 Minutes into the Future*, both of Scott's films represented enormous missed opportunities for the UK's declining cinema industry.

7
PUNK: BIRTH

If one single individual could link the many disparate threads connecting drab '50s Britain and the explosion of pop culture in the '60s with the second coming of psychedelia in 1988 and Cool Britannia, it would be John Peel. Emerging out of a post-war black and white world where he was at school with Michael Palin and, like all young men then, did his National Service, by the early '60s he had emigrated to the US where everything, abruptly, erupted into colour.

Amongst other things, he was in the room when Ruby shot Oswald, he landed a radio show in Texas because of his 'Liverpool accent', he had an absurdly young teenage wife (like Jerry Lee Lewis), he floated around the North Sea on Radio London presenting *The Perfumed Garden* and he managed a fine early psychedelic group, The Misunderstood. Radio 1 claimed him in 1967 and he toured the UK in a van living the rock 'n' roll lifestyle, much of this diligently recorded by him in *International Times* and *Sounds*. He did all the early festivals, started his own record label (Dandelion), hit once with Medicine Head and missed with everything else... did he seriously think anything called *1917 Revolution* – by Beau – would make the charts? Everyone listened to Peel. His stints on *Night Ride*, *Sounds of the Seventies* and *Top Gear* were an enduring rite of passage for successive generations, a religious experience with Peel as the high priest administering the sacraments. He was even exported via the BBC World Service.

For years anyone wanting to know what was happening in the counterculture or just anxious to spot a coming trend could do so just by tuning into his show. David Bowie, Marc Bolan, Roxy Music, Dr. Feelgood and The Damned were all given crucial early breaks, as were many others from dub reggae to industrial noise exponents to the wild diversification of styles from the late '80s onwards. Throughout it all he was defiantly low tech, remaining on radio. He didn't transfer to TV and there was no grand move into film. His loss in 2004, aged 65, was like a death in the family.

Like Peel, a small number of broadcasters, musicians, actors and writers acted as midwives at the birth of the new post-'60s counterculture. Alchemists at work on the fringes, turning base metal into gold and for the main resolute, defiant, outsiders. Acting singly rather than collectively, and often in isolation, few of these trailblazers were taken up by film or TV, but between them they created much of the audio, written and visual framework that appeared after 1975 and remains highly regarded to this day.

Amazing as it may seem in the digital age, before Charlie Gillett – who taught film studies at Kingsway College – nobody remembered anything about rock and pop. As Warhol, Richard Hamilton and many other exponents of pop-art declared, it was mass-produced and largely disposable: so why keep a documentary record? Going against this, in 1972 Gillett wrote *Rock File*, which diligently listed every hit single that the UK had had since the charts started in the early '50s and illustrated, simply and economically, everything that a few years earlier would have quietly faded away. By virtue of this simple action an entire generation of would-be musicians and cultural archaeologists were given an immediate historical perspective of what had sold, what the main trends had been, and, importantly, as they rifled through jumble sales and charity shops for copies of old records, what might be valuable (and what might not). Hired by BBC Radio London and given his own show, Gillett also provided early exposure for acts like Ian Dury and Jona Lewie, both of whom exuded a unique type of English drollness. Second only to John Peel, and like him low key and self-deprecating, Gillett also ran Oval records from 1974, whose occasional and eclectic output – stretching from semi-forgotten Bayou bluesters like Johnnie Allan via new-wave act Holly and The Italians to Jah Wobble's Invaders of the Heart – rarely, if ever, sold. However, the list of bands and singers he discovered and recommended to others was very lengthy.

Like Gillett and Peel, Ian Dury was a typical product of the '60s, teaching at various art schools from 1967, exhibiting at the Institute of Contemporary Arts (ICA) and even doing commercial design work for *The Sunday Times*. Around 1970, whilst at Canterbury School of Art, he moved into music, initially jamming and declaiming with former members of The People Band, some of whom had previously been in Pete Brown and The Battered Ornaments. Out of this emerged Kilburn and The High Roads, and by 1972, Dury had found his voice, which, crucially, was the opposite then of what everyone else was doing. As was his image: defiantly anti-fashion and dressed midway between a '30s costermonger and a '50s biker (Gene Vincent was a great favourite).

Managed by Charlie Gillett and then Tommy Roberts (whose shop 'Mr Freedom' had become by the early '70s the McLaren/Westwood HQ), the venture failed. But Dury persisted. By 1977 he had a deal with Stiff, a new writing partner (Chaz Jankel, formerly in straight rock outfit Byzantium) and a new group, inherited 100 per cent from '60s pirate radio operator Ronan O'Rahilly and, embarrassingly, previously known as the Loving Awareness Band: not that this was advertised as such at the time. By now his affairs were handled by Peter Jenner and Andrew King, who started out managing Pink Floyd and had considerable prior experience of handling wayward talents like Syd Barrett, Kevin Ayers and Roy Harper. A period of great success followed between 1977 and 1981, after which it all fell apart again and Dury faded somewhat. Given his character, a carefully honed cockney/wideboy construct, and his lyrical style, a surrealist take on rhyming slang, this was perhaps inevitable as such a persona – outside mainstream Saturday night comedy – was too particular to last.

Reunited with Jankel, Dury did the theme music for the TV

series *The Secret Diary of Adrian Mole Aged 13¾* ('85), after which he got a couple of starring roles in Farrukh Dhondy's excellent BBC drama *King of the Ghetto* (with Tim Roth) and the now barely seen UK road movie *Rocinante* ('86). By the end of the decade, though, he had faded away and earned his living via one-off prestige gigs, occasional guest slots on other bands' albums and medium-scale acting parts. Ultimately his importance came down to the way in which he extracted his songs and appearance from everyday surroundings, and how easy it was doing this in London at that time – not making a tremendous living out of it, but managing somehow to get from one year to the next whilst making his way in the scene.

Throughout much of this period Dury lived in very cheap temporary housing in Oval Mansions (near Charlie Gillett, hence the name of Gillett's record label) and, like a magpie, found odd bits of discarded clothing and jewellery in charity shops and customised them into his ensemble stage outfit. He pioneered the use of razor blade earrings. The Sex Pistols were great admirers. His singing style (he couldn't, in a conventional sense, sing) with a hunched demeanour, menacing delivery and rasping voice had many imitators, not least John Lydon. As Nik Cohn once pointed out about Buddy Holly: in the late '50s teenagers saw Holly live with his simple songs and average singing and thought '*I* could do that, too.' Similarly, in the '70s a new generation saw Dury live and reached the same view. Or if not 'do that', at least 'do' something similar.

Like Ian Dury, Ken Campbell specialised in outré entertainments and had little time for convention. In his case that meant avoiding repertory company work and touring the UK in a van, like a band, with members of his own experimental theatre project. Like Dury, too, he went way back, appearing in a supporting role in *Poor Cow* ('67) and even at one point doing a magic act on *The Dusty Springfield Show*. By the '70s he was based in Liverpool where he assembled *Illuminatus!*, a vast, sprawling adaptation of a US conspiracy theory/sci-fi/counterculture novel by two former contributors to *Playboy* magazine, Robert Shea and

Robert Anton Wilson. Reckoned on publication to be 'the biggest sci-fi cult novel to come along since *Dune*', this had set designs by Bill Drummond, whose subsequent career, through punk, new wave, the rebirth of psychedelia and British art provides a cultural continuum across six decades. Campbell's version was nine hours long, obliging the audience to spend the entire day in the theatre. But it transferred – incredibly, as the opening production – to the National Theatre in 1977. Having done the undoable once, Campbell did it a second time with a stage version at the ICA of *The Hitchhiker's Guide to the Galaxy*, in which the audience moved around the auditorium on a hovercraft. Around this time, he almost 'made it' with a starring role in the BBC TV series *Law and Order*, but then failed an audition for *Doctor Who* (deemed 'too dark') and was restricted instead to a long list of minor TV and film parts in material like *The Tempest*, *Breaking Glass*, *The Bride* and *A Zed & Two Noughts* that he used to subsidise his own more experimental work. Still, like his protégé Drummond, he saw it through to Cool Britannia and in 1998 did *Macbeth* in pidgin English, deadpanning that it was a 'great improvement' on Shakespeare's original. Campbell was interested in whatever was 'out there', whatever was on the fringes that couldn't be accommodated in mainstream culture. A big fan of the *Fortean Times*, he could often be found at their annual Unconvention in the company of writers like Brian Aldiss.

Aldiss was a great author of dystopian sci-fi (and also, with *A Soldier Erect*, wrote arguably the best personal memoir of active service in WWII). In 1977 he published *Brothers of the Head*, about a pair of conjoined twins forming a punk band. It took 28 years before anyone made it into a film. Aldiss, though, was not writer of choice for fans of punk, new wave and industrial music: for the cognoscenti this crown was firmly worn by JG Ballard. Originally, like Aldiss, dystopian, Ballard's *Crash*, *Concrete Island*, *High-Rise* trilogy (1973–5) wrenched entirely believable, albeit extreme, plots out of the fabric of UK urban life at this time – derelict inner-city areas, semi-complete motorways, obsessions with modern technology and casual violence. Specifically, these were set in locations in and around north Westminster and North Kensington, an environment rich with dramatic and cinematic possibilities: as can be seen in the film *Leo the Last* ('70). Available in paperback – and very widely read – Ballard's work directly inspired John Foxx, Joy Division, Hawkwind, The Creatures and Gary Numan through to The Manic Street Preachers. Even Madonna (with *Drowned World*) and Buggles (with *Video Killed the Radio Star*, a no 1 hit in 1979, and inspired by Ballard's story *The Sound Sweep*) got in on the act.

High-Rise ('75) was a particular favourite of Joy Division singer Ian Curtis. Immediately optioned for a film, with Nic Roeg due to direct, the production fell apart amidst the financial difficulties then prevalent. Had it been completed, surely an ideal choice for supporting feature on its release would have been *Towers of Babel*, the 1981 surreal comedy set in a tower block with Ken Campbell and music by Georg Kajanus of Sailor and, previously, Eclection. Instead it took until 2016 (41 years, eleven years longer than Aldiss had to wait) to appear and when it did, with music by Clint Mansell of late '80s act Pop Will Eat Itself, it amazed contemporary audiences at how relevant it still appeared to be. What, exactly, had we done with the intervening years? And why did something 40+ years old still seem so fresh?

But apart from Peel, Gillett, Dury, Campbell and Ballard, one of the key instigators and influences of the trends that would erupt in the UK in the mid-'70s was the fashion boutique at 430 King's Road SW10. The building itself isn't that remarkable: an end-of-terrace shop with two floors of residential above. It may have been on the King's Road (albeit its 'wrong end'), but there were tens of thousands of similar looking properties across London, and many more beyond. Nevertheless, it was out of this address that much of the new clothing and music of the '70s would appear before being picked up and disseminated by others throughout society as a whole.

Nik Cohn spotted it first: operated by Michael Rainey as 'Hung on You' and 'simultaneously the last fling of dandyism and the first intimation of Hippie, of strangenesses to come'. When

'Swinging London' faded Rainey sold up to Tommy Roberts, who ran it as 'Mr Freedom' from 1969, selling retro '40s stuff and kitsch material generally and, indicative of what was to come, with an inflatable sex doll stuck on the front of the shop.

Malcolm McLaren and Vivienne Westwood arrived in 1970 selling '50s records from a back room... stuff that was difficult to find back then and thus chiming in with what Charlie Gillett and *ZigZag* proprietor Pete Frame were doing in rediscovering rock's recent history. They took over the lease and renamed it 'Let it Rock' in 1971 with a business plan built around supplying '50s clothes to films, such as *That'll Be the Day* and *Tommy*, as well as selling to a tiny section of the public. In many ways this was quite a radical step. Given that 1971 was 'peak hippy' they were deliberately the opposite: flash, retro, glamorous. They had a pop-up boutique at the Wembley Rock and Roll Festival at Wembley in 1972, but then became tired of the unthinking conservatism of the Teddy Boy crowd. The shop was relaunched as 'SEX' in 1974 and did some leather costumes, daubed with swastikas for Ken Russell's *Mahler* the same year. By now McLaren wanted to go the whole hog and manage a band as well. On a trip to New York he signed up The New York Dolls (who broke up a few months later), but more importantly he saw Richard Hell in his prime, replete with ripped clothes, safety pins, hair spiked up into greasy spires and garage-band music. On his return to London he began assembling a group that would replicate this image in the UK.

McLaren's journey to King's Road notoriety started in Stamford Hill in the early '60s as one of the young mods who congregated at places like the Super Cinema, in its latter guise as the UK's first bowling alley. Marc Bolan was another, as were Bernie Rhodes, at that point a close friend of McLaren's, and Johnny Moke. By the late '60s Rhodes was sharing a flat with John Pearse, owner of 'Granny Takes a Trip' (488 King's Road), in whose basement Moke was running his first bespoke footwear shop. It was quite a small scene. McLaren meanwhile moved on to Croydon Art College where he made another significant friendship – Robin Scott. A writer/musician (very vogue at that time), Scott released an album in 1969 on which he was backed by Mighty Baby, formerly The Action. One of the better-rated bands on the London scene, their journey took them, in the space of three years, from mod icons, all RAF roundels and scooters, via the esoteric interests of their guitarist Martin Stone to Crowley, Gurdjieff and Sufi Islam by the early '70s. Scott later managed bands on the London pub-rock circuit (Roogalator being the best known) and had his own label, Do It, named after a track by The Pink Fairies. In April 1979, as M, and unrecognisable as the acid-folk performer of a decade earlier, he hit No 2 in the UK charts with *Pop Muzik*, a brilliant satirical send-up of the industry and its foibles. In time, McLaren would follow this path too with his own recording career.

Like many King's Road boutiques and smart shops elsewhere, 'SEX' attracted numerous teenagers wanting Saturday jobs or just interested in crossing boundaries. Some were dedicated to the cause. At one point, sales assistant Jordan commuted in from Seaford in Sussex, a round trip of 120 miles. The idea of using non-musicians to form a band actually came from McLaren's old friend Rhodes (he wanted one of his own too and got The Clash). It was also Rhodes who found John Lydon when McLaren's outfit needed a singer and Rhodes, again, who provided the idea for Westwood's first big selling T-shirt 'You're Gonna Wake Up One Morning and Know What Side of The Bed You've Been Lying On!' in late 1974.

Thus, like a jackdaw collecting good ideas, McLaren, without ever being truly original, formed The Sex Pistols out of the urchins who gathered at 430 King's Road. Part Fagin and part Serge Gainsbourg, he moved, like a shark surrounded by a shoal of pilot fish, through the music industry, booking gigs, making demos, hustling for record deals and most importantly (and again, a tactic used by Rhodes) coaching his band members to give absurd agitprop replies to questions whenever interviewed so that their 'working-class' credentials could be openly displayed, something that Sex Pistols Lydon and Matlock and Terry Chimes (in The Clash) all found embarrassing. Political rhetoric was very '70s, of course, but did anyone ever really think The Clash were Maoists?

As to how to make a really big impression... McLaren and Jamie Reid, who did poster and gig advertisements, drew inspiration from material like Gainsbourg's *Torrey Canyon* EP (from '67), with its ransom note-style lettering, and may also have been influenced by Pauline Smith and her Mail Art: the circulation of peculiar private works by post, including material from the supposed Adolf Hitler Fan Club, news of which made headlines in 1974. Whether McLaren, Rhodes, Reid and Westwood did this consciously is hardly the point: the important thing is, at a time when the gruesome exploits of the Yorkshire Ripper were front page news and political terrorists used similar items to make their case, they chimed with the zeitgeist, and were assured of notoriety.

Looking at 430 King's Road today it is instructive to realise that you don't need to occupy very much space to change the way people think.

But whatever their collective and long-term importance, few of the acts that emerged like Dury from London's pub-rock and punk scenes of the '70s enjoyed much film or TV exposure. Perhaps this was hardly surprising given the scale of the decline in UK film activity post-1970. But there were some exceptions. *Marc*, final act in the all-too-brief life of Marc Bolan, was a six-part Granada TV series commissioned after an upturn in his popularity. Produced by Muriel Young, whose other pop-magazine show credits included *Discotheque* ('68) and *Lift off with Ayshea* ('70), Bolan's selection by her as host was a deft choice. He understood intuitively what adolescent viewers wanted and didn't talk down to them. He featured a new group each week, with The Jam, The Boomtown Rats, Radio Stars and Generation X appearing, as well as more established names like David Bowie and Thin Lizzy. This was an intelligent music series for discerning teenagers at a time when the UK didn't really have anything comparable.

It turned out to be a fitting conclusion to Bolan's career. Starting out as a miniature early '60s mod from Stamford Hill, Bolan, like legendary DJ Jeff Dexter, originally worked as a fashion model. But music beckoned and from 1965 he moved through all the genres fashionable at that time, changing his style every

18 months or so: firstly, a Bob Dylan protest singer, then electric guitarist in the garage band John's Children (whose singer Andy Ellison later fronted the Radio Stars), then the ultimate hippy in Tyrannosaurus Rex before briefly enjoying the much bandied about 'new Beatles' accolade as leader of glam rockers T. Rex. Along the way he also knocked out a slim volume of sub-Tolkien verse, *Warlock of Love* ('69). Unlike long-standing friend David Bowie, though, he never saw himself as 'an all-round entertainer'. Instead, like so many during this time – Peel, Dury, McLaren and Strummer among them – his inspiration was the brashness and energy of '50s rock and roll. Like contemporaries Slade, he was big in the UK but not the US, and like them got only one major film role (*Born to Boogie*, '72) and was glimpsed in a couple of others (*London Rock*, '70 and *Stamping Ground*, '71).

His final LP *Dandy in the Underworld* (No 26 UK) was launched at The Roxy, Covent Garden, in April 1977, after which Bolan and T. Rex headed out on tour with The Damned as their support act. With his direct, simple approach and penchant for catchy two-minute-long songs, it's a shame he wasn't around longer and that a car crash on Putney Common claimed him in September 1977, his demise understandably bringing the Granada TV series, and by association its exposure for new bands, to an end.

Mention should also be made of *Bloody Kids*, an early effort from Stephen Poliakoff, whose career started as writer-in-residence at the National Theatre in 1976, at only 24 years of age. This led to an early success with *Hitting Town*, part of the Thames TV series *Plays for Britain*. Set on a housing estate near Paddington, with Mick Ford and Deborah Norton and about an incestuous relationship between a brother and sister, it was a production that Mary Whitehouse tried to have banned.

In *Bloody Kids*, the drama is about a couple of young boys misbehaving in the nondescript, deadbeat environment between Southend-on-Sea and Canvey Island. This area, very much part of the East End diaspora, had a significant musical resonance in the '70s as the birthplace of bands like Dr. Feelgood, Eddie and The Hot Rods and The Kursaal Flyers. Directed by Stephen

Frears midway between his two major feature successes *Gumshoe* and *The Hit*, the production didn't have a happy history: Richard Beckinsale, a major '70s TV star – *Rising Damp, Porridge* – was cast in the leading role but died halfway through the shoot and had to be replaced by Derrick O'Connor. Gary Holton who, like Steve Marriott, Davy Jones, Jack Wild and Phil Collins, had learnt his acting skills via the London stage adaptation of *Oliver!* co-stars as the leader of a gang of punks. Holton, an accomplished pop/rock actor-singer, had previously fronted The Heavy Metal Kids, a much fancied pre-1976 UK act, most of whom had started out in The Mickey Finn, formerly a significant London mod group. Taking their name from characters in William Burroughs' 1962 book *The Soft Machine*, The Heavy Metal Kids never made it despite an immense amount of press and TV coverage and an album on Atlantic produced by Dave Dee. Holton's performance in *Bloody Kids* suggests he would have had a substantial acting career, had he not died, at only 33 years old, in 1985.

The film itself is bleak but entertaining and came with a soundtrack by George Fenton. Seen now, it is very much a time capsule of the era. When shown on ITV in March 1980 it attracted an audience of 15m, a level of popularity that suggests it really should have had a cinema release.

8
PUNK: FLOWERING

Like the music, clothes and fanzines, punk cinema – when it arrived – was strictly DIY. Peter Whitehead might have recorded the first 'Summer of Love' in all its glory in *Tonite Let's All Make Love in London*, but his equivalent in London in 1977 was a 25-year-old West German MA student, Wolfgang Büld. *Punk in London* was one of five music documentaries he made between 1977 and 1980. This critical period produced no home-grown Pennebaker, nor did anything on the scale of *Monterey Pop* or *Woodstock* appear. Unlike the US, where Czech émigré musician Ivan Král caught the zeitgeist in his films *Night Lunch* ('75) and *The Blank Generation* ('76), documentarists and cultural historians who wish to learn what the London club scene circa 1977 was like have to rely on a solitary German student who captured as much as he could for posterity. Büld's films are time capsules recording the talented people who, in those days, operated on tiny budgets and suddenly found themselves propelled into the limelight.

Made with a handheld 16mm camera and simple recording techniques, this is very low-tech film. London looks a truly drab place – as it was – and the colour (exclusively reliant on natural light) is washed out, meaning that the material, shot in places like The Red Cow, Hammersmith and the Rough Trade shop in Ladbroke Grove, looks like it was filmed in a pond. But emerging out of this muddy soup are some serious creative figures: The Adverts, X-Ray Spex, The Lurkers, The Jolt, Miles Copeland III,

Chelsea, Wayne County and The Electric Chairs, The Jam, The Killjoys, The Subway Sect and The Stranglers. The US presence is particularly intriguing and shows how much punk owed to the New York scene of a few years earlier. One key figure in this was Wayne County, a performance artist and drag act, who first appeared on stage with Patti Smith in 1969, and arrived in London in 1971 to appear in Andy Warhol's *PORK* at the Roundhouse. As early as 1972 he had assembled a 'punk' group called Queen Elizabeth (in order to maximise outrage) and had signed to Main Man, who managed David Bowie, only to find that none of his recordings got released. Miles Copeland III (whose father was a senior CIA officer at one point) eventually signed County, having worked in London since 1974 running the BTM label and handling bands like Curved Air and Renaissance. Copeland even had a subsidiary label – Deptford Fun City – and his career at this point reads as if it may have been the inspiration for the central character in Paul Theroux's 1976 novel *The Family Arsenal* about a US diplomat (for which read CIA man) hiding out in a forgotten 'squatted' street in south London.

Also observable here are Poly Styrene (aka Marianne Elliott-Said, the Bromley person never regarded as being part of the 'Bromley contingent', and originally a reggae/soul act), Kevin Rowland (pre-Dexys and long before his adoption of 'Celtic' rock) and Vic Godard, singer of Subway Sect and one of the most intriguing and underrated of all the early punk acts. Rather than just impersonate The MC5 or The New York Dolls, Godard went for a kind of louche cabaret-type drollness, something of a dangerous stance at the time given the violence that attended most live gigs. Büld also filmed The Clash (in Munich), only for the group and its management, being displeased with the footage, to demand that it be removed from the film.

Parking the moral outrage that attended the emergence of punk (and was deliberately fanned by McLaren and Rhodes), less than half of the acts here actually enjoyed any significant commercial success and punk itself got little exposure. An attempt by ITV to showcase it on *Revolver*, presented with throwaway insolence by

Peter Cook, lasted for only a handful of programmes in early 1978. *Time Out* might have thought Büld's film 'quite interesting', but it only got a limited distribution and still isn't listed in *Halliwell's*.

For a modest upgrade from his debut, Büld directed *Bored Teenagers*, a West German TV drama, in which he follows The Adverts touring West Germany and meeting young kids. With music by TV Smith (the group's singer), the title comes from the song the group performed on *The Roxy, London WC2* sampler album and later released as the b-side of *Gary Gilmore's Eyes*, the only substantial hit they would enjoy: No 18 in the UK in September 1977. Smith and his partner, Gaye Advert, had arrived in London from Bideford in Devon in 1976, formed the group in March 1977, and with punk sweeping the UK, were snapped up by Stiff. Advert had statuesque gothic looks which helped their image.

The cast were not widely known, though Karl Scheydt had appeared in *Beware of a Holy Whore* ('71) and many others for Rainer Werner Fassbinder. The film, however, does include Steven Conolly – a roadie with The Clash – whose appearance in this inspired the 1981 hit single *I'm in Love with a German Film Star* (No 25 February '81) by The Passions. *Bored Teenagers* survives today as an adequate homage, by Büld, to English punk at its apogee. The best scenes are the live footage. For their part, The Adverts never found wide-ranging success despite Smith's obvious songwriting skills and after a brief spell on RCA broke up in late 1979.

Producer Barbara Moorse went on to make *Trance* ('82) with Rheingold, a West German new-wave/electronic act, about teenage fan obsession. Almost the ultimate gothic horror with nudity and cannibalism, she surpassed it with *Loft* ('85), mixing anarchism, surrealism and torture in a plot set in a dystopian future. Inventive material like this, though, was beyond the UK film industry in the mid-'80s. Büld's subsequent career included *Feel the Motion* ('85), which by comparison with Moorse's efforts is a very conventional West German pop film – set in a car repair garage – with various bands (Limahl, Katrina and The Waves, Meat Loaf) doing a turn – yet another, and in this case very late, example of a feature made for teenagers where a string of bands and singers perform their latest hits. For this, Büld had wanted Billy Idol and Motörhead, but EMI, who funded it, insisted on choosing the acts.

In terms of legendary venues punk produced few: most of the places where the new groups played were the same places that had already offered live music for a decade or longer. The same was true, more or less, of the Roxy, a tiny bar with a basement stage area in Covent Garden. Originally gay club Chaguaramas, it had first staged live music in 1970–71, hosting acts like Egg and Dada. Back then, record producer Tony Ashfield, a producer of very elegant smoochy soul reggae who had a big UK hit with John Holt's *Help Me Make It Through the Night* (No 6, '74), held the lease. In late 1976 Andy Czezowski took over with Don Letts as DJ, Letts playing a great deal of dub reggae on the sound system, and the venue began staging punk acts. Like McLaren and Westwood, Letts and Czezowski had started out a couple of years earlier selling retro stuff, in their case at 'Acme Attractions', a shop owned by jukebox dealer John Krivine.

The Roxy functioned for barely two years but a live compilation album, *The Roxy, London WC2*, of the various bands that played there (the most prominent of which were The Adverts, Eater, X-Ray Spex and the Buzzcocks) was released by Harvest in July 1977 and reached No 24 in the UK charts. A month later another compilation on Philips, *New Wave*, peaked at No 11, this showcasing, among others, The Ramones, Patti Smith, The Runaways, The Boomtown Rats, Talking Heads and The Damned. Nothing like this had burst on the UK scene since skiffle in 1956 or Merseybeat in 1963.

Inevitably some sort of film followed. What emerged made Wolfgang Büld's efforts look like a masterclass in auteurism. Essentially a home movie, *The Punk Rock Movie* was filmed at the club by Letts over three months in 1977 on an 8mm camera. Production costs were met by Peter Clifton, an Australian with many late '60s and early '70s music documentaries to his credit, including *Popcorn* ('69), *Rock City* ('72), *The London Rock 'n' Roll Show* ('73), which contains early footage of Vivienne Westwood hawking her line of vintage '50s clothing, and the Led Zeppelin opus, *The Song Remains the Same* ('76). The footage – we see The Clash, The Sex Pistols, Wayne County and The Electric Chairs, Generation X, Slaughter and The Dogs, The Slits, Siouxsie and The Banshees, Eater, Subway Sect, X-Ray Spex, Johnny Thunders and The Heartbreakers and Alternative TV – is blurred to the point of being utterly indistinct, the sound is muffled and the lighting non-existent. Andy Czezowski co-produced.

An early version was screened at the ICA in late 1977, but, despite Clifton's heavyweight credentials, the film had only a very limited release in 1978-9. No subsequent follow-ups were made, even if this might have been possible given the transient nature of the material. With the Roxy now shut, Letts went to Jamaica with John Lydon in 1978 and whilst there shot *Ranking Movie* (basically filmed auditions of acts that Richard Branson's Virgin were considering signing), which got a few showings a year later before disappearing from sight: a tiny bit of it appeared at later reissues of *The Punk Rock Movie*, whilst the negative is now held at the BFI.

A priceless museum piece at best, although some of the groups seen in Letts' film became successful, others just folded. After a couple of years Letts too turned his hand to music as part of Big Audio Dynamite from 1985-90 with Mick Jones, ex-The Clash, and Dan Donovan, son of '60s photographer Terry Donovan. Their debut, *This Is Big Audio Dynamite*, charted at No 27 in the UK in late 1985 and featured much sampling from spaghetti westerns, but subsequent releases were less successful. Andy Czezowski returned to club management, opening The Fridge in Brixton in 1984 with the help of £5,000 from Joe Strummer. A legendary venue for trance and electronica, its reputation quickly surpassed that of the Roxy and it remained open for 26 years (and, indeed, is still open today under different ownership), during which time the premises that had hosted Chaguaramas and the Roxy became a very conventional sportswear shop. And Krivine? He moved on from 'Acme Attractions' to start the hugely successful Boy fashion label.

But for a BBC ban, the original version of *Scum*, filmed as a *Play for Today* in mid-'77 with Ray Winstone and Phil Daniels, might have been seen before the cinéma vérité offerings of Wolfgang Büld and Don Letts. Instead it had to be remade in its entirety for cinema in order to get it out to audiences. There isn't much music to speak of in *Scum*, but it is definitely a youth-oriented film depicting the casual violence of the '70s and it eventually went out as a double bill with *Quadrophenia*. As such, it reflects much of the youth and punk culture of that time.

About the goings-on in a borstal, *Scum* is brutal, violent and graphically depicts non-consensual homosexual activity. For the film version Winstone and Daniels (by this point the best known of the young actors and a rising star) are joined by Mick Ford and Julian Firth. During the transition from TV to film, the Winstone character was toughened up: in the original play he has a gay relationship with another inmate. This was omitted in the film. Following their success with *That Summer*, Davina Belling and Clive Parsons produced. Both the TV and film versions were directed by Alan Clarke from a script by Roy Minton.

The message being pushed by Minton is that the Borstal system doesn't work, but as far as the plot is concerned no clear alternative to it is suggested. In fact, borstals were abolished in 1982 (after the film had reached cinemas, but before it, or the original *Play for Today*, were shown on TV) and because of this the storyline seemed slightly dated even at the time. In popular culture it takes its place alongside Brendan Behan's *Borstal Boy* and Alan Sillitoe's *The Loneliness of the Long-Distance Runner*, which contains at least one scene (the riot in the canteen) that is repeated in *Scum*. Juvenile delinquency had provided a rich seam of material in music, too, with The Faces' *Borstal Boys* ('73) and Sham 69's *Borstal Breakout* ('77) both reflecting a hardening of youth culture at a time when football hooliganism was very common and street crime rising. When finally shown on TV by Channel 4 in 1983, Mary Whitehouse brought a prosecution – which failed – because of a male rape scene. Clarke was an important director whose career never really got going and had ground to a halt by the end of the '80s.

With *Scum* a success, HandMade did a quasi-sequel, *Scrubbers* in 1982, exploring very similar themes but set in a girls' borstal. Roy Minton did the script for this, too, having in the aftermath of *Scum* worked on a TV series, *Horace* ('82), which broke new ground by having a central character with learning disabilities. Mai Zetterling directs, though few would argue this to be the high point of a career which began in Sweden with Ingmar Bergman's *Torment* ('44), included *Frieda* ('47), *The Lost People* ('49) and an adaptation of the Kingsley Amis novel *Only Two Can Play* ('62), before moving behind the camera in Sweden and Denmark, notably with *Flickorna/The Girls* ('68).

The cast are mainly TV and theatre stalwarts. There are no major stars. Among those appearing in supporting roles are Honey Bane and Pauline Melville. Bane, a singer-actress, was quite a character. Serving a stint in detention at the age of 15, she started a singing career with Donna and The Kebabs doing ska-type stuff... it subsequently emerged that her backing band were the fiercely political anarchist outfit Crass, who without her would produce *Christ The Album* (No 26, '82). After Bane had a couple of minor hits in 1981, she moved into acting in the play *Demonstration of Affection* with Richard Jobson (late of The Skids). Melville, a black, radical stand-up comedienne, was one of several participants in *Alternative Cabaret*, who released a 1981 LP on Original records, the same label that produced a double album adaptation of *The Hitchhiker's Guide to the Galaxy*. By association, *Scrubbers* is also a film for Bowie completists, featuring in key roles two of his exes: Eva Mottley (late '70s) and Dana Gillespie (late '60s).

Scrubbers was not as shocking or visceral as *Scum* and Zetterling may have been trying to make a documentary-style *Cathy Come Home* piece that would condemn the incarceration of young women but it is let down throughout by the script. With Minton's original screenplay rewritten by others, what remains constantly opts for cheap, predictable melodrama. Some of this may have been inevitable, given the nature of the plot. After all, far fewer women are detained in prison than men (then and now) and the circumstances inside jails and borstals that accommodate women offenders are generally much less violent and disruptive than those that handle male criminals. Thus, compared to most women-in-prison films, say *Caged Heat!* ('74, Jonathan Demme with music by John Cale), as 'entertainment' this is insufficiently manic, though we do get, rather in the style of the UK soft-core films of the period, some lesbian scenes. The use, at one point, of early '70s stock library music is a disappointment, too, as well as highly incongruous. Given that the film's composer was Michael Hurd (a considerable figure in post-war classical music, and a long-standing collaborator with Zetterling), one suspects that this was another missed opportunity. All in all, *Scrubbers* was much less successful than *Scum*, though, for once, Mary Whitehouse didn't prosecute. Perhaps, like Queen Victoria, she didn't 'get' lesbianism.

For a great example of the production history of a film being as interesting, or more so, than the film itself, *The Great Rock N' Roll Swindle* still divides opinion and remains marginalised by cinema buffs – not taken seriously and unmentioned in many reference works. It seems that Malcolm McLaren, obsessed with getting to the top of the music industry, made plans for a feature film about, and with, The Sex Pistols from very early on in their career. Certainly, footage of them was being shot and edited together by Julien Temple around the time they signed to EMI, and, after that label dumped them and A&M did likewise, a bit of this appeared as *Sex Pistols No 1* ('77), which is a decent enough effort. (Today it plays like a music video made by college students.) But McLaren wanted much more than this. He commissioned a script – *Rock Around the Contract* – from Peter Cook, then dropped that and commissioned another by Graham Chapman and Johnny Speight to be called *Anarchy in the UK*, with the action, à la *Jubilee*, taking place in derelict bits of London.

By July 1977, with the band relaunched by Virgin and scoring two hit singles – *God Save the Queen* (No 2 UK) and *Pretty Vacant* (No 6 UK) – in quick succession, McLaren had raised £500k for his film project, the same amount that it cost Brent Walker to make *The Stud*, and arguably enough to make a decent film. A great admirer of *Beyond the Valley of the Dolls* – manic, tasteless, but a big US box office hit in 1970 – McLaren brought in Russ Meyer to direct. Meyer promptly announced that the feature envisaged would cost twice McLaren's budget (which may have been true in Hollywood) and insisted that Roger Ebert, who had written *Beyond the Valley of the Dolls*, provide a new script. This incarnation, now known as *Who Killed Bambi?*, finally moved into production when 20th Century-Fox signed up as executive producer and agreed a distribution deal. Obviously, the group would star, but the main acting part went to James Aubrey, who had played one of the major roles in the ITV dysfunctional family drama *Bouquet of Barbed Wire* ('76) and was a name of some substance then. Alas: shooting ended after only one day in October 1977 when, as predicted by Meyer, McLaren's money dried up.

Somehow the film survived the failure of The Sex Pistols to break through in the US, Lydon quitting the group immediately after their abortive tour, the carnage of Vicious's solo career and Lydon refusing to have anything further to do with McLaren. The truth was that by early 1978 the band had become a cartoon-like franchise from which McLaren could milk a good living and by then too much money was attached to the film project to allow it to fade away. But who would pick up the baton? It seems that McLaren parried a suggestion of funding from Larry Parnes, by then owner of the Cambridge Theatre in London where *Chicago* was starting a successful run, sensing loss of control in the venture if he agreed. Instead McLaren approached both Pete Walker (an active auteur in the basement of UK cinema since the mid-'60s) and Jonathan Kaplan, but both declined, Walker making *Home Before Midnight* (with Aubrey) and Kaplan doing *Over the Edge* with music by The Cars, The Ramones and Cheap Trick instead. Having – legally – lost control of the group in March 1979, McLaren, now resident in Paris (where he was employed by Barclay records to dub soundtracks on soft-porn films), devised his own approach to the script and brought back Julien Temple to direct (he was cheaper than Meyer) with Don Boyd, who had done *Scum*, as producer.

Built around monologues from Malcolm McLaren in which he patiently explains his business strategy to lesser mortals, footage of The Sex Pistols (of whom only Cook and Jones remained by the time it was shot), the remainder of the cast includes worn-out '50s regulars like Irene Handl, Liz Fraser and Jess Conrad, as well as Mary Millington – the UK's first authentic porn star and at that point top billed in *Come Play with Me*, the longest-running film in British history. (Millington committed suicide shortly after shooting her scenes, thus appearing here with Vicious and Nancy Spungen as one of a trio who were dead by the time the film was released.) Intended, it would seem, as a satire on the entertainment industry, it comes nowhere near the level of *The Girl Can't Help It* and ends up instead as an idiotic, updated and deliberately obscene version of *The Tommy Steele Story*. Indeed, McLaren's persona of a provocative and cynical Svengali owes more than a little to Tin Pan Alley pop hustler Larry Parnes in his incarnation as manager of Tommy Steele, Billy Fury, Marty Wilde and Terry Dene. The film did okay business in the UK but The Sex Pistols, in all their permutations, had completely gone by the end of 1980.

But any opportunity to make money was seized by McLaren and Branson. During the death-throes of the group they released the albums *The Great Rock N' Roll Swindle* (March '79, No 7, and an early trailer for the film), *Some Product – Carri on Sex Pistols* (August '79, No 6) and *Flogging a Dead Horse* (February '80, No 23). The problem of the band no longer having a singer didn't matter either. Ronald Biggs, former Great Train Robber and a minor criminal (despite the UK media constantly portraying him otherwise) living in exile in a Brazilian favela, stepped up for *No One is Innocent* (July '78, No 7). Edward Tudor-Pole, aka Tenpole Tudor and once mooted as a replacement for Lydon, handled the vocals for *Who Killed Bambi* (April '79, No 6) and *The Great Rock N' Roll Swindle* (October '79, No 21), whilst the Pistols Cook and Jones managed *Silly Thing* between them. Some effort, too, was put into making Sid Vicious an acceptable act in his own right – and he duly scored successes with *Something Else* (March '79, No 3) and *C'mon Everybody* (June '79, No 3) and the album *Sid Sings* (December '79, No 30). Just as the earlier truncated careers of Buddy Holly and Eddie Cochrane had been milked by record labels after their demise, these were, in true Joe Meek style, posthumous 'death disc' releases, Vicious having died in February 1979, but as an exercise in razor-sharp marketing and making the best of limited resources, all of this really took some beating. Even one of McLaren's old art school friends, Fred Vermorel, got in on the act with his partner Judy, producing the April 1979 single *99% is Shit* (which has a rambling spoken introduction by Vicious) and releasing it as the Cash Pussies. (The musicians used were Alternative TV.)

The film also spawned a soundtrack LP (June '80, No 16) that was basically a reissue of the album of the same name released a year earlier. In the strangest tie-in of all, though, Michael Moorcock wrote the paperback 'book of the film', which includes characters from Hawkwind and Motörhead. Earlier, the demise of The Sex Pistols was accompanied in true Andy Warhol style by an instantly available paperback book charting their rise and fall. Written by McLaren's fellow provocateurs Fred and Judy Vermorel, it sold heavily and was subsequently reissued as *Sex Pistols – The Inside Story* in 1987.

A visual account of the final stages of their career, though, can be found in *DOA* – which shows their last moments as a gigging band – and was assembled for cinema release by Lech Kowalski and Chris Salewicz (an *NME* journalist). This is a documentary about The Sex Pistols on their only US tour, which lasted from 27 December 1977 to 14 January 1978. Kowalski and Salewicz followed them with hand-held 16mm cameras to each of the locations they played – venues deliberately chosen by McLaren to cause maximum disruption and difficulty and where their appearances were in front of small audiences, as little to no publicity for the tour had been organised. The executive producer was Steve Menkin, whose later career included a wide range of sensational and exploitative features and documentaries.

What the film offers is valuable contemporary footage of a number of bands (The Clash, Generation X, The Rich Kids, Sham 69, X-Ray Spex, The Dead Boys) alongside cinéma-vérité material of hangers-on, McLaren and the Pistols on the road in various, unlikely settings and Sid Vicious and Nancy Spungen together as a couple and both clearly very much taken with each other. This is then intercut with straight-to-the-camera pronouncements by virulent anti-counterculture types of the time, notably Mary Whitehouse and Jonathan Guinness (Monday Club and son of prominent Nazi Diana Mitford). The juxtapositioning of the dreadful reactionaries with the swirling chaos of youth is understated and possibly the best part of the film. But looked at today one might well reflect that as Whitehouse, Mitford and their disciples won the political battles, were McLaren, Lydon and (many) others winning the cultural battles of equal importance? Sadly, unlike *Tonite Let's All Make Love in London*, the film today features in very few reference works and barely achieved a cinema release at the time.

Apart from generalised documentaries and the antics of The Sex Pistols, the only other leading punk act to attempt feature film exposure – the door never knocked for The Jam, The Stranglers or The Damned – were The Clash. To be sure, out of all the bands that emerged in 1976–7 The Clash were the ones who were confidently expected to emulate the '60s greats (Stones, The Who and so on) and, as such, were given immense amounts of coverage and latitude by the serious media. Inevitably, a film project was sought for them and, once they had dented the US charts in 1979, was finally delivered by Jack Hazan and David Mingay in 1980 as *Rude Boy*. Documentarists, prior to this they had done *A Bigger Splash* about David Hockney and Hazan had even been one of the cameramen at the 1970 Isle of Wight Festival. Over two hours long, *Rude Boy* shows The Clash on a Rock Against Racism tour with a young roadie and recording the *Give 'Em Enough Rope* album, which made No 2 in the UK.

Other than the band themselves, the main role – of their roadie – is played by Ray Gange, a personal friend of Strummer's, whose day job normally found him behind the counter at 58 Dean Street, the legendary mecca for film soundtrack collectors. Gange also co-wrote the script. Also seen here are the writer and literary critic Elizabeth Young, as Gange's girlfriend, and Caroline Coon, a counterculture veteran who by this point was managing The Clash. Michael White produced. One of the few people to survive the worst years of the UK film industry, White's other credits included *The Rocky Horror Picture Show*, which made money, and *The Hound of the Baskervilles*, which didn't. Somewhere along the way he must have thought that *Rude Boy* would do well in cinemas. Alas, most of the material seen on the screen was improvised, with the group and Caroline Coon evidently thinking it would do for them what, say, *Gimme Shelter* had done for The Rolling Stones. Actually, it turned out to be rather self-conscious and rambling. Their behaviour was boorish and the film was promptly disowned by its subjects on release.

But to take the adage that the camera never lies – does it show them as they actually were? After all, their ambition from the beginning was to combine the radical-chic politics of The MC5 with the money of the Stones. (Not that this ever impressed The MC5, whose guitarist Wayne Kramer opined 'Boy, this punk thing... it's so phoney. They're not for real tough guys.') Consequently, in real life, although cheerfully comparing themselves with the characters in *The Magnificent Seven* – outlaws who would ride into town and put everything right – they signed as quickly as possible to CBS, went out on tour at £1,000 a night (a huge sum then) *before* releasing any records and booked Richard Hell as their support act. Yes, the man who in New York circa 1972 devised the entire punk style was relegated by them to a subsidiary role, given a Mini and demeaned by being told to follow their tour bus, on which, replete with drugs, groupies, drink and hangers-on, The Clash relaxed between gigs. Later, *The New York Times* would observe about Strummer 'his surest goal is to become a person of privilege'. (The paper might have added that as a boarding school-educated son of a UK diplomat he already was one.) Despite it all, the film was liked in Europe and The Clash became, from 1980, a big draw in the US. This brought them a minute non-speaking part in Scorsese's *King of Comedy*, but this film lost a packet and they folded as a band shortly afterwards.

In a final twist, The Clash left in the can another film, one they had started on their own after *Rude Boy* turned out to be not quite up to their expectations. A 50-minute long, black and white gangster parody, part-*Performance*, part-*The Sweeney*, part-Cagney/Bogart, this was *Hell W10*, directed and written by Strummer with other members of the group in acting roles. The film is silent with ornate Edwardian style dialogue cards and was presumably intended as a comedy. No sound was recorded and only sufficient footage was shot, in 16mm with poor camera work and lighting, to produce a supporting feature. It was never formally released and the other participants were Martin Degville, a drag queen, clothes designer and former flatmate of Boy George, and Tony James, previously of Generation X. Both Degville and James were later in Sigue Sigue Sputnik, a band who were briefly big circa 1986, and the film itself could be seen as more about them and their appearance than anything to do with The Clash.

9

PUNK: DEATH

As an illustration of how rapidly music and fashion evolved in the '70s, *Jubilee* filmed at peak punk in the spring and summer of 1977, but by the time it premiered in early 1978, the main protagonists of the new scene (The Sex Pistols) had disintegrated. Similarly, McLaren's *The Great Rock N' Roll Swindle* only emerged when the parade had passed. Three years after his debut production, Wolfgang Büld returned to the UK and this time took his format of extended live music sequences and hand-held camera interviews around the country with a small crew that included Dick Pope – a cameraman who had worked on *World in Action* documentaries for Granada TV. The end result, *Punk and Its Aftershocks* ('80) remains fairly conventional in approach and the film itself got only a small showing and remains relatively unknown.

No longer 100 per cent London centric, in this Büld ventures to Coventry to report on the 2-Tone phenomenon, a soul and dance movement that echoed the success enjoyed in 1967-8 by racially mixed outfits like The Equals and Geno Washington and the Ram Jam Band. Music of this type had disappeared by the '70s when the skinhead culture (which originally welcomed them) narrowed and became overtly racist. Captured for posterity here are Madness, The Selecter and The Specials, with The Boomtown Rats, The Jam, The Sex Pistols, The Clash, Secret Affair, The Pretenders, The Police and Gary Numan. The ska acts were filmed in 1979-80, but most of the footage clearly predates this. Premiered in Switzerland, it was renamed *British Rock* for its limited distribution in the UK.

After *Punk and Its Aftershocks* Büld returned to Munich, where he completed *Women in Rock* ('80) for West German TV, with footage of The Slits and Siouxsie and The Bansees, and made *Hangin' Out* (released February '83) with Nena, at that point riding high after the success of her hit *99 Red Balloons* (No 1 UK and No 2 US). Co-produced by Stein Films, who had an impressive roster of West German productions, this was ostensibly a parody of a typical German music comedy-romance of 20–30 years earlier. The critics were damning, but at least, unlike Büld's earlier outings, it was a fairly big hit. Büld had actually wanted Trio (whose 1982 hit *Da-Da-Da* was even bigger than Nena's) for the film, but they withdrew to make an album. After *Punk and Its Aftershocks*, Büld never directed in the UK again.

The final example of DIY cinema to emerge in the punk period, *Rough Cut and Ready Dubbed*, was part-funded by the BFI and ended up being the only film project to be given money by the Ken Livingstone era GLC. An award-winning music documentary filmed over several years between 1978 and 1981, the footage shows Stiff Little Fingers, A Certain Ratio, The Cockney Rejects, Patrick Fitzgerald, Johnny G, The Purple Hearts, The Selecter, Sham 69, The UK Subs, Garry Bushell, John Peel, Charles Shaar Murray and Tony Wilson.

Watching Wilson is particularly rewarding: a considerable figure who hosted the Granada TV series *So It Goes* (from '76) and ran Factory Records (from '78 and home to Joy Division, New Order and later The Happy Mondays), he was based in Manchester, not London, thus demonstrating how the centre of gravity of the UK scene was beginning to shift away from the capital. Like Peel, he was a lucid, quasi-father figure to many of his bands and their followers and a northerner with years of enduring influence.

Made by Hasan Shah and Dom Shaw, *Rough Cut and Ready Dubbed* is amateur DIY stuff shot on 8mm and later blown up to 16mm, the end product being a step down in quality from even Wolfgang Büld, full of blurred and grainy images. But it has an abiding charm. All the various post-'76 tribes are shown: punk, mod, skinhead and 2-tone. One thing noticeable nearly 40 years on is how the accents of some of the teenage London exponents are voices that have now all but vanished from everyday life – a flat, deadpan cockney of a type that is now hardly heard. Hasan Shah has few other credits, but Dom Shaw carried on with music documentaries as well as working with Mike Leigh.

Highly rated on its brief release in 1982 and made for virtually nothing, *Rough Cut and Ready Dubbed* nevertheless shows punk in decline. Intriguingly, none of those featured in it saw the coming economic collapse in live and recorded music that would accelerate from the mid-'80s onwards via venue closures, taping, loss of venues and, eventually, the internet. All the participants talk throughout about a continuing '70s style vibrant scene, of bands, gigs and small labels.

The petering out of punk, though, was not just a matter of bands breaking up and fashions changing. It was also to do with a rapid coarsening of its culture. A style that had seemed colourful and creative in 1975–6 became within a few years very conventional and just another commercially marketed fad. But at the same time the UK remained a violent society and aspects of this, and the impact that these changes had on the youth of the time, were picked up in a couple of productions made by Central TV, a Birmingham-based ITV franchise launched in 1982.

The first of these, *Made in Britain*, was directed by Alan Clarke and deals with a bitterly confrontational and racist skinhead – so adversarial that he exhibits mental health issues – who, having been completely failed by the education system, is unable to get work and ends up in a detention centre, but still refuses to conform. Visually, the appearance of the main character illustrates what many of the skinheads actually looked like by the early '80s; how the original mod culture of the mid-'60s, with its fondness for Italian and French clothes and black music, had spiralled down to this threatening level. The logical conclusion, in many ways, of Alex in *A Clockwork Orange*.

David Leland wrote the script and *Made in Britain* won an

award at the International TV Festival, but Clarke's career faded away in the late '80s. As political changes in the UK media took place, there was less demand for his work – productions of his type, usually based on working-class characters and communities hitting back at a right-wing establishment, were no longer fashionable. The film itself remains unforgettable due to a blistering debut by a 20-year-old Tim Roth, playing Trevor, the main character. Just prior to filming this Roth was dallying with music, playing trumpet – there were a lot of trumpet players around in 1981 – as one of The Casual Labourers, who got as far as releasing a cassette album recorded live at The Africa Centre, Covent Garden. We can only speculate what would have happened to his career if they had been offered a deal and Roth had then turned down *Made in Britain*...

Musically, by the early '80s many skinheads were following bands like The UK Subs and Sham 69. The soundtrack here features music by a similar act, The Exploited, culled from their LP *Troops of Tomorrow*, which reached No 17 in the UK charts. From Edinburgh, their 1981 debut *Punk's Not Dead* sold well (No 20 UK), but by the '80s and '90s punks were a permanently anarchic sub-tribe, who were increasingly left behind, following much the same trajectory as the mod to skinhead changes of a few years earlier, and, like the Teddy Boys before them, ossified as relics of an earlier time.

Central TV followed up *Made in Britain* with *Oi for England*, a drama from Trevor Griffiths. A revolutionary leftist with many TV and stage credits, through the '70s he produced adaptations of Gramsci (*Occupations*, '74, directed by Michael Lindsay-Hogg), dramatised the early life of Lenin and knocked out an entire drama series, *Bill Brand*, for Thames TV about how the Parliamentary process ultimately compromises genuine socialists. With credentials like these he was a shoo-in for Warren Beatty's *Reds* ('81), on which he worked for several years at the end of the decade. A defiant counterblast to what was happening politically then in both the US and UK, when released *Reds* was a box-office success and should have propelled Griffiths's career to new heights. In fact, with the death of TV drama and the continued contraction of the UK film industry, he did comparatively little work after the mid-'80s.

Oi for England is set in Manchester in the aftermath of the 1981 urban riots with a plot about a struggling punk group who are tempted to support right-wing causes by a sinister individual played by Gavin Richards. In illustrating the manipulation of working-class communities by cynical extremists, it is an effective companion piece to *Destiny*, the 1978 TV play about the rise of the National Front. Tony Smith directed and Margaret Matheson produced, both of these having previously done the original TV version of *Scum*.

As part of general efforts to alert people to the dangers of the ultra-right, the screenplay was subsequently adapted and staged at the Royal Court Theatre and even performed in clubs with groups like The 4-Skins, an outfit led by Hoxton Tom McCourt, who was something of a libertarian and preferred the original, sharper clothing worn by the late '60s suede heads, as seen in the film *Bronco Bullfrog*, to the SS stormtrooper-style garb of late-period skinheads. There was an 'Oi' subsection of punk too, championed by Garry Bushell. Various compilations of this material were released, but they were not heavy sellers. Central TV subsequently produced *Auf Wiedersehen, Pet* and the long-running satirical puppet show *Spitting Image*, but in terms of hard-hitting political drama *Oi for England* remains their finest hour.

During the 'Swinging Sixties', films shot in Swinging London carried on appearing a couple of years after the film production had moved elsewhere, for purely practical reasons if no other: films took a long time to fund, cast, shoot, edit, dub and release. Thus, the collapse of The Sex Pistols in January 1978 and the shifting of UK music into terrain frequented by ska, 2-tone and 'new romantic' synthesiser bands did not end the momentum that had built up around the careers of Lydon, Vicious, Cook and Jones. Once The Clash had broken into the US charts in 1979–80, the idea of making a punk-based film appealed in LA. *All Washed Up!* by Nancy Dowd, one of the few women working as screenplay writers in Hollywood and who had landed an academy nomination for *Coming Home*, moved into production as Lou Adler's follow-up to this film. Filmed in early 1982 as *Ladies and Gentlemen, The Fabulous Stains*, and entirely US-set, Adler directed. One of the great producers of US music, his prior successes included working with Jan and Dean, Johnny Rivers, Barry McGuire, The Mamas and The Papas, Scott McKenzie, Spirit, Merry Clayton and Carole King. By 1975 he had moved into film as executive producer of *The Rocky Horror Picture Show* and in 1978 had a massive success with the Cheech & Chong stoner farce *Up in Smoke*, which he also directed.

Filmed in Canada, *Ladies and Gentlemen, The Fabulous Stains* stars Diane Lane, Laura Dern and Marin Kanter as three bored teenage girls living in the fictional US 'rust belt' town of Charlston. A UK band – The Looters – are appearing locally with a long forgotten glam rock outfit (played by The Tubes), so the girls go to the gig, are blown away by the show, form their own band (The Stains) and then persuade The Looters to keep them as a support act for the rest of their tour. As in all good show-business musicals they then ascend to stardom, leaving their once superior benefactors crumpled and defeated in their wake. The boys break up ignominiously. The girls are triumphant. An appreciation of fantasy is required to accept the likelihood of this happening in real life.

The line-up of The Looters attracts some attention today: Ray Winstone (vocals), Steve Jones (guitar), Paul Simonon (bass) and Paul Cook (drums). Was this how The Sex Pistols might have ended up if they'd managed to replace Lydon and Vicious? Perhaps. Caroline Coon, Simonon's girlfriend and a throwback to the 1967 era, acted as technical adviser – presumably to ensure some authenticity re the UK 'punk' input. The end result is curious.

In 1982 Dowd had her name taken off the credits, objecting to the finished item being packaged as more of a teenage brat-pack and rites-of-passage drama than her script had intended and the film was barely released. It only became known some years later after screenings on various cable channels and late-night slots, still lacking a listing in many reference works. Subsequently, Lane, Dern and Winstone went on to become stars and Simonon remained in The Clash until their final collapse in 1985-6, after which he applied himself to painting with some success. A soundtrack album finally reached the public twenty-six years later, with four tracks by The Looters, two by The Stains (both sung by Diane Lane) and one by The Tubes, using the pseudonym of The Metal Corpses. Some of the arrangements were done by Barry Ford, a UK drummer once in Kilburn and The High Roads.

John Lydon's own film debut came in *Order of Death*. Given his extraordinary status as 'spokesman for a generation' between 1977 and 1980 he would probably have ended up in feature films irrespective of any acting ability. The media – nice and nasty – couldn't get enough of him at one point. Set in New York, and about a deranged serial killer who targets police officers, Lydon signed for the role after completing the Public Image Ltd album *Flowers of Romance* (No 11 in the UK in May '81).

Filmed in late 1981 with an understanding that PIL would also do the soundtrack and Virgin would distribute, Harvey Keitel, in a role tailor-made for him, co-stars as a hard-bitten NYPD detective. The source is a novel by Hugh Fleetwood, a UK writer based in Italy. Roberto Faenza, who had dropped into London back in 1967 to do *Escalation/Ascenso*, part of which was filmed at the Roundhouse, co-wrote the script and directed, with the remainder of the cast led by Nicole Garcia and Leonard Mann, the latter with many credits in spaghetti westerns and giallo thrillers. Essentially this is a decently made Italian–American crime drama with a plot that develops into a peculiar psychological drama between Lydon, as the suspect, and Keitel, almost on the same lines as the interplay between Jagger and Fox in *Performance*. Virgin by this point were beginning to explore the wider entertainment and leisure world beyond music and record shops and would shortly launch their own film production company, so, in one sense, this was a low-risk debut project for them. But the snag is that Lydon doesn't really convince as an actor.

By late 1982 shooting and editing was almost complete. At

this point the Italian producers (who renamed the film *Copkiller*) abruptly brought in Ennio Morricone to do the score, with the PIL contributions eventually being shunted to their July 1984 LP *This is What You Want... This is What You Get*. The title was lifted from a line of dialogue spoken by Lydon in the film and the album failed to sell. The group broke up around that time and the film only had a few cursory showings in the UK at places like The Scala, King's Cross. Lydon is deadpan (at best) throughout, with an accent that at times sounds rather like Peter Cook. His subsequent screen career consisted mainly of TV commercials, and if he had any other offers of acting work they are not known about.

The collapse of The Sex Pistols, and the gruesome end of the bass player Sid Vicious, was portrayed in *Sid and Nancy*. Made only seven years after the events it portrays, its making proved, if nothing else did, that the punk moment had well and truly passed. Written and directed by Alex Cox, who left the UK for Los Angeles in 1977 and eventually made *Repo Man* ('84) – a considerable art-house hit and, possibly, a brilliant film – *Sid and Nancy* explores the life and times of Vicious (aka Simon Ritchie) and stars Gary Oldman in the title role with Chloe Webb as his equally doomed girlfriend, Nancy Spungen. Oldman found Ritchie/Vicious an uninteresting character, didn't identify with the music and declined to do the film at first, eventually signing up mainly because of the money on offer. For Margaret Matheson, who acted as executive producer, *Sid and Nancy* was a natural progression from *Scum*, *Destiny* and *Made in Britain*, whilst for Eric Fellner, in day-to-day charge of the production, it was a first feature credit, his previous work amounting to some videos for Duran Duran and Kajagoogoo. (Today he ranks as just about the biggest and most commercially successful producer in the UK.) The remainder of the cast includes David Hayman, from *A Sense of Freedom*, in fine form as Malcolm McLaren, and an interesting gallery of cameos from Edward Tudor-Pole, Sallie Anne Field, Nico, Courtney Love and Iggy Pop.

The accuracy of the film was much disputed by John Lydon, a long-standing personal friend of Ritchie's, but, with so many of the characters portrayed still living, some liberties had to be taken. What reached the screen was never going to be a documentary. Rather, it was a semi-fictionalised road-to-ruin rock and roll morality tale; a classic story of a charismatic but damaged young man ascending to stardom and sudden death. Whatever the disputes, though, the essentials are all correct and, in one sense, Oldman was right about Vicious: he wasn't by any means likeable and was trouble to be around. He was jailed in 1976 after blinding a girl by throwing a glass at the stage at the 100 Club, this occurring after a couple of other serious assaults. Vivienne Westwood, who sent him a book about Charles Manson as reading material whilst he was in prison, and Malcolm McLaren grotesquely amplified his career by bringing him into The Sex Pistols in early 1977, despite the fact that he couldn't play bass guitar. (He replaced Glen Matlock, who composed much of the group's early repertoire.)

But... in one of many similarities to the management style of the '50s Tin Pan Alley hustlers that he emulated, McLaren simply didn't care. Vicious looked the part: slim, young, slightly cadaverous and doomed–looking, with a fine shock of dark hair. Usually dressed in the latest garb, he was actually quite handsome when not completely out of it on hard drugs, an on/off addiction to which caused him constant problems. More importantly, he had stage presence and could sing – when he wanted to – fairly well. After The Sex Pistols disintegrated in January 1978 Vicious released an extraordinary version of *My Way* (which reached No 7 in the UK charts in August '78) and then departed for the US, where he stabbed Spungen to death in the Chelsea Hotel, New York, a couple of months later, the most notorious of many notorious episodes to have occurred in this legendary building run by owner Stanley Bard as a bohemian refuge. Released on bail in February 1979, he died of a drug overdose the following day. After his demise, whoever inherited his estate enjoyed further successes when the album, *Sid Sings*, made No 12 in the UK charts and a couple of Cochrane covers, *Something Else* and *C'mon Everybody*, both got as high as No 3, all in 1979–80.

Joe Strummer, available in early 1986 after the final collapse of The Clash, did much of the music for *Sid and Nancy*, albeit his contributions were mainly uncredited to avoid contract issues with CBS. Cox also used Pray for Rain, a band formed specifically to do evocative soundtracks and named after a superb 1967 Box Tops track, for five numbers, whilst The Pogues, a late UK punk offshoot, provided another seven, one of which, *Haunted*, was a modest UK hit in 1986. Oldman, as Vicious, sings in the film too. Not all of this material appears on the soundtrack album. The critics liked it and it just about broke even on overall sales and quickly became a deserved cult hit. It may not, as John Lydon would insist, be scrupulously accurate, but as an updating of the classic rock and roll-lifestyle myth it is exceptionally well done, and was a huge step up in career terms for Oldman, who made *Prick Up Your Ears*, another study of a doomed young man (Joe Orton), immediately afterwards. Cox subsequently did two films with Joe Strummer, *Straight to Hell* and *Walker*, neither of which were hits.

Yet by the time *Sid and Nancy* reached audiences, many might have concluded, with respect to Lydon, Strummer and Weller, that the crown for being the most successful figure to emerge from UK punk after 1977 surely resided with Adam Ant, aka Stuart Goddard. Briefly one of the McLaren stable of artistes, he partly owed his breakthrough to McLaren advising that he copy the African tribal drumming of *Burundi Black* (a minor '71 hit) on his 1980 single *Dog Eat Dog* (No 4 UK). Despite splitting from McLaren, who replaced him as singer of the Ants with Annabelle Lwin and renamed the group Bow Wow Wow, he had five chart albums and a dozen hit singles between 1979 and 1984 and when the gold discs stopped raining down, moved seamlessly into acting, doing *Entertaining Mr Sloane* on the London stage and then heading for Hollywood. Here he fell in with 25-year-old fellow Brit and producer Cassian Elwes, whose debut film, *Oxford Blues* with Rob Lowe as an undergraduate amidst the dreaming spires, had just been a biggish hit. For his first US production Elwes opted for *Nomads*, with John McTiernan directing and Adam Ant in a co-starring role.

Both the plot and the cast are interesting. McTiernan provided his own script, set in a typically affluent American suburb where the locals are tormented by an 'urban tribe' of young outcasts. The narrative structure isn't straightforward, but one of the residents, a French anthropologist, finds out that there is more to them than expected and parallels are duly drawn with the various indigenous peoples he has previously studied. (In some ways, comparisons could be made here with McTiernan's colossal later success, *Predator* ('87), where typically mainstream US characters encounter an unexpectedly savage adversary.) The lead roles are played by Lesley-Anne Down and Pierce Brosnan (who replaced Gérard Depardieu). It was Brosnan's first starring role and the first time he had been seen in a film on UK screens since his small but influential appearance in *The Long Good Friday*. The urban interlopers (or 'nomads') are played by Adam Ant, as the leader of the gang, supported by Mary Woronov (once in *Chelsea Girls* and a Warhol acolyte), Josie Cotton, at that point signed to Elektra as a kind of high school/trash/garage guitar act, and Frank Doubleday, previously seen as a heavy in films like *Assault on Precinct 13* ('76) and *Escape from New York* ('81).

Much of the dramatic tension in the film was due to a rock music soundtrack mainly provided by Ted Nugent, ex-The Amboy Dukes and definitely on that basis alone a candidate – like several others – for the backstory that inspired *Spinal Tap*. No one rated *Nomads* as a great film, but it was entertaining, original and had a visceral power and got McTiernan selected by Arnold Schwarzenegger to do *Predator*. Elwes continued on his way and after *White of the Eye* ('87, a rare Donald Cammell film, with a Nick Mason soundtrack) had produced over 60 US features by 2018. Adam Ant's other film credits included *World Gone Wild* ('87), *Spellcaster* ('88 – top billed), *Trust Me* ('89), *Sunset Heat* ('92), *Love Bites* ('93), *Desert Winds* ('94), *Cyber Bandits* ('95, with Martin Kemp of Spandau Ballet) and *Drop Dead Rock* ('96, with Debbie Harry). He was the only UK musical figure to emerge out of the punk period who managed to assemble a half-decent acting career.

10
COMEDY

If *Quadrophenia* was a final farewell to the mod era, the emergence of Derek and Clive in 1976 was another signing off: the valedictory work of Peter Cook and Dudley Moore, two of the finest satirists of their time, whose careers, individually and collectively, stretched from the Royal Court Theatre, to *Saturday Night and Sunday Morning*, to guying Harold Macmillan at the Establishment Club, to predicting the emergence of a Blairite politician in *The Rise and Rise of Michael Rimmer*. After considerable successes in film (*Bedazzled*), TV (*Not Only... But Also*) and stage reviews (*Behind the Fridge*, a Hemdale-funded venture), like many of their contemporaries they seemed to disappear at the end of the '60s. But, unlike many, they returned via a trio of LPs whose production and sales eventually led to an accompanying film, *Derek and Clive Get the Horn* in 1979.

The material had its genesis in routines they improvised in 1972, whilst in New York doing *Behind the Fridge*, and intended, not unsurprisingly, given their deliberately obscene nature, for private distribution. Others spotted a clear commercial potential, however, and re-recording of the dialogues for Island ('76) and subsequently Virgin ('78) resulted in a couple of hit LPs, *Derek and Clive Live* ('76, No 12) and *Come Again* ('78, No 18). The film shows them making their final Virgin LP and was directed by Russell Mulcahy, whose only prior credit at that point had been the promotional video for The Saints, *I'm Stranded*, an Australian punk single that predated by a couple of months anything released in the UK.

It's a tour de force. The plot, in so far as one exists, has Cook and Moore playing delusional, racist and sexist lavatory attendants spewing out a blizzard of conspiracy theories and foul language. The setting is not specified, but in one's imagination it could easily have been one of the large underground urinals used as cruising cottages by the gay community. An intended cinema release was abandoned after the British Board of Film Censors refused to grant it a certificate and a planned straight-to-video release was blocked when all the available copies were impounded by the police.

In the midst of this uproar, Cook and Moore returned to the US, where they hosted early editions of the TV show *Saturday Night Live* and were greatly admired by a new generation of edgy, taboo-breaking comedians. They also tried to regenerate their film career with *The Hound of the Baskervilles* (July '78). Directed by Warhol associate Paul Morrissey, who had previously done the horror comedies *Flesh for Frankenstein* ('73) and *Blood for Dracula* ('74), this, sadly, despite a huge ensemble UK cast, most of whose talent was wasted, got terrible reviews. Michael White produced and Moore did the music in silent film style. Looking back, one wonders if this wasn't a missed opportunity. Could not Morrissey have made *Derek and Clive Get the Horn* instead? Perhaps as a vile, abusive satirical drama – possibly set in a bleak, JG Ballard-type dystopian London landscape – in the style of *Chelsea Girls* or *Trash?*

It was very much a last hurrah, as by early 1979 Moore was in Hollywood making *10*, which made him into a mega-star, whilst Cook remained in the UK and declined into alcoholism. There are few listings in official reference works today about *Derek and Clive Get the Horn*, but its scabrous and ribald approach makes for an interesting comparison with some of the films subsequently produced to showcase the new 'alternative' comedy talents arriving on the UK scene at this point. Whatever the conclusion, as a duo Cook and Moore went out in style.

Like them, and similarly originating in the UK satire boom of the early '60s, *Monty Python* had long mixed comedy, music and social comment. Eric Idle, Terry Jones and Michael Palin were all in *Do Not Adjust Your Set* ('67) with the Bonzo Dog Doo-Dah Band, whilst Graham Chapman and John Cleese worked on films like *The Rise and Rise of Michael Rimmer* and *The Magic Christian* (both '69). The ensemble also had a recording deal, with Charisma, where they nestled alongside Rare Bird, The Nice, Lindisfarne, Genesis, Clifford T Ward, Bo Hansson (and his *Lord of the Rings* concept album) and Hawkwind. Sales of their material on vinyl were healthy, with *Another Monty Python Record* (No 26 UK '71) and *Live at Drury Lane* (No 19 UK '74) both having decent chart runs.

After a successful and award-winning five-year TV run from 1969, they were ready by 1976 to diversify into other projects, with the first, *Jabberwocky* ('77), being directed by Terry Gilliam and co-written by him with Charles Alverson, a US writer who had arrived in the UK in 1969 and who had worked with Gilliam in the mid-'60s at the US satirical magazine *Help!* Given the collective popularity of the Python team, and that they were also liked in the US where both their preceding films, *And Now for Something Completely Different* and *Monty Python and The Holy Grail* had done well, raising funds for an original screenplay wasn't too difficult. Sanford Lieberson and John Goldstone (*The Final Programme*) produced.

For *Jabberwocky*, Gilliam cast Michael Palin in the lead and surrounded him with the cream of British situation comedy actors (Harry H Corbett, Warren Mitchell, John Le Mesurier, Rodney Bewes). Also seen here, in a rare co-starring role, is Max Wall, a former variety and music hall artist whose career stretched back to the '20s. Rediscovered decades later, Wall's deadpan non sequiturs were seemingly taken for a kind of proto-stoned hippy wisdom by younger audiences. Later credits in his career included starring in the absurdist farce *Ubu Roi*, touring with Mott the Hoople in 1972 (at 64 years old) and recording the Ian Dury song *England's Glory* for Stiff in April 1977. The plot of *Jabberwocky* takes Lewis Carroll's poem and twists it into something that resembles instead

Hieronymus Bosch. Visually, this is a world of derelict castles and crumbling buildings, where, with some parallels with the UK of the '70s, we have an incompetent civil service and a dithering leader (Wall as Bruno the Questionable). The art direction is one of the strong points, so much so that Stanley Kubrick later asked Gilliam for help in that area prior to shooting *The Shining*. Which turned out to be impossible: Kubrick's requirements were too exacting.

The film, of course, reflects very much the time when it was made and would not have been done in this style ten years earlier, when Lewis Carroll themes were popular in both music and film, and executed then in a quirky, dreamy, English eccentric way. There is much to enjoy, particularly the good comic underplaying and sense of the grotesque, with the style more Mervyn Peake than Carroll, an interesting juxtaposition given that Peake illustrated Carroll's work in the '40s. Not an outstanding box-office hit, it was liked on the student circuit, but looked down on by some mainstream critics as little more than 'an intellectual Carry On'.

Moving to EMI, the Python team reunited for *Life of Brian*, which they worked on throughout 1977–8, only for the film to fall into disarray when EMI pulled out after reading the script, fearing that the backlash from a full-on religious satire would damage the company. With a heavy interest in the US market, where religion was taken very seriously, this was hardly surprising and they had, of course, dropped The Sex Pistols a little earlier as soon as public outrage became noticeable. Once again, as with *The Long Good Friday*, George Harrison came to the rescue, funding it himself via HandMade Films. Written mainly by John Cleese and Graham Chapman and directed by Terry Jones, it was filmed in Tunisia using the same locations as Zeffirelli's *Jesus of Nazareth*. This is a very, very different film to Jarman's *Sebastiane*, but makes some clever points nonetheless and could be regarded as the high-water mark of the '60s satire boom.

Essentially a mistaken identity comedy about Jesus, in this version of the New Testament the three wise men go to the wrong manger and worship the wrong child: Brian, not Jesus, whose subsequent life, as a result, constantly involves him being mistaken for the Messiah. The film also dabbles in political satire (à la *Citizen Smith*, the 1977–80 BBC TV series), notably in its portrait of hair-splitting leftism as the Judean People's Front and the Popular Front of Judea debate the merits of the Romans. The finale – at the crucifixion – is staged like a scene from Kubrick's *Spartacus*, except that the cast here are performing *Always Look on the Bright Side of Life* as an uplifting cockney-style sing-a-long. As time went by this became an internationally popular anthem, even at one point being covered by US punk band Green Day. Reissued in 1991, it reached No 3 in the UK charts and was one of the pieces of music selected for the 2012 UK Olympic Games. Its author, Eric Idle, had some skill as a songwriter, having worked on the 1978 Beatles parody *The Rutles: All You Need is Cash*, with Neil Innes (ex-Bonzo Dog Doo-Dah Band), Ollie Halsall and John Halsey (both ex-Timebox).

Life of Brian came with a brilliant Shirley Bassey-style title song, done in the style usually associated with biblical epics. Except... it wasn't Shirley Bassey, but Sonia Jones, who also released her own disco music at this time. When the film was planned, the role of Jesus was offered to George Lazenby, still best known at this point for his solitary outing as a Carnaby Street-era Bond and a few Far East Kung-Fu productions. He declined and the part – not significant in the film as a whole and not treated satirically – went to Kenneth Colley, whose CV included parts in *Performance*, *Flame*, *Pennies from Heaven* and a range of Ken Russell films. The very idea, though, of Lazenby as Jesus and a brassy theme song was asking for trouble. Premiered in the US in August 1979, and the top grossing UK release of that year, it opened to massive controversy with attacks on it raining down from the likes of Mary Whitehouse, demonstrations outside cinemas and bans on its screening in many locations.

After this, Gilliam and Palin wrote *Time Bandits* ('81), a fantasy about a boy from a house in a soulless new cul-de-sac, who escapes the day-to-day drudgery and has adventures in other dimensions and across time. This is a highly inventive and fully realised alternative world, the first of three created by Gilliam, the others being *Brazil* ('85) and *The Adventures of Baron Munchausen* ('89). All were notable and welcome exceptions to the fare offered by the UK film industry during a period of accelerating decline. The starring roles are played by two memorable figures from the peak years of UK cinema, Sean Connery (hats off to him for this and *Zardoz*) and David Warner, a pioneer of absurdist/escapist drama in *Morgan – A Suitable Case for Treatment* ('66) and *Work is a Four-Letter Word* ('68), supported by John Cleese, Shelley Duvall and a raft of reliable UK character actors in guest slots.

Time Bandits was a big hit commercially. Unlike other fantasy films and film franchises in later years (for instance *Harry Potter*, set in the type of retro boarding-school Britain that appeals to tourists), there is a political point being made here about stifling conformism, the unpleasant nature of much of the modern world and the essentially wicked proclivities of modern corporate management and technological progress: Warner plays the Devil as a successful capitalist. It also bears comparison with another sci-fi fantasy that was hugely popular then, Douglas Adams' *The Hitchhiker's Guide to the Galaxy*. Adams had worked with the *Monty Python* team in 1974 and produced the original radio-play version of his work in March 1978 (which was broadcast with a soundtrack that included a couple of Pink Floyd tracks from their 1975 album *Shine on You Crazy Diamond*; Adams was a friend of Dave Gilmour). Various adaptations followed, the most memorable/notorious at the ICA from enfant terrible Ken Campbell in May 1979. Like *Time Bandits*, *The Hitchhiker's Guide to the Galaxy* was astonishingly successful. Its plot was similar too – focusing on the absurdity of day-to-day life and a release from that, for its simple central character, into a world of freewheeling fantasy.

Harrison produced – another feather in his cap – via HandMade Films and also wrote and performed the main theme, *Dream Away*, with Mike Moran; it appeared on Harrison's 1982 album *Gone Troppo*, which didn't sell. Moran had been at the Royal College of Music with Rick Wakeman in the late '60s, subsequently going on to work with John Kongos, Barry Ryan,

David McWilliams, Jimmy Helms, David Dundas, Peter Sarstedt and Lulu. The remainder of the score was done by Trevor Jones, whose other credits included *Life of Brian* and *Excalibur* and who would later make contributions to *The Dark Crystal* and *Labyrinth*. There was even a Dutch synthesiser band, Time Bandits, who took their name from the film and were signed by CBS. Their debut album has an image of a digital watch, a motif in the film. But... despite its box-office success, no *Time Bandits* soundtrack album appeared.

After a final sketch-based film – *The Meaning of Life* ('83) – the Python members went their separate ways, breaking up and pursuing solo careers rather like one of the big '60s rock bands. By the time they split, UK comedy was awash with what was then termed 'alternative' comedy, a style that had emerged in the late '70s and came together from the intertwining of three distinct ingredients: the network of agitprop; counterculture theatre groups; and performers established from the late '60s onwards, the worthy benefit concerts they tended to perform at and an intrusion into the UK of raw US comedy clubs.

Some of this had been around for years. The early poetry scene had yielded The Scaffold and Pete Brown. Notable, too, was the immense popularity Woody Allen enjoyed in the UK throughout the '70s, whilst many of the cognoscenti also cited Lenny Bruce as a major influence. One early UK practitioner who pulled these threads together was John Davidge, now long-forgotten, who did stand-up from 1967 and later appeared at Bernard Manning's Embassy Club. In 1970, as John Paul Joans, he had a hit single, *Man from Nazareth* (No 25 UK), backed by the musicians who later became 10cc, and further releases included a benefit record for the striking miners ('72), before he faded from the scene. Like Davidge, much of the new energy came from outside London, with two performers in particular standing out – John Cooper Clarke, a poet who interspersed his verse with comic asides and who was easily the most iconoclastic and the most tied to punk; and Alexei Sayle, the most versatile, mixing comedy, acting, surreal monologues and political commentary. Both had depth and both emerged defiantly out of the '60s counterculture. They illustrated, too, the extent to which comedy was 'the new rock and roll', with both of them playing the 1982 Glastonbury Festival. Thus, like bands and singers before them, it was expected that both would seamlessly transition into TV and film.

John Cooper Clarke affected the image of Bob Dylan circa 1966, wiry and with unkempt black hair bursting like a psychedelic bubble out of his head. From Salford, his father had been a semi-pro comedian on the northern pub circuit. Cooper Clarke Jnr actually had his early work published in *Grass Eye* (a minute circulation 'alternative' paper) as far back as 1970. Then, like Davidge/Joans, he had an early stint in Manning's club – which he even compèred at one point – after which he finally reached a wider audience via Rabid records in 1977, the same indie label that produced Jilted John, aka Graham Fellows, aka John Shuttleworth. CBS signed Cooper Clarke a year later and had a success with the album *Snap, Crackle and Bop* in 1980 (No 26 UK). After this, he was one of many turns in *Urgh! A Music War* ('81), before Channel 4 and the Arts Council funded *Ten Years in an Open Necked Shirt*, a 1982 film which co-starred Linton Kwesi Johnson. It bears comparison with Dylan's *Don't Look Back*, or, given the footage shot in and around Manchester, anything by Shelagh Delaney (*A Taste of Honey*, *The White Bus*, *Charlie Bubbles*). But it was poorly distributed and few people saw it. Which was a shame, as the final sequence with Cooper Clarke narrating *Beasley Street* against tracking shots of ruined terraced housing was deeply moving. He might have done more had he not explored the dark side, spending the rest of the decade in a squat in Lambeth, battling heroin addiction with Nico.

Alexei Sayle originated from Liverpool and after a spell at Chelsea Art School worked in graphic design. His image was part nightclub bouncer, part political activist and part anarchic observer of society. He was compère of the Comedy Store from its opening in Soho in 1979. (The original started in LA in 1972, the exporting of it to the UK replicating, during the same period, how punk copied the New York street and music culture.) After an early leading role in the utterly obscure *Repeater* ('79), much of his early film exposure reflected his background as a left-wing activist with Communist parents: *Fundamental Frolics* ('81, a filmed benefit concert for the disabled); *Whoops Apocalypse* ('82, an LWT comedy about nuclear incineration); *Live a Life* ('82, a documentary about the unemployed, filmed at the Rainbow); and *The Secret Policeman's Other Ball* ('82, a fundraiser for Amnesty International).

Sayle's breakthrough came with *The Young Ones*, a 1982 BBC TV series about students sharing a house that he starred in and co-wrote with Ben Elton. It featured a different band each week (Madness, The Damned, Motörhead, Dexys Midnight Runners and so on) and Sayle duly moved into music himself with *'Ullo John! Gotta New Motor?* ('84, No 15 UK). After this he appeared in *The Supergrass*, a determined 1985 attempt to bring together all the 'alternative' comedy players in a big-budget crime-caper film. With Rowan Atkinson, Mel Smith, Pamela Stephenson, Griff Rhys Jones and Ben Elton co-starring, it was a UK success and boasted a superior soundtrack, on Island, from Keith Tippett, PP Arnold, Grace Jones and Frankie Goes to Hollywood. Since then, he has mixed stand-up with comedy albums, film parts – *The Bride* ('85), *Siesta* ('87), *Indiana Jones and the Last Crusade* ('89), *Carry On Columbus* ('92) – script-writing (*Itch*, '91), novels, short stories, TV and radio monologues, whilst remaining recognisably the same figure who appeared 40 odd years ago.

Many of Sayle's fellow players in *The Supergrass* were first noted in the popular BBC2 TV series *Not the Nine O' Clock News* (October '79; it would have gone out earlier but was postponed due to the General Election), which, like the Comedy Store, was copied wholesale from a US source, in this case a faux newspaper, *Not the New York Times*. The wider public got another dose of them in *Boom, Boom, Out Go the Lights*. Both shows were presented in a traditional satirical sketch format, which could, in fact, have been done many years before, though its admirers were at pains to claim it had more credibility than, say, *The Two Ronnies*. The two stars of the show, Rhys Jones and Smith (whose demeanour was not unlike that of Barker and Corbett), later had the Mike Hodges feature

Morons from Outer Space ('85) built around them and which co-starred Jimmy Nail. Hodges' follow-up to *Flash Gordon* ('80), this was a piece of nonsense about an alien spaceship crash landing on the M1 and its crew getting involved in a music concert, a plot with echoes of *Popdown* ('68) and *Toomorrow* ('70). Like both of these, it failed at the box office, but the TV careers of Rhys Jones and Smith remained unaffected.

Occasional commercial successes also emerged from the political left, one such example being Dario Fo's *Accidental Death of an Anarchist*. A popular Italian play about a true incident, the subject was played as broad farce, rather than tragedy. Staged successfully in the UK in 1980, filmed by Thames TV in 1983 and finally shown on Channel 4 in 1985 (with as many references as possible to Thatcher's Government worked into the story), it starred Gavin Richards who had toured for years in the Belt and Braces Theatre Group, a Ken Campbell-type ensemble, doing political rock musicals.

But neither dramas like this nor revolutionary activism were ever going to generate widespread commercial success or supplant mainstream TV and film. Instead, support for good causes, some of which had roots in the counterculture of the '60s and the satire boom, remained for many the preferred way of expressing a difference with the prevailing views of the time. Amnesty International, in particular, started a long series of fundraising stage reviews, TV programmes, films and albums with *A Poke in the Eye* ('76), which was sufficiently popular to produce *The Secret Policeman's Ball* ('79) and a set of sequels that ran through to 2012. Devised by John Cleese, other early participants included Terry Jones, Michael Palin, Graham Chapman, Tim Brooke-Taylor, Peter Cook, Jonathan Miller, Rowan Atkinson, Billy Connolly, Pete Townshend, Eric Clapton, Jeff Beck, Phil Collins, Tom Robinson, Sting and Julien Temple. *The Secret Policeman's Other Ball* ('82) included Bob Geldof who, ultimately, with *Band Aid* ('84) and *Live Aid* ('85), brought this approach to a culmination as he – and the colleagues he mustered – single-handedly responded to famine and poverty in Africa. For *Live*

Aid the line-up was tremendous, featuring Status Quo, The Style Council, The Boomtown Rats, Adam Ant, Ultravox, Spandau Ballet, Elvis Costello, Nik Kershaw, Sade, Sting, Phil Collins, Howard Jones, Bryan Ferry, David Gilmour, Paul Young, Alison Moyet, U2, Dire Straits, Queen, David Bowie, The Who, Elton John, Paul McCartney, Black Sabbath, Judas Priest, Simple Minds, The Pretenders, The Thompson Twins, Eric Clapton, Led Zeppelin, Duran Duran, Mick Jagger, Keith Richards and Ronnie Wood, together with any number of comedians, actors and celebrity presenters. In terms of scale and audience figures, this was massive and outstripped earlier efforts such as George Harrison's *The Concert for Bangladesh* ('71).

What is striking today is how much success was enjoyed by some of these newcomers and how prolific a few of them were. Ben Elton knocked out 14 bestselling novels (often on fashionably dystopian themes) over 23 years, collaborated with Andrew Lloyd Webber on musicals, did a jukebox musical of his own based on the hits of Queen and wrote innumerable TV series. Rowan Atkinson devised the *Blackadder* series ('83, for six years, with Elton) and then cleaned up internationally on both TV ('90) and film ('97, directed by Mel Smith) with *Mr Bean*, a blundering comic civil servant whose misadventures provided an immensely successful sequel in 2007. He continues to play variations of this character in the Johnny English franchise, a set of Bond parodies that started in 2003 and continues to run. Compared with this level of stratospheric success, Cooper Clarke and Sayle remain much the same today as they always were, whilst alongside them a new generation of comedians emerges who are as acerbic and observational about society's failings as their predecessors.

As noted, much of the 'new comedy' of the '70s and '80s originated in the US, where, complementing the club appearances, TV shows and albums that the genre produced, were a couple of important and influential films. The first of these, *Americathon*, was adapted by Phil Proctor and Peter Bergman from a play 'set in the near future' and represents the culmination of their work in the subculture of US political comedy. Starting out in the Firesign

Theatre comedy revue back in 1967 they had previously produced a string of albums culminating in *What This Country Needs* ('75), as well as scripting the rock western *Zachariah* ('71). What they present in *Americathon* is a bizarre dystopian farce set in 1998, in which the US has gone bankrupt, people are destitute and the Governor of California (an overly-optimistic man who quotes positive affirmation slogans) has become President. In short, a grim version of an American future where the country has no oil, everyone wears sports clothes and political debate is conducted at imbecile level. Written and filmed in late 1981, long before Trump, it turns out to have been an uncannily accurate version of what was to come. Lorimar produced, and, had they been more astute, they might have sent this out as a raucous supporting feature to *Being There* ('79), a great success for them at the same time, which explores, in a serious vein, the possibility of a simpleton becoming President.

Directed by Neal Israel, who wrote the 1978 TV movie *Ringo* (with Ringo Starr, George Harrison and various others), *Americathon* has a cast led by Harvey Korman, from the ensemble usually used by Mel Brooks, and Peter Riegert, later seen in *Local Hero*. A huge range of comedy and music figures guest or co-star, including Meat Loaf and, bizarrely, the Del Rubio triplets. Elvis Costello appears too, playing the Earl of Manchester, his inclusion a confirmation of his popularity in the US where he had six Top 30 albums between 1978 and 1984.

The end product, though, failed to generate warm reviews. Roger Ebert called it 'puerile exploitation', quite a put-down from the author of *The Great Rock N' Roll Swindle*. Today it is an obscure work and usually unlisted in reference books of the period. One might conclude that Proctor and Bergman's style worked in small theatres and clubs, and even on TV, but didn't particularly translate to film. For instance, *J Men Forever*, a comedy pastiche that they wrote around the same time as *Americathon*, with music from UK heavy rock outfit Budgie and US satirists The Tubes, is less impressive than Carl Reiner's film-noir spoof *Dead Men Don't Wear Plaid*. A UK equivalent of them isn't immediately obvious.

A soundtrack album was released on CBS with five songs by Elvis Costello and a contribution from Nick Lowe. There was no UK release at the time for either the film or the soundtrack, something which wasn't the case with *This Is Spinal Tap* in 1984.

A brilliant cinéma-vérité spoof documentary, *Spinal Tap* is a flawless parody (as anyone who was around at the time will testify) of the pedestrian, conventional rock bands that still existed throughout the punk/new-wave period... aimlessly traversing the US on annual promotional tours as they tried to nudge their latest nondescript album through the lower reaches of the Hot 100. The film portrays one such dinosaur, an absurd, massively self-regarding relic that is ripe for debunking: Spinal Tap, a fictional UK band that started out doing psychedelic pop, before peddling grossly inflated and overblown stadium rock whilst constantly changing its drummer.

Christopher Guest, a British national, long resident in the US and half-brother of Anthony Haden-Guest, one of the key swingers in '60s London, co-wrote and co-starred, having previously done a lot of work on US TV for the likes of Chevy Chase. In fact, Spinal Tap as an ensemble character first appeared in a TV special in 1979; making the feature-length version of their escapades took five years with authenticity being key. One of their many drummers was played by Rick Parnell, ex-Atomic Rooster, whilst on keyboards could be found David Kafinetti, formerly of Rare Bird. A great deal of speculation ensued about what band Spinal Tap were based on. Given their psychedelic origins and subsequent denim-clad excesses, Status Quo? Or just on the turnover of drummers, Gentle Giant? (Who arose out of another psychedelic outfit, Simon Dupree and The Big Sound.) Or were they Parnell's very first outfit – Horse – a rather drab, heavy blues rock ensemble who put out an album on RCA in 1970? It is interesting to note that the film satirises ill-educated and pretentious UK rock stars, rather than any of the US bands/musicians who fell into the same category. This was a clear example of the UK's cultural heritage being pillaged for commercial success by others: and in the case of Atomic Rooster and Rare Bird somewhat unfair as both were decent acts. And, of course, the thought occurs as to why something like this really wasn't being made in the UK.

Rob Reiner directed and the film was successful commercially. Culturally, though, it was a massive step forward and led to the fly-on-the-wall observational comedy of the '90s and beyond. The ensemble playing by the cast is brilliant, with plenty of absurd pomposity and self-regarding nonsense on display. Michael McKean and Harry Shearer, both of whom had been in the US TV series *Laverne and Shirley*, co-star. The film eventually became such an 'in joke' that the actors actually went on tour as Spinal Tap, playing to packed houses. Their 1992 album on MCA, *Break Like the Wind*, featured Jeff Beck and Nicky Hopkins and even yielded a couple of minor hit singles. *Spinal Tap*, though, set the gold standard for works of this type and still seems a fresh, relevant portrait when watched today.

11

RACE

Race featured significantly in the plots of a couple of UK films during the kitchen-sink era, notably *Sapphire* ('59) and *Flame in the Streets* ('61), only to fade away into the background when the 'Swinging Sixties' erupted. But whilst British cinema produced neither a Sidney Poitier nor a James Earl Jones, it did, eventually, have sufficient space for Frankie Dymon Jr, whose supporting feature *Death May Be Your Santa Claus* ('69) was arguably the UK's first and only example of a 'Black Power' film. Shot in the same locations as John Boorman's *Leo the Last* ('70), another neglected film portraying the rising inner-city black community, it was hardly seen anywhere. Dymon was a colleague of Michael X and had been in Godard's *Sympathy for the Devil* ('68), but after the commercial failure of his film he quit the UK for West Germany where he made a funk album, *Let it Out* ('72), before vanishing from the public eye.

The commercial success of reggae in the UK – where music of this type produced 38 hit singles between 1967 and 1972 – led, inevitably, to a feature film portraying that scene. *The Harder They Come* was filmed in Jamaica in early 1972 and got a release in the US a year later via Roger Corman. Chris Blackwell, uncredited, put up production funds and it came with music by Jimmy Cliff (who starred), Desmond Dekker and The Maytals, but the UK distribution was quite restricted and it mainly played the late-night circuit. Blackwell's biggest black star would eventually turn out to be Bob Marley, but in terms of film work Marley, other than documentaries, was restricted to providing a bit of the soundtrack to the Swedish *Love Is Not a Game* ('71), which starred singer Johnny Nash (then, despite being a US soul singer, the most successful reggae act internationally) and again was hard to see anywhere outside its country of origin.

The big breakthrough – commercially – in terms of non-white cinema came with the Hong Kong-produced Kung-Fu films, specifically from 1971 when Bruce Lee became the first genuine ethnic minority film star in the world. Made on far lower budgets than US or European features, the audiences for Lee's big hits *The Way of the Dragon* and *Enter the Dragon* in 1972 and 1973 produced such stupendous returns on modest investment that other producers quickly cashed in, notably Hammer with *The Legend of the Seven Golden Vampires* and the Bond franchise with *The Man with the Golden Gun*, both of which were filmed wholly or partly in Hong Kong.

In the latter case this was somewhat ironic, given that in popular mythology the view long prevailed that George Lazenby made the biggest mistake in his life by walking away from the Bond franchise in 1970 and that his career ended after this. Even at the time this wasn't true. Though *Universal Soldier* ('71) was a misfire (but by no means as bad as some held at the time), after this Lazenby did a superior giallo thriller *Who Saw Her Die* ('72) and on the strength of these and his outing as 007 in *On Her Majesty's Secret Service* ('69), by the summer of 1973 he had signed up for a trio of films with Kung-Fu legend Bruce Lee, at that point the biggest star in the world. Alas, Lee died a few days after the contract was agreed, but the films went ahead anyway and were still big-budget Hong Kong productions.

After the success of the first film, *The Shrine of Ultimate Bliss/Stoner* ('74), the second, *The Man from Hong Kong*, was eagerly awaited. Set in Australia, it co-stars Jimmy Wang Yu (the most potent Hong Kong star post-Lee) and is a well-made fast-moving crime thriller with excellent car chases and extended, very violent, fight sequences. Much of it is shot in the Australian outback, with Lazenby as an organised crime boss and Yu playing the policeman from Hong Kong sent to arrest him. As such, it would not be wrong to regard it as the missing link between Carnaby Street, as personified by Lazenby in 1969, and *Mad Max*, given that we also find in the supporting cast Hugh Keays-Byrne and Roger Ward (both subsequently in *Mad Max*), Frank Thring (who would appear in *Mad Max: Beyond Thunderdrome*) and Bill Hunter (previously, with Thring, in Mick Jagger's *Ned Kelly*). Lazenby is physically robust, holds his own in the fight sequences and the film is entertaining. It did well at the box office.

The main title theme was by UK group Jigsaw. Like Slade, they had an ancestry that went back some distance, with most of them originally in The Mighty Avengers, an Andrew Loog Oldham act with three Decca singles in 1965–6. They evolved, after a name change, into a mod soul band on MGM in 1967–8 and from there morphed into a 'progressive' group with a concept album on Philips in 1970. Subsequently embracing commercial pop, their song *Sky High* is the main theme in *The Man from Hong Kong* and reached No 9 in the UK and No 3 in the US. The remainder of the score was by Noel Quinlan, originally guitarist and singer in Australian garage band The Jet Set back in the '60s.

Lazenby and Yu made a follow-up, *A Queen's Ransom* ('76), with Lazenby playing an IRA assassin planning to kill Her Majesty on a state visit to Hong Kong. All three Lazenby Kung-Fu films were hugely popular in Hong Kong, Taiwan, Korea, Japan, the Philippines, Australia, Malaysia and selected parts of the US, so much so that by the end of the decade he was one of the most widely viewed actors in the world. In the UK, though, such works played to largely ethnic minority audiences on the late-night fleapit circuit in decaying inner urban town centres and were barely noticed by the critics. Many of these had all-night Kung-Fu screenings, where the vast number of Hong Kong-produced features could be watched alongside many of the US blaxploitation works of the period.

Attempts to make a UK feature with a black crew and cast continued and eventually led to the BFI-funded *Pressure*

('75). Written and directed by Horace Ové, who had made a documentary about a reggae festival staged at Wembley in 1970, this drama, set on the streets of Ladbroke Grove, waited three years to get a limited release due to it depicting (accurately) scenes showing police violence. *Pressure* starred Herbert Norville, later seen in *Scum*, and Oscar James, subsequently in a supporting role in *Black Joy*, and it would be the latter film, directed by Anthony Simmons, that became the first widely seen UK example of black cinema in 1977.

Simmons, despite winning various prizes at European film festivals, was a respected but underused UK director whose feature *The Optimists of Nine Elms*, with Peter Sellers as a streetwise busker in a run-down Battersea, had been a modest success in 1973. *Black Joy*, with a budget of £150,000, was his follow-up to this, with Elliott Kastner (*Villain*, *Zee and Co*) producing, and was adapted from a play, *Dark Days and Light Nights*, by Jamal Ali. Ali, originally Clifford Agard, a British Rail wages clerk from Guyana, was regarded by Simmons as 'the Damon Runyon of Brixton', and had, indeed, set up a black theatre project in the area.

What we get on the big screen is a gentle culture-clash comedy where a naïve young man arrives in Brixton from Guyana and various misadventures ensue. This is SW9 in the '70s with squatters, conmen, feral kids, music venues (formal and not) and lots of brown and orange interiors. *Black Joy* remains worth watching today as a faithful record of how London looked nearly 50 years ago: glum and derelict, with an abundance of empty buildings and abandoned cars. Trevor Thomas stars with Norman Beaton (who in an earlier career in the mid-'60s had once been guitarist in The Scaffold) and Floella Benjamin (from *Hair*, *Jesus Christ Superstar*) in supporting roles. Beaton was voted best actor of 1977 by the Variety Club of GB for his performance here: not an Oscar, nor even a BAFTA, but recognition nonetheless.

The Playboys, a small-scale UK reggae group, appear in one scene and Chris Rea did the score. From Middlesbrough, Rea had been with Magnet records since 1974 and enjoyed his commercial breakthrough shortly afterwards with *Fool (If You Think It's Over)*,

(No 30, October '78). Rea always had ambitions to do film work and his later credits would include *Cross Country* (Canada, '83), *Into the Darkness* ('85, shot in Malta and Manchester) and *Auf immer und ewig* ('86, West Germany). An official soundtrack album was released on Ronco and made No 26 in the UK charts. Consisting mainly of US soul hits, it also had two tracks by The Cimarons (a UK–Jamaican group and later early exponents of Rock Against Racism), including their version of the title song *Black Joy*. They'd been putting out material since 1969 and by this point had released no fewer than 33 singles, a prolific output that was typical of many reggae acts.

In some ways resembling a UK version of a US blaxploitation film, *Black Joy* was released with an X-certificate, as was *Saturday Night Fever* a little later. Its portrayal of the black community in Brixton in the '70s is important, however hackneyed it may seem today. An accurate illustration of its time and as unjustly neglected as *Leo the Last*, it represents a world that has now passed and been supplanted by a greatly gentrified inner city. The immediate future, though, would be bleak. Serious rioting took place in Brixton a few years later, causing further destruction to an already blighted area.

A more direct comparison with *Saturday Night Fever* might be *The Music Machine* ('79), one of many films in the strange career of James Kenelm Clarke. Starting out leading an easy-listening orchestra in the late '60s, Clarke also dabbled in library music for film and TV, with one of his compositions making it into the US hippy road movie *Two-Lane Blacktop* ('71). In 1973 he directed the BBC Man Alive documentary *Twinkle Twinkle Little Star*, about the search for a clean, wholesome British teenybopper act that could rival The Osmonds, after which he scored the lesbian vampire shocker *Vampyres* ('74) and directed *Got It Made*, an X-certificate drama set in Norwich. Neither were great films, but they led to a trio of efforts attempting, with mixed results, to make a legit film star out of glamour model Fiona Richmond: *Trauma* ('76), *Hardcore* ('77) and *Let's Get Laid* ('78). The latter two of these did good business on the sex-cinema circuit.

Combining an ability to shoot cheaply and quickly with a modest cast, and fully clued-up about the use of incidental music and main title themes, Clarke was – with hindsight – an obvious possibility (if not the best choice) for the role of executive producer of *The Music Machine*, a 1979 Brit imitation of *Saturday Night Fever*. Directed by Ian Sharp, who had done the 1978 BBC documentary *The Record Machine* with Debbie Harry, The Mekons and The Slits, *The Music Machine* is about a disco-dancing competition and stars Gerry Sundquist, who had just appeared with Nastassja Kinski in *Passion Flower Hotel* (78), and Patti Boulaye. Filmed at The Music Machine – a major London live music venue – it yielded a soundtrack LP on Pye assembled by Frank Ricotti (whose credits stretch back to 1968 and *Hair*) and Trevor Bastow. The decision to cast Boulaye, who had recording deals with Anchor and Polydor around this time, was interesting, as few black actresses had leading roles in UK films either then, or for some years afterwards. The supporting cast is led by Michael Feast, like Ricotti another *Hair* veteran, but no one would claim the end result is great drama. Unlike *Saturday Night Fever* itself – an X-rated release when it stormed the world in 1977, and a good companion piece to Scorsese's *Mean Streets* – the end result is dingy, clichéd and very clearly aimed at young adolescents. Nor did the soundtrack chart, unlike several other disco compilations around this time. *The Music Machine* had no lasting artistic impact, but deserves some credit for its portrayal of a mixed-race relationship and also serves as a reminder of just how popular disco remained in the UK in the late '70s.

Curiously, much of the film's interest today lies in our recognition of the significance of the building where most of the action takes place. Formerly a BBC-owned theatre, the programmes recorded there from the '50s through to 1970 include *The Goon Show* and the debut album from *Monty Python's Flying Circus*. Reborn as The Music Machine in 1977, it became one of about a dozen sacred temples across London hosting over the next five years just about every major punk and new-wave act. By the '90s it was being managed by Sam Taylor-Johnson and subsequently voted the most promising young artist at the 1997

Venice Biennale. It is no exaggeration to say that from its music-hall beginnings in 1900 to the present this has been a cultural hub of some reckoning... within which its disco period was, perhaps mercifully, rather slight.

By contrast, *Blacks Britannica* provides a very serious look at black culture in the UK. Just as Wolfgang Büld had explored the UK's nascent musical scene, David Koff did likewise when tackling the country's social and political mores. A US documentary maker, with the eye and attitude of an anthropologist, he had lived in Sierra Leone, Ghana and Kenya in the '60s prior to pitching up in the UK and releasing *White Man's Country* ('70 – with music from Peter Frampton), the first of a trio of films charting the iniquities of colonisation in Africa.

In 1977 – Silver Jubilee year – Koff was commissioned by Boston TV station WGBH to make an hour-long programme about race relations in the UK. Approaching this in the same way that he would have done a field trip, what emerged was *Blacks Britannica*, arguably the best film of its type, and one that really ought to have been forthcoming from the UK itself. Mixing rare archive footage and extensive interviews, Koff portrays Britain as a society that is deeply oppressive towards black people. It created controversy on both sides of the Atlantic and was attacked by one US TV executive as having a 'Marxist agenda'. An official of the British Information Service (the PR wing of the Foreign Office) duly intervened, on the basis that the film was 'dangerous' and insisted that if it were shown the UK Government should be granted an equal amount of time to put 'the counter case', whilst *New York Times* critic John O'Connor said the film 'not only documents the growing militancy, but, quite clearly, the structure and tone endorse it'. To Koff's dismay, WGBH buckled under the pressure and dropped the transmission, deeming the film too overtly political.

The main sticking point for the (many) objectors appears to have been that among those taking part are Darcus Howe, nephew of CLR James, like Frankie Dymon Jr a one-time member of Michael X's UK Black Panthers and later editor of *Race Today* magazine. Musically, Steel Pulse are both seen and heard. From

Handsworth, they were a significant reggae act at the time and their LP *Handsworth Revolution* was released on Island in August 1978 and rose to No 9 in the UK charts.

As a piece of serious intellectual filmmaking, well-argued throughout and extremely even-handed, *Blacks Britannica* is on a par with the writing of Frantz Fanon or Jürgen Habermas. In Europe, where Fanon and Habermas were studied closely (and where Can even paraphrased Habermas in the lyrics of their 1976 hit *I Want More*), none of this would have been exceptional. But in the UK *Blacks Britannica* was banned and not finally seen until 1989. The treatment meted out to this film in 1978, and later years, effectively indicates that anything of this type was automatically regarded as 'Marxist', that nothing like it would be made in the UK, and if it were made, certainly not broadcast. Today it is occasionally screened at places like the Institute for Race Relations.

Despite the difficulties that attended the distribution of both *The Harder They Come* and *Pressure*, film and TV companies began exploring the possibilities presented by the inner-city black communities in earnest after the commercial breakthrough of Bob Marley in 1975-6 in the UK and US. A slew of documentaries about black music and culture quickly appeared, mainly screened in the emerging network of community cinemas that existed around London. Starting with *Roots Rock Reggae* (filmed in Jamaica in 1977 by Jeremy Marre, with Jimmy Cliff and Bob Marley), others in this field included: *Rockers* (Jamaica, '78, with various local stars such as Gregory Isaacs, Burning Spear and Big Youth), which was shown with subtitles due to its patois dialogue; *Reggae in Babylon* (made in the UK by the indefatigable Wolfgang Büld in 1978 with Alton Ellis, Steel Pulse, Aswad and Matumbi); *Reggae Sunsplash 2* (a 1979 West German concert film shot in Jamaica); *Heartland Reggae* ('80, a concert film featuring Marley, Dennis Brown and Marcia Griffiths); *Bob Marley* ('81, more concert footage); *Land of the Look Behind* ('82, Marley again and Gregory Isaacs); *Bob Marley and The Wailers: The Bob Marley Story* ('84, the official version, narrated by Darcus Howe); and *Bullwackie* ('85, with Horace Andy, Sugar Minott and Lone Ranger).

In terms of drama, *Babylon* ('80) has a very superior set of credits for a film that got a relatively minor distribution and is barely remembered today. Partially funded by the National Film Finance Corporation, Gavrik Losey produced after previously working on *That'll Be the Day*, *Stardust* and *Flame*. Franco Rosso directed and co-wrote the script with Martin Stellman, who had just done *Quadrophenia*. It was Rosso's follow-up to a documentary, *Dread, Beat an' Blood*, about Linton Kwesi Johnson. The ensemble cast in *Babylon*, which includes Trevor Laird, Karl Howman, Mel Smith and Victor Romero Evans, is led by Brinsley Forde, something of a veteran having by this point racked up credits in *Leo the Last* ('70), *Here Come the Double Deckers* ('70, TV with a soundtrack LP on Capitol) and *The Georgian House* ('76, TV). As well as acting, Forde had a parallel career in the reggae band Aswad, who recorded for Island and CBS through the '70s and '80s.

Set in Deptford and Brixton, this is a story about rival sound systems, police harassment and gang violence that, accurately, given their condition at the time, makes its surroundings look like the Bronx. The cinematography, from Chris Menges (*The War Game*, *Kes*, *Gumshoe*) brilliantly captures the juxtaposition of decay with the vibrancy of emerging home-grown, non-white culture. What we get is a close-up vision of the economic hinterland of the black music scene, the endemic white racism and the restricted opportunities that were available to those still deemed, in the '70s, to be temporary visitors from overseas.

This was a subculture with enormous popularity among the young black community, as well as a niche appeal to their white counterparts. It was also regarded as politically okay. *Babylon* produced a soundtrack LP released by Chrysalis in 1980 that featured material by Aswad and Dennis Bovell, who also worked with The Slits and The Boomtown Rats at this point. The line between what constitutes the soundtrack and what you get to hear in the film itself is actually quite fine, as among those appearing as themselves in *Babylon* are Mikey Dread, King Sounds and Jah Shaka.

Burning an Illusion, made by the BFI after *Pressure*, opens with a scene that many young people today might find quite remarkable: a voice-over from the main character about how she is 'doing okay, 24, with a job and a flat of my own'; in summary, personal circumstances that were still entirely possible in 1981. A very well-made drama about a young black woman's love life and her politicisation, *Burning an Illusion* was directed by Menelik Shabazz, a 26-year-old Barbadian, and won the Grand Prix at the Amiens International Film Festival. Set in North Kensington, the plot concerns the main character's plans to get married and how these are abruptly curtailed when her boyfriend is arrested on trumped-up charges and jailed. She reacts against this, identifying herself as an African and finding the value of political protest.

The leading role is played by Cassie McFarlane, 23 when it was filmed, and already at that point noted for her appearances in several TV plays. Her performance here was reckoned by some to make her the best new actress of 1981. In fact, she waited five years after this for any more film or TV work, which illustrates how even the most promising careers could run into the sand in the UK at this point. During this pause she appeared instead as one of the Radical Alliance of Poets and Players. In 1982 this ensemble released a Dennis Bovell-produced EP, *Wicked City*, on Y records, then home to The Pop Group, Pigbag and Sun Ra. Victor Romero Evans, a lovers-rock singer who released his own album in 1982, co-stars with McFarlane and also sings on the soundtrack, which additionally features Janet Kay, Pablo Gad, Samantha Rose and Judy Mowatt. Of these, Janet Kay was the best known, having reached No 2 in the charts in June 1979 with *Silly Games*. She appears in *Burning an Illusion* as the singer in an outfit called The Government, who in real life also included Victor Romero Evans. They released a trio of reggae singles on minor labels as well as acting in a couple of productions written by Farrukh Dhondy: the play *Mama Dragon* ('80), a drama about various misfortunes suffered by the black community that is not unlike this film; and the TV series *No Problem!* ('83), about West Indian siblings living in Willesden Green whose parents have retired and returned back home.

The vogue for lovers-rock, a very accessible and smooth soul-reggae with its own extensive 'below the radar' scene, is worthy of some comment too. Its greatest exponent would turn out to be Sade, who to a certain extent emulated the sound a few years later in the white market with immense success – but was she actually 'better' than either Kay or Mowatt?

All in all, *Burning an Illusion* was an accurate depiction of what it was like to be young and black in the UK – and even in London – in the '70s and early '80s. The limited success and exposure of many of those who appeared in the production, compared, say, with better-known white stars and groups, is an interesting demonstration of how marginalised the black community was at that time. It also reflects the indifference of the wider community to the black community: 1981 was the year of the New Cross fire, in which 13 young black people died, an event for which no prosecution was ever brought.

With so many UK films about the black community being banned, unreleased or poorly distributed, it seems fitting to refer to *Downtown 81*, a US-made documentary that suffered (albeit unintentionally) a similar fate. Throughout the '70s and '80s, the UK very much followed the lead of New York and other US cities in how it dealt with a new urban environment that arose from surroundings dominated by empty plots and derelict land. It was a time when defunct industrial buildings were converted into studio and living space, gang violence and graffiti proliferated and the middle classes escaped to the safety of the suburbs. Much of the music arising from this milieu was first recorded on film in *The Blank Generation* ('76), an Amos Poe production with Television, Blondie, Patti Smith, The Ramones and Talking Heads among others, and subsequently showcased on *TV Party*, a cable TV show hosted by Andy Warhol associate Glenn O'Brien. A couple of years later, O'Brien wrote and produced *Downtown 81*, a study of New York and its contemporary counterculture. Edo Bertoglio, a Swiss fashion photographer for *Vogue*, who also did photo shoots of LP sleeves for the likes of James White and Blondie, directed.

The story centres on the day-to-day tribulations of Jean-Michel

Basquiat, a 19-year-old black graffiti artist and musician. Anne Carlisle, a writer and actress, co-stars and the sharp-eyed will spot Giorgio Gomelsky, one-time '60s mover and shaker at Marmalade records, in a minor part as Basquiat's landlord. Well-made and shot in an engagingly informal way (it remains very watchable), the action takes place in a desolate, semi-abandoned inner-city zone of the type also common then in similar UK locations. The film illustrates, in fact, the similarities between the UK and US scenes in the '80s: graffiti, hip-hop music, unfashionable urban areas. Music by Blondie, Kid Creole and The Coconuts, Dillinger and The Specials is prominently featured, the last three of whom were all significantly more popular in the UK than the US. Creole, who emerged out of the Haitian street culture of New York, cultivated a '40s Zoot Suit-style image and had two hit LPs and four hit singles in the UK in 1982–3. Granada TV even built a film around him: *There's Something Wrong in Paradise* ('84), with the band on a tropical island run by a totalitarian government. Pauline Black and Peter Straker co-starred.

And, if Creole travelled in one direction across the Atlantic in search of success, Malcolm McLaren, visiting New York in 1981 to scout for a support act for Bow Wow Wow, was heading in the opposite. Liking what he heard and saw, McLaren assembled an album, *Duck Rock* (No 9 UK, '83), that pulled together the vestiges of urban hip-hop seen in *Downtown 81* and came with a cover designed by Basquiat's fellow graffiti artist, Keith Haring. The film soundtrack was put together by Vincent Gallo, who, like Basquiat, was a member of the band Gray, who provide three tracks. But, despite the best efforts of O'Brien and Bertoglio, funding ran out and *Downtown 81* was never completed. We can only speculate what the ending may have been.

Spotted early on by UK pop artist Stan Peskett, who recognised before many others that graffiti could be a mainstream art form, Basquiat was heavily promoted by Andy Warhol and Robert 'Groovy Bob' Fraser exhibited his work in London a couple of years later, alongside that of Keith Haring. Basquiat died in '88 of a heroin overdose, at the rock-and-roll age of 27, but his influence on urban culture was immense. Gallo later became a significant US actor/director with strong right-wing political affiliations. At the time he was making *Downtown 81*, O'Brien also produced *Subway Riders* ('81), directed by Amos Poe with Robbie Coltrane, another US production with a noticeable UK influence. Carlisle for her part later had leading roles in *Liquid Sky* ('82) and *Perfect Strangers* ('84, directed by Larry Cohen), after which she concentrated on performance art and photography.

Eventually, after Basquiat and his story had been dramatised in *Basquiat* ('96), with David Bowie (as Warhol), Dennis Hopper, Gary Oldman, Courtney Love, Willem Dafoe, Christopher Walken and many others (you couldn't move for people who wanted to be in it), money was found to knock *Downtown 81* into sufficient shape to allow it to be released. With French photographer and designer Maripol as co-producer, it finally appeared in 2000 with a soundtrack on Virgin following in 2001. Whilst it remains both eminently viewable and relatively obscure, as a document recording a crucial time and place in cultural evolution it is essential viewing. The cultural cross-pollination that it shows between the UK and the US at this point is so marked that one may wonder who was influencing whom.

12

BEYOND ENGLAND

Throughout this period, one thing was certain: however bleak the rest of the UK might have been, Northern Ireland was worse. It had more violence, more unemployment, worse housing and more inner-city dereliction... nowhere in Britain was as miserable as parts of the six counties of Northern Ireland in the '70s and '80s. In the '60s the area gave birth, musically, to Them and Taste, but had a limited cinema profile. Nobody made films in Ulster. Billy Connolly ventured there in 1976 with his concert film *Big Banana Feet*, but few others followed. In many ways the area was the ultimate teenage wasteland with only one decent record shop, Good Vibrations, in a semi-derelict building in Great Victoria Street, Belfast. The shop also operated its own label, whose main act, The Undertones, emerged in the summer of 1978 and were promptly snapped up by US major Sire (home of The Ramones, Talking Heads and Patti Smith) a few months later. John Peel loved them and between 1979 and 1981 they had four hit singles and three chart albums. Running them a close second were Stiff Little Fingers, signed by Rough Trade in September 1978, who had one hit single and five chart albums between 1979 and 1983. Not surprisingly, the filmmakers quickly visited the source of this success.

An early cinematic work was *Shellshock Rock* (April '79), a 46-minute documentary made locally for £5,000 by John Davis with Stiff Little Fingers and many other local groups. Plans for a soundtrack LP came to nothing and the film was banned at its own premiere in the Republic of Ireland, where very conservative attitudes still prevailed. Like the hand-held footage assembled by Wolfgang Büld, *Shellshock Rock* is a film made by a figure on the periphery of the industry. Davis later did two others in the same vein – *Protex Hurrah* ('80, featuring Protex) and *Self-Conscious Over You* ('81, with The Outcasts) – but neither of the bands showcased in these reached the levels of success enjoyed by Stiff Little Fingers and neither film is widely seen today. By the mid-'80s Davis had moved on from low-budget music documentaries to a road movie about Studs Terkel travelling across the US (*Route 66*, '85).

Feature directors arrived with Tony Luraschi's *The Outsider* (November '79) about a US Vietnam veteran who volunteers for the IRA. A scene showing a British army officer torturing an Irish prisoner caused outrage outside Northern Ireland and the film got dropped from the London Film Festival as a result and it was hardly seen subsequently, despite decent reviews and a strong cast. A slightly better fate awaited *Looks and Smiles* (August '81), which Ken Loach shot in black and white in Sheffield from a Barry Hines book: Hines had written *Kes*, the adaptation of which remains one of Loach's greatest successes. The cast in this is minor, but the astute will spot among them Roy Haywood (from *Bronco Bullfrog*). It's desperately bleak stuff: unemployment, the limitations of working-class culture, routine violence... very much *The Loneliness of the Long-Distance Runner* revisited, except that in the earlier Courtenay/Sillitoe masterpiece the central character had the cultural highs of the '60s to look forward to. Here a descent into pointless and degrading poverty with army service in Northern Ireland beckons.

TV began producing Troubles-based drama too. *Iris in the Traffic, Ruby in the Rain* (November '81) starred Jake Burns, singer in Stiff Little Fingers, who also provided the music. Written by Stewart Parker, whose career reached a peak with *Blue Money* ('85), this was a BBC *Play for Today* set in Belfast, about the differing misfortunes affecting two young women on a drab winter's day. Eventually an entire series appeared from Yorkshire TV – *Harry's Game* (October '82). Based on a 1975 novel by Gerald Seymour, an ITN journalist who had covered the Vietnam War and political extremism in Europe, this centred on political assassination in Northern Ireland and was filmed in Leeds and Belfast. Starring Derek Thompson (a Belfast boy, late of mid-'60s folk trio Odin's People and subsequently an actor in Rock Follies, The Long Good Friday and the hospital drama Casualty), the production was graced with music from Clannad, active on the Irish music scene since 1973 and led by their singer Enya.

A big-budget, widely distributed feature (by Warners and Goldcrest) finally arrived with Cal (August '84). Adapted from a Bernard MacLaverty novel, this is a love drama set in Northern Ireland against a backdrop of sectarian killing, starring Helen Mirren and John Lynch. The score came from Mark Knopfler, following his work on Local Hero and Comfort and Joy, both of these also taking place in what was seen by many as the geographical fringe of the UK.

Between 1975 and the time the UK reached its cultural nadir (1986), 1,446 people were killed in Northern Ireland. Had such a level of violence existed in England, the equivalent of 43,000 would have died and in the US 240,000. In this context it is difficult to see why the events were constantly referred to as either a low-intensity conflict or some type of marginal political episode. At the point this narrative ends, a solution was still over a decade away and studies of the subject would continue in films like A Prayer for the Dying ('87), Hidden Agenda ('90), The Crying Game ('92) and In the Name of the Father ('93). Perhaps in such circumstances a gallows sense of humour was appropriate. No Surrender, made by Channel 4 in December 1985, from a script by Alan Bleasdale, has rival groups of Catholics and Protestants clashing in a dismal Liverpool working men's club, with each faction having inadvertently booked the venue on the same night as the other. Played as deadpan comedy, its cast included Elvis Costello.

Looking back, it is notable that however highly prized Ulster bands like The Undertones and Stiff Little Fingers were in the late '70s, none matched the level of success then enjoyed by Dublin's The Boomtown Rats. And all of them were eventually eclipsed by

U2. A major chart phenomenon from 1981 onwards, and quite possibly the biggest band in the world since 1987, U2's success was grounded in a different, less bloody Irish culture and in a country where economic and social progress accelerated rapidly throughout this period.

In the meantime, the remainder of the UK, particularly London, felt the impact of events in Belfast and Derry. As time wore on, the dramatic possibilities that these raised were exploited in film and TV. *The Long Good Friday* was an early example. Made by Euston Films after their tremendous success with *The Sweeney*, it was originally intended for TV. Alas... it failed Lord Grade's quality control, with the self-proclaimed saviour of the UK film industry taking against a plot which had the IRA running rings around a true-blue London gangster boss. After their bombing campaigns on the UK mainland, selling a film in which Sinn Féin outwit the Brits was always going to be difficult and, with the cultural freeze that descended after the 1979 General Election, best avoided by those with wider interests at stake. Grade and Thames TV demanded heavy cuts; the producers and director declined and it became, after he had intervened to save both *Monty Python's Life of Brian* and *A Sense of Freedom*, another George Harrison rescue job. Purchased for less than it cost to make, plans to show it on TV were dropped and it was given a cinema release in 1981 by Harrison and HandMade instead.

Regarded by many as the toughest UK crime drama made up until that point (though surely not the best – that accolade remained firmly with either *Get Carter* or *Performance*), it was produced by Barry Hanson who had a major TV success with *The Naked Civil Servant* ('75). John Mackenzie directed and had arisen from the same cultural soil as Hanson. Starting as an assistant to Ken Loach, he branched out on his own, directing *Unman, Wittering and Zigo* ('70), *Made* ('72) and *A Sense of Freedom* ('79). The cast is led by Bob Hoskins, who did an early stint in Ken Campbell's roving community theatre company, even playing King Lear at one point in a Hull arts centre run by Hanson. By 1979, after his TV success with *Pennies from Heaven*, Hoskins was a recognisable 'name'. Helen Mirren co-stars after roles in *Savage Messiah, O Lucky Man!* and *Caligula* had made her possibly the most interesting UK actress of this time. Supporting parts went to Dave King, a '50s comedian/singer who was very effective here as a bent police officer, and Derek Thompson fresh from *Rock Follies*. As the gangland boss Hoskins is somewhat mannered and melodramatic, playing the character as a George Walker-type figure with grandiose redevelopment plans for his old manor that can only be realised with US money, represented here by Eddie Constantine – known for his appearances in a huge roster of giallo and European art films.

The score was by Francis Monkman, formerly keyboardist and synthesiser player in Curved Air, whose other credits included *King, Queen, Knave* ('72) and who, throughout this period, ran Brian Eno a close second in the composition of incidental music for TV, radio and film. Some may consider *The Long Good Friday* to be overrated, but it was back then a rare example of a UK film with a contemporary plot. It made Hoskins a star, but didn't really address the wider political issues. In the version released, the IRA role was downplayed, but most notably the film didn't allude to why the locations shown so effectively were falling into dereliction in the first place. Instead, as entertainment it provides an efficient crime drama set in a traditional London locale shortly before it was swept away by the glass towers of the new financial district.

The economic changes taking place across the UK were also the subject of *Blue Money*. Filmed in North Kensington, the film follows the adventures and misadventures of a group of casual workers who are trying to glue together what we would now call 'portfolio' careers. The script was by Stewart Parker, a Northern Irish journalist who wrote a column on pop music for *The Irish Times*. As significant a figure on the Ulster scene as Terry Hooley, the founder of Good Vibrations records, Parker also wrote *Iris in the Traffic, Ruby in the Rain*, lifting the title from a 1971 Van Morrison single of the same name, which had been a significant hit in the US.

The starring role was taken by Tim Curry, a box-office name

of some substance in the early '80s, a period when he was active in theatre, music and TV. Globally famous after *The Rocky Horror Picture Show*, he commanded leading film roles in *Times Square* and *Annie*, played Mozart in the Broadway production of *Amadeus* and released a trio of Michael Kamen-produced albums on A&M, one of which (*Fearless*, '79) was a reasonably big US success. Back in the UK, he accepted the lead in *Blue Money*, an LWT production about a taxi driver who dreams of being a big recording star. Written so that Curry could showcase his full range of abilities, it allows him to do many impersonations, including at one point a pretty good Billie Holiday. Debbie Bishop and Billy Connolly co-star and the film is basically a crime-comedy caper with a great deal of music, mainly from Curry.

Richard Hartley supervised the soundtrack, which features Curry and Bishop. Bishop, in fact, was a well-known singer herself for a few years, often as a backing vocalist for Freddie Mercury and Spandau Ballet and, a little later, she landed a co-starring role in *Sid and Nancy*. A film of this scale should really have been much more widely seen in the UK, where it disappeared after limited TV screenings. It played cinemas overseas.

The peculiar seedy/glamorous milieu of snooker, and the career of Belfast-born Alex 'Hurricane' Higgins, served as the basis of *Number One* ('85). The huge popularity that the sport enjoyed, both live and on TV, owed much to the steady growth of television ownership from the '50s onwards. This produced changes in how people conducted their lives, particularly how much time they spent at home and what they watched in their living rooms. One aspect of this was a massive increase in viewing figures for a number of niche sports, especially as the volume of daytime TV increased. Before snooker (and later darts) took off, wrestling attracted huge audiences throughout the '60s and '70s and even featured as a central part of the plot in the 1968 film *The Touchables*. Wrestling leached into popular culture too with Judge Dread, formerly wrestler Alex Hughes 'The Masked Executioner'. Between 1972 and 1976 Dread enjoyed seven Top 30 hits and a chart album all delivered in a hybrid cockney/cod-reggae style that wasn't a million miles from Ian Dury. He was actually the biggest selling 'reggae' act pre-Bob Marley. (And, of course, for those looking for a slightly more elevated cultural connection, there was Led Zeppelin manager Peter Grant, whose *entrée* into the entertainment world, before he acted as doorman at the 2 I's Coffee Bar, came as heavyweight wrestler 'Count Massimo'.) By the '80s, wrestling had faded slightly and the new vogue TV sport was snooker, with its reverential, almost funereal commentaries emanating from vast sports halls and theatres across the UK. The difficulty of following the game on black and white TV counted for little and its practitioners quickly became huge stars, none more so than Higgins, whose George Best-type prominence lasted from 1972 until the late 1980s.

Number One, a fictionalised version of Higgins' career, was scripted by GF Newman and is a gritty, downbeat piece, quite like Newman's other works, which stretched from the anti-police drama *Sir, You Bastard* ('70) to the TV series *Law and Order* ('78). Les Blair, who had worked with Mike Leigh on *Bleak Moments* back in 1971, directs. The cast is very strong. Bob Geldof plays the Higgins-type lead: a down and out Irishman in London who takes to playing snooker to make a decent living. Mel Smith, Alison Steadman, Phil Daniels, Alfred Molina, Ian Dury and Ray Winstone all have supporting roles. Nor is the film London-centric; some of the action takes place in Sheffield and Blackpool. For Geldof this was his first major acting role after *The Wall*, in the aftermath of which he turned down *Flashdance*. Again, his performance suggests that he could have done more work in this area had he wished. (Other than fourth billing in the French *Mauvaise Fille* in 2012, nothing has transpired since.)

Number One was a well-made feature-length production that should have reached a much bigger audience than it ultimately attracted. The main title theme was composed by David Mackay and Joe Fagin, both well known at that point for doing the score for the hugely popular series *Auf Wiedersehen, Pet* (1983–4, starring Gary Holton, Timothy Spall and Jimmy Nail). The music here is very much hewn from the same cloth. The UK's dalliance with snooker also produced a couple of years later *Billy the Kid and the Green Baize Vampire* ('87), a musical with Phil Daniels, directed by Alan Clarke of *Scum*.

Ireland and the Irish were one thing, and whilst the tribulations of 'John Bull's other island' had always been part of the tapestry of UK culture, issues to do with Scotland had tended to be less explored. Although occasionally portrayed in comedies such as *Whisky Galore!* ('49) and serving as a background for historical dramas, Scotland as a place, and the lives of its people, were almost completely absent from the run of UK kitchen-sink dramas that appeared from the mid-'50s. Leaving aside *The Wicker Man* ('73) and similar supernatural thrillers, it was not until the late '70s that a distinctly Scottish genre of drama emerged, initially via *A Sense of Freedom*.

A gangster drama, this had the same mix of decent acting, realistic violence, stylish decor and heavy social comment that had featured in *Performance* ('68), *Get Carter* ('70) and *Villain* ('71), a line of descent that led, eventually, to *The Squeeze* ('77), *The Long Good Friday* and *McVicar* ('80). All of these were very London-centric, even *Get Carter*. (In the original book, Caine is a London-based gangster going north – actually to Scunthorpe – to 'sort out' a family matter.) Ultimately, the genre arose out of the huge publicity, from the London media, that surrounded the rise and downfall of the Krays and their dalliance with celebrities and politicians.

Much less attention was shown to hard provincial criminals. *A Sense of Freedom* is one of a very few that did and was directed by John Mackenzie, five years after he had done the dour drama *Made* with Roy Harper and Carol White. Based on the autobiography of Glasgow criminal Jimmy Boyle, it follows his career from his 1967 conviction for murder through to his (eventual) rehabilitation in prison. Both Boyle's book and the film appeared whilst he was serving a life sentence in Barlinnie Jail – an event that would be hard to imagine now. After his release in 1981 he became a writer, sculptor and artist of some repute, something, again, that it is difficult to envisage today.

Shot by Mackenzie in difficult circumstances with much

obstruction from the authorities (the prison scenes eventually had to be filmed in Dublin), it was ready for release in 1979 but was only eventually shown in February 1981, after George Harrison had intervened – as part of his one-man rescue mission in UK cinema – and snapped it up for HandMade Films. Jeremy Isaacs, the leading TV producer of the day (he did *The World at War*) and, like Mackenzie and Boyle a Scot, produced and some might see the end product as confirming the rise of a particular type of Scots self-assertion, if not actual nationalism. In fact, 'northern' ultra-realist dramas were relatively common at this time: Alan Bleasdale did *The Black Stuff* ('78) set near Middlesbrough (and later a TV series showing the grim impact of mass unemployment) and Willy Russell produced *Educating Rita* ('80), both of which depicted the north as a complete dead end and somewhere to be escaped from. Another, somewhat more left-field example, was Bertrand Tavernier's dystopian 1980 sci-fi thriller *Death Watch*, which with a stellar cast (Romy Schneider, Harvey Keitel, Harry Dean Stanton and many others) was filmed on the Clyde. As one critic noted '...a fascinating snapshot of the City of Glasgow in the late '70s... soot blackened ...'.

David Hayman, later memorable as Malcolm McLaren in *Sid and Nancy*, plays Boyle alongside a cast of seasoned Scottish actors led by Jake D'Arcy and Sean Scanlan. Hayman was a very significant figure in Glasgow, well known for his performances at the Citizens Theatre and provides a visceral tour de force here. *A Sense of Freedom* stayed local for its music, too, with a main theme by Rory Gallagher and Frankie Miller. Both were adept at a kind of gritty blues rock and were veterans of this denim-clad scene that thrived outside London. Miller, a second cousin to Boyle and a drinking partner of Sean Scanlan, worked several times more for Mackenzie, doing an acting turn in his 1979 BBC *Play for Today, Just a Boys' Game*, as well the soundtrack for *Act of Vengeance* ('86, with Charles Bronson). The film, though, remains relatively unknown, unlike *McVicar*, which covers similar ground. It is barely listed in written reference works and Miller and Gallagher's efforts on the soundtrack were denied any official release.

Hayman's co-star Jake D'Arcy also appeared in *Gregory's Girl* ('80), which for most audiences across the UK was quite possibly the first explicitly Scottish film they would have seen. A production by Davina Belling and Clive Parsons, it was funded by the National Film Finance Corporation and Scottish TV. Bill Forsyth wrote and directed. After editing documentaries through the '60s and '70s, this was his follow-up to *That Sinking Feeling* ('79), another Scottish-set comedy. Most of the cast were recruited from the Glasgow Youth Theatre, with the major roles being played by John Gordon Sinclair (who briefly became a star at 19), D'Arcy, Dee Hepburn and Clare Grogan.

Set in Cumbernauld – a new town still being developed at the time the film was being shot – this is a youth/school courtship drama that makes for an interesting comparison with *Here We Go Round the Mulberry Bush* ('67). But compared with the earlier film, which also dealt with adolescents longing for exploratory sexual relationships and kickstarted the descent into the tatty suburban sex films of the '70s, this is all rather chaste. The plot centres on Gregory (Gordon Sinclair) and his interest in Dorothy (Dee Hepburn), a keen female soccer player. A worldwide success that won many awards, the overall tone is very matter of fact and no great visual style emerges. Audiences clearly found this attractive after the social-realism approach of preceding decades with their gritty northern characters, mumbled, cynical, understated dialogue and vague inconclusive plots. Looked at this way, for all its charm *Gregory's Girl* can be seen as a turn towards the conservative and away from the experimental and the visionary. In fact, very 'on trend' with the mood of the times.

The soundtrack was done by Colin Tully, formerly saxophone player in Cado Belle, a Scottish funk/rock outfit who had made a bit of a splash a couple of years earlier. No commercial release followed, however, which, given the film's popularity, seems a curious oversight, particularly as Clare Grogan enjoyed a major singing career with Altered Images, scoring five hit singles and three chart albums between 1981 and 1983. In a strange footnote, with life imitating art, John Gordon Sinclair also got in on the act with a voiceover promo single with the reigning Miss Scotland (Georgina Kearney) for the 1982 Scottish World Cup Squad. This reached No 5 in the UK charts in June 1982. Alas, although Scotland made it to Spain (unlike England), they got knocked out in the group stage.

Unusually for a film from this period it - eventually - spawned a sequel, Gregory's Two Girls ('99), still in Cumbernauld with Gordon Sinclair as a middle-aged school teacher. Bill Forsyth directed again, having returned to the UK after a spell in Hollywood.

Long before that, though, in the wake of the acclaim that attended Gregory's Girl, Forsyth got backing from Goldcrest and David Puttnam for Local Hero, a 1983 drama about a US oil tycoon who tries to buy up land in Scotland for an oil production terminal. With oil money pouring into Scotland in the '80s, this was a big political issue and disputes about the provenance of such funds and their ultimate destination were helping to fuel the rise of the Scottish National Party.

But Local Hero is no Mike Leigh or Ken Loach exposé and not even a Powell and Pressburger Edge of the World-type drama. Instead, it's whimsical, pleasant and a good example of a decently made medium-sized film. Burt Lancaster stars, with Peter Riegert (from Americathon) in support. The remainder of the cast (Denis Lawson, Fulton Mackay and Peter Capaldi) were reliable and well-known faces from UK TV. The film points up the contrast between the brash commercialism of US business life and the gentle pace of a small Scottish coastal town.

The soundtrack was done by Mark Knopfler and Vertigo released it as an LP, winning several awards. Knopfler, born in Scotland, began his rise to mega-stardom, as many did, on the London pub-rock circuit in the early '70s and was assisted on this project by fellow members of his group Dire Straits (formed '77 in Deptford) and Terry Williams (ex-Love Sculpture and Rockpile). Gerry Rafferty takes the lead vocal on one number, and because of the prominence of Dire Straits at the time, the album sold well, reaching No 14 in the UK.

The film did pretty good business, too, and with that and

Forsyth's earlier success (*Gregory's Girl*), big things were expected of his subsequent career. But *Comfort and Joy* ('84), a Glasgow-set drama about a hapless DJ getting embroiled in battles between owners of rival ice-cream vans, was thought by some to show evidence of a falling away in originality. Bill Paterson's portrait of the DJ makes for an interesting comparison now with Steve Coogan's later creation, Alan Partridge, but the film was only mildly amusing rather than laugh-out-loud funny. It came with music by Clare Grogan and Mark Knopfler. After his move to Hollwood, Forsyth made an effective crime drama, *Breaking In* ('89), with Burt Reynolds and Casey Siemaszko.

Immediately prior to his successes with *That Sinking Feeling* and *Gregory's Girl*, Forsyth had worked on a number of documentaries made by fellow Scot Charles Gormley, who spent much of the '70s in the Netherlands, where he had eight screenplay credits between 1970 and 1975. Returning to Scotland in the early '80s, Gormley directed *Living Apart Together* ('82), his first feature. Most of it is shot on natural locations across Glasgow, many of which no longer exist, and it stars musician BA Robertson as Ritchie Hannah, a singer-songwriter returning to the city after the death of a friend.

The plot has the main character's long-suffering wife Evie (Barbara Kellerman, also seen in *The Quatermass Conclusion*), tiring of the upheaval in her marriage and using the opportunity to walk out, leaving Robertson to care for their children. He goes in search of her with the help of his manager's assistant, Alicia (Judi Trott), and then starts an affair with Trott when it becomes clear that his wife is not ready to return home. Peter Capaldi and John Gordon Sinclair both make early appearances in supporting roles. The film itself is basically a character study that looks at the damage that a public media profile can cause when inflicted on private lives, and the vulnerabilities that lurk behind a macho facade.

Shot in early 1982 and released later that year, *Living Apart Together* was made for Channel 4 and produced by Gavrik Losey. It makes for an interesting comparison with *Breaking Glass*, or, indeed, Losey's earlier productions *That'll Be the Day* and *Stardust*, all of which are far better known. Like fellow Scots Maggie Bell and Frankie Miller, Robertson avoided both the glam-rock and prog-rock excesses that bedevilled many UK acts in the '70s and had a somewhat unusual career. Signed by US label Ardent in 1973 (the home of legendary outfit Big Star), he had returned to the UK by 1975, where, after a spell on Arista, he had five hit singles on Asylum between 1979 and 1981, delivered in a kind of shrewdly satirical pop style (not unlike Big Star). These included *Kool in the Kaftan* (No 17 UK, March '80), which featured a sitar and was an early reversion to the type of material that had been prominent in the UK charts in the '60s. During this time, he also did a turn in *The Monster Club* ('81) alongside veterans The Pretty Things.

In this film Robertson – who wrote the entire score – performs a number of songs with co-star Trott, none of which was formally released despite Robertson's success around this time and the presence on the tracks of Carol Kenyon, noted for many sessions with Heaven 17 and Dexys Midnight Runners. In 1986 he did the soundtrack for *Heavenly Pursuits*, a Tom Conti–Helen Mirren comedy drama directed, again, by Gormley. Set in Scotland and made by Channel 4, it got a reasonable cinema distribution. But once more, no official release of the soundtrack followed.

The idea that a specifically Scottish, rather than British, identity might be emerging, particularly among young people, was addressed in *Restless Natives* ('85). A comedy set in Scotland, this is about two young 'underemployed' men, to use the parlance coming into vogue, who don masks (one a clown, the other a wolfman) and hold up tourist coaches in the Highlands. The media latch on and they duly become folk heroes in the tradition of Rob Roy.

Well, it's certainly very different to *Gregory's Girl*. Based on a novel by Ninian Dunnett, whose parents Dorothy and Alistair were respected Scottish literary figures, this is shot in drab and depressing locations and stars Vincent Friell, who later went on to appear in *Trainspotting* ('96), and Joe Mullaney, fresh from the BBC series *Maggie*, about a teenage girl growing up in Glasgow. Michael Hoffman directed, having previously made *Privileged* ('82, Hugh Grant). Although no heavy political message is relayed by the dialogue and action, an underlying anti-UK theme is apparent. Generally, the plot and characters have an amoral undertow, albeit one that reflects the times. As one of them says: 'without money you can't do anything'.

Restless Natives had limited box-office takings, which seemed to indicate that the brief mini-genre of Celtic comedies, emanating mainly from Bill Forsyth, had ended. An EMI production, the soundtrack was by Big Country, the band fronted by Stuart Adamson from Dunfermline and formerly of The Skids. Big Country were on a roll in the decade from 1983, with their debut LP, *The Crossing*, reaching No 18 in the US. The film title track was duly released on the flip of the single *Look Away* (No 7 UK and No 5 US). Despite all this and the investment in the film itself, EMI declined to release Adamson's score and one wonders today why such a high proportion of these films – *A Sense of Freedom*, *Gregory's Girl*, *Living Apart Together* as well as *Restless Natives* – lacked an official soundtrack album. Apparently, there was an unwillingness to make even a minimal investment in their release, even though those composing and performing the material were well known at the time.

13

ART AND POLITICS

Reflecting the social and cultural views of their time, a high proportion of the diminishing numbers of TV and film productions made in the UK in the '70s and '80s were either overtly political or strove to achieve cutting-edge artistic integrity. In terms of the soundscape that accompanied such efforts, quite a bit of it was culled from the work of Brian Eno, who, by the end of the '70s, was the most sought-after figure in UK film soundtrack work.

An art school student in the '60s, Eno had studied under Roy Ascott, an early pioneer of cybernetics: the use of tape loops and computer-generated compositions. (Ascott, who also tutored Pete Townshend, had in turn studied under Richard Hamilton, the father of British pop art, as did Bryan Ferry some years later, the connecting threads here illustrating on a microscale some of the continuities in the English counterculture.) After a spell with Ferry in Roxy Music (1971-3), Eno went solo with the album *Here Come the Warm Jets*, which, unusually for something left-field, charted (No 26 UK) and between 1975 and 1985 he released 18 albums of ambient library music, extracts from which appeared in 22 film and TV productions ranging from horror, *Land of the Minotaur* ('76), to science-fiction parody, *Alternative 3*, ('77) to TV's *Creation of the Universe* ('82 – you couldn't get bigger than that), to Nic Roeg's *Castaway* ('86). Complete scores by him were rare, his material being used instead for either evocative or dramatic purposes. In this respect his output resembled that of

'60s library music specialists Reg Tilsley and Basil Kirchin.

Originally a non-musician, Eno mainly composed on a synthesiser, reflecting in this how the technology of the time triggered a move away from the set-piece orchestras, bands and singers that had characterised the work of Barry, Legrand, Morricone and others in the '60s. Although electronic music had been around for over a decade via the BBC Radiophonic Workshop and Stockhausen, it wasn't until the Minimoog appeared in 1970 that its use became widespread. Walter/Wendy Carlos's score for *A Clockwork Orange* ('71) was the first big-seller to showcase the instrument, after which Tangerine Dream made it part of the mainstream with a couple of chart albums on Richard Branson's Virgin label in 1974 and 1975. In demand as a producer, Eno worked with Bowie, Talking Heads, Devo and U2, as well as the early version of Ultravox, whose founder John Foxx – like him a '60s art-school graduate – later ran him a close second in album sales and was selected by Antonioni to score *Identification of a Woman* ('82).

Leading the way in this field was *Radio On*, released in 1979 and very much hewn from the imagination of Wim Wenders, who had established himself as an interesting European auteur with a penchant for road movies and films that explored the boundaries between the visual and aural. After successes with *Summer in the City* ('70, dedicated to The Kinks) and *Alice in the Cities* ('74, music by Can), he agreed to a collaboration with the BFI and National Film Finance Corporation in which Wenders himself took a back-seat role. In *Radio On* his company co-produce and he is officially Assistant Producer, with his cameraman Martin Schäfer as cinematographer. Chris Petit (who did film reviews for *Time Out* and wrote for *Melody Maker*) directed.

Lisa Kreuzer (whose many West German credits included *Alice in the Cities*, *Kings of the Road* and *The American Friend*, all for Wenders) and Sandy Ratcliff (*Family Life*, '71, and a model once regarded as 'the face of the '70s') are the most notable figures in a cast led by David Beames, whose other credits during this time included *Destiny* and *Giro City*. Sting, then bass guitarist in

The Police, appears in a small supporting role. Beames plays a DJ working for a factory broadcasting network who drives out of London to visit the location where his brother is supposed to have committed suicide. Filmed, fashionably, in black and white, and relatively cheap to make, the plot seems to echo the novels of JG Ballard, including as it does much imagery of motorways, the built environment and people on the periphery. As such, it ended up being the closest the UK actually got to making a Ballard-type film in the '70s. The funding issues that beset the industry then blocked any adaptations of Ballard's work being made. *High-Rise* was due to be filmed in 1978-9, possibly as a UK rival to *The Towering Inferno*, but never got started and only a truncated version was managed of *Crash*, shot in 1971, with Ballard himself in the main role and Gabrielle Drake (brother of hippy folk singer Nick) as the actress around whom the story revolves. Despite the visual similarities, though, *Radio On* lacks the clear plotting of Ballard's work and trying to discern any overall meaning to the film is difficult.

The soundtrack includes music by David Bowie (*Heroes*, delivered, very chicly, in German), The Rumour, Kraftwerk, Ian Dury, Wreckless Eric, Lene Lovich, Devo and Robert Fripp. Stiff Records owned the rights to five of these and one wonders if they paid towards the film's production costs in exchange for some publicity for their artistes. Of their roster, Lovich, a Charlie Gillett discovery, made quite an impact in the late '70s, also starring in *Cha Cha*, a film about the local punk scene in the Netherlands.

Considering it was unashamedly an art-house film, *Radio On* was a reasonable success with mainstream critics, which was more than was usually the case with BFI-funded work. But it soon faded and audiences today would be bemused by the X-certificate rating that it was given. Petit later did film and TV work with Ballard and subsequently collaborated with Iain Sinclair, another Ballardian-style writer.

For his follow up to *Radio On*, though, Petit opted to adapt *An Unsuitable Job for a Woman*, a 1977 PD James detective novel set in Cambridge. After the *succès d'estime* of his earlier film, a bigger budget was available and, reflecting this, the cast includes Billie Whitelaw, Paul Freeman (*The Long Good Friday*, *Raiders of the Lost Ark*), Pippa Guard and Dominic Guard. Don Boyd and Goldcrest co-produced with, despite the increased funding, help from the National Film Finance Corporation. It was one of 25 films that received NFFC money between 1977 and 1986, the others including *Black Joy*, *Radio On*, *Gregory's Girl*, *Memoirs of a Survivor* and *Britannia Hospital*.

An *Unsuitable Job for a Woman* is an interesting example of the type of 'quality' UK film that began dying out in the '80s. Like *Radio On*, it centres on a supposed suicide, with a central character, Pippa Guard, as private detective Cordelia Gray, investigating the murky details. James's book was sufficiently popular to produce a sequel, *The Skull Beneath the Skin* in 1982, which many thought implausible, after which the notion of a series with the same characters was abandoned. Petit's film, though, kickstarted a run of TV adaptations of James's other works, thirteen appearing in the decades after 1983, including a 1997 remake of this with Helen Baxendale. The involvement of heavyweights like Boyd (*Scum*, *The Great Rock N' Roll Swindle*) and Goldcrest (*Chariots of Fire*, *Gandhi*) stemmed from James being regarded by some as the natural successor to Agatha Christie, whose output kept many film and TV companies ticking over nicely from the '30s onwards. In fact, James was nothing like Christie. Her work was literary and her finest novel, *The Children of Men* ('92 and a brilliant 2006 film), is a dystopian masterpiece.

The soundtrack, which like many from this era remains unreleased, features music by Chaz Jankel, who, after huge successes with Ian Dury and The Blockheads, was now recording as a solo artist for A&M. In the immediate aftermath of the film Petit moved to Berlin, where he made *Flight to Berlin* ('83) and *Chinese Boxes* ('84), both for Wenders. But by the end of the decade he was, ironically, back in the UK doing TV adaptations of Christie's Miss Marple.

As an illustration of the type of film made as a BFI production at a time when the BFI was fast becoming the last-chance saloon of

UK film funding, *Crystal Gazing* ('82) provides a perfect example of that mini-genre. Laura Mulvey and Peter Wollen co-directed, Wollen having previously done the screenplay for *The Passenger* ('75) and the film has an interesting set of credits, including a script with one scene written by Keith (father of Lily) Allen and leading roles played by Gavin Richards (from *Accidental Death of an Anarchist*), Lora Logic (of X-Ray Spex and Essential Logic) and Jeff Rawle (the star of a '73 TV *Billy Liar* adaptation). Wollen and Mulvey warmed up for this by making *Amy* ('80), which looked at the career of '30s aviation heroine Amy Johnson through a feminist perspective accompanied by music from X-Ray Spex and Lora Logic.

In *Crystal Gazing* various characters, including a science-fiction illustrator, a saxophonist who busks and appears on *Top of the Pops*, an analyst of satellite photography and a PhD student, intersect in a recession-hit London amidst a worsening economic situation. At the time, Mulvey stated '...It's about the contrast between the 1960s and the 1980s. But that was one aspect of the original script which diminished tremendously, the project was very much taken over by events here and now. As we actually made the film the moment of making it became more and more important – we wanted to inscribe the present, Thatcherism, cuts, unemployment into it ....' This was an admirable point of view, but, even then, were the travails of cultural types likely to be of interest to the 95 per cent who do not work in those fields? Although *City Limits* (the magazine that split from *Time Out* in 1981, when *Time Out* stopped being a co-operative) reckoned it was an '...Effervescent and largely successful black comedy... it's great to see the Left dancing so wittily on the graveyards of past and present ....', the film, like many in this period, was barely released, which seems a shame given its potential.

The music was by Lora Logic, one of many talents to emerge in the aftermath of the 1976 punk explosion. Some of it can be heard on her solo album *Pedigree Charm*, where she was assisted by Ben Annesley and Philip Legg (from Essential Logic) and Charles Hayward (from This Heat). John Altman (whose credits stretched from 1969 blues rockers Jellybread to *Erik the Viking* via *The Rutles*, *Just a Gigolo* and *Life of Brian*) and Mike Ratledge (ex-Soft Machine) were also involved. Indeed, the Softs had also scored the 1977 Wollen-Mulvey *Riddles of the Sphinx*, which was also BFI-funded and waited until 2013 for an accessible release. Today, *Crystal Gazing* comes across as a buried time capsule and some might say it illustrates the pointlessness of winning the artistic battles if you lose the political. It was ignored by the mainstream.

Another study of diverse characters struggling with the political changes of the early '80s came with *Meantime* ('83). Filmed in Haggerston, then a flat, featureless, forgotten part of London, crowded with nondescript housing estates and a few boarded-up Victorian buildings, one would hardly recognise it as the hip, expensive area it is now. The birthplace of the Krays, who held sway in local pubs there well into the '60s, the same streets can be glimpsed in the background of the 1971 Richard Burton gangster film *Villain*, and even further back in the Mike Sarne and Rita Tushingham juvenile delinquency drama *A Place to Go* ('63). An utterly miserable comic farce, *Meantime* is about a dysfunctional family holed up in a badly maintained block of '40s utility flats (Bryant Court), whilst a few yards away the demolition crews are at work flattening parts of the neighbourhood.

Written and directed by Mike Leigh, and an example of the working-class drama that he championed, this is less well known than his legendary success *Abigail's Party* and even today is not listed in many reference works. Which is rather surprising given that it has a cast to die for – Tim Roth, Gary Oldman, Phil Daniels and Alfred Molina. Oldman had first been noticed in *Remembrance* ('82) as one of a group of RN sailors having a night on the town prior to going on a major NATO exercise. Filmed during the Falklands War and with a decent score that included contributions from Brian Eno and Phil Collins, it also featured John Altman (who played George Harrison in *Birth of The Beatles*) and Timothy Spall. Entered into the Taormina Film Festival, it won a prize and as a result, unlike *Meantime*, it got a reasonable cinema distribution.

Like *Remembrance, Meantime* is a Channel 4 film and is typical of the productions made by the company in its early years. Oldman was almost destined to play the role of the skinhead in Leigh's film: from New Cross, he supported Millwall and had been rejected by RADA. In an irony to beat all others, given that he would reluctantly make his name in *Sid and Nancy*, some of the scenes in *Meantime* are shot in and around Fellows Court, a council high-rise building in London E2 where Sid Vicious and his mother had lived a couple of years earlier. For their part, Roth, Daniels and Molina all came from low or lowish income families and their subsequent careers were good examples of the social mobility that existed in the UK in the '70s. They progressed into acting because of the opportunities open to young people then and they came from the same background as the characters they portray. For Roth in particular this was another stepping stone in his career. An outstanding talent, he chose his future parts well and was much admired a little later in the stylish crime drama *The Hit* ('84) alongside Terence Stamp and John Hurt. *Meantime* features music by Andrew Dickson, a long-standing Leigh collaborator, who came out of the folk music and theatre scene of the '60s and '70s, and George Khan, who had played with both Pete Brown and His Battered Ornaments and Kilburn and The High Roads.

Channel 4 was also behind the documentary series *Play at Home* ('84) about key bands of the period and their home towns. Various people, including Don Coutts and Peter Orton, produced or directed selected episodes, and, among those it featured were The Angelic Upstarts, Big Country, The Creatures, The Specials, Echo and The Bunnymen, XTC and, most interestingly of all, in an episode inscrutably subtitled 'The Word Came Out of L.A.' Son of 'Leaving the 20th Century', New Order and their relationship with Tony Wilson, Manchester and Factory records.

As was the case with many major figures active from the '60s through to the '80s, Wilson's own broadcasting career illustrated how rapidly the long overhang of the '60s came to an end. He presented *So It Goes* on Granada TV from July 1976 to December 1977 and kicked off with a piece about Peter Blake, UK pop-artist in chief since the early '60s and creator, among much else, of the *Sgt. Pepper* album cover. Then, as fashions changed at breakneck speed, he ended the series with a programme on The Clash. Noting the impact made by the Edinburgh-based independent label Fast Product, he launched his own, Factory, in late 1978 and had some initial success with Orchestral Manoeuvres in the Dark (who quickly moved elsewhere) and Joy Division, before really hitting it big in 1981 with New Order.

On screen, Wilson behaves rather like any record company executive, albeit in his case one who fancied himself politically. At one point he is sitting (naked) in the bath and being interviewed (also in the bath) by an 18-year-old female journalist (who keeps her clothes on), whilst talking knowledgeably about capitalism and Trotsky. Only 33 when this was shot, he already looks decidedly paunchy and middle-aged. Later we catch up with him being hassled by the members of various minor Factory acts (The Durutti Column, A Certain Ratio and Section 25) about non-payment of royalties and retainers: something usually associated with the likes of Malcolm McLaren rather than Wilson, who gets a benign press generally. An exception to this coverage came from *Private Eye* who noted, at the time, that he appeared to have a penchant for names and imagery that invoked the Third Reich, whilst maintaining firmly that this interest was no more than an affinity with industrial chic. (Factory even had a representative in Berlin, Martin Reeder, throughout the '80s, who managed to work successfully in both halves of the divided city.) In all probability, Wilson was being ironic and provocative, and displaying the same knack for causing outrage as Malcolm McLaren.

In 1982 Wilson started his own club (The Haçienda, the name lifted from a Situationist slogan) which had bars named after the UK's Soviet spies. Bernard Manning, no less, compèred the opening night... another provocative/ironic gesture... and bombed completely. In fact, Manning's own club, the Embassy (five miles away) operated with much less hype and for certain types of acts seeking a break was somewhat more accessible. Sadly, like many venues, The Haçienda didn't survive to enjoy the full glory of

Cool Britannia, closing in 1997 after its licence was revoked. It was subsequently demolished and replaced by a block of flats. The footage preserved of a New Order concert at its peak is priceless.

In tone, with its mix of politics, music, 'northern' irreverence and the avant-garde, this is a bit like something John and Yoko might have knocked out 15 years earlier... and would again be common 15 years further down the line from Wilson's only other big act, The Happy Mondays, and a host of other guitar bands. Following their involvement with *Play at Home*, Peter Orton became one of the most prolific directors of UK TV comedy from the 90s onwards and Don Coutts subsequently did *After Dark*, a Channel 4 discussion series which had Wilson and Colin Wallace (a witness to the secret activities of the UK Government in Northern Ireland during the Troubles) on its opening night in 1987. A welcome addition to the limited political output of the UK media, it lasted until August 1991. Wilson himself died in 2007, but had the privilege during his own lifetime of his story, and that of the entire Manchester scene over 30 years, being made into a film *24 Hour Party People* (2002, starring Steve Coogan).

Tackling difficult and even taboo subjects was something UK TV drama became noted for in the '60s and, until its decline started in the mid-'80s, productions like *Brimstone and Treacle* appeared with a reasonable frequency. With more than a little similarity to *Theorem*, Pasolini's 1968 account of a man (Terence Stamp) insinuating himself into a family, this had originally been a 1976 BBC *Play for Today* starring Denholm Elliott and with Michael Kitchen (*Unman, Wittering and Zigo* and *Dracula AD 1972*) as the interloper. Written by Dennis Potter, regarded by many as the country's finest TV dramatist, *Brimstone and Treacle* concerns a suburban couple whose daughter is severely disabled after a car crash. A diabolical young man comes into their life and ingratiates himself with the parents, only to rape their daughter at the first available opportunity.

Because of the rape scene, the BBC dropped the play in 1976 just before transmission and only belatedly broadcast it in 1987. In the meantime, Potter had a considerable UK TV success with the series *Pennies from Heaven* ('78), which he then adapted into a 1981 MGM musical with Steve Martin and Christopher Walken. He had also been signed up to do the screenplay for *Gorky Park*. With its author now bankable (in cinema terms), funding was raised for a feature film adaptation, to be directed by Richard Loncraine (who did *Flame*) and produced by UK/Palestinian publisher Naim Attallah, who owned the glamorous and successful Quartet books imprint.

For this version Elliott remained in situ, but Kitchen was replaced – after David Bowie had turned down the part – by Sting, with the supporting roles taken by Joan Plowright and Suzanna Hamilton (later in *1984* and *Wetherby*) as the mother and daughter. Like much of Potter's writing, the tone is slightly uncertain, veering from shocking drama to black comedy: perhaps with hindsight it was significant that as a writer he was one of many talents to emerge from the '60s satire boom, first having been noted as a contributor to *That Was The Week That Was*.

Michael Nyman, one of a very small number of composers working in original film scores in the UK, did the soundtrack, which included music from The Police, Squeeze, Sting and The Go-Gos. A good choice, Nyman had an album, *Decay Music*, produced by Brian Eno and released by Island in 1976 and his much-liked soundtrack for *The Draughtsman's Contract* had appeared on Charisma in 1982. Sting's version of *Spread a Little Happiness* was a No 16 UK hit for him, but *Brimstone and Treacle* only did modest business and Naim Attallah pulled back from any further productions. Potter continued to be in demand, though, notably for Nic Roeg's *Track 29* ('88) and many TV commissions up until his death in 1994.

For those in search of highbrow political drama Channel 4 provided *The Ploughman's Lunch* ('83). A study of the emasculation and rightward shift of the UK media during the Falklands War, this was written by Ian McEwan and directed by Richard Eyre. As such, it provides a perfect example of the intersection of theatre, politics, fiction and cinema in the mid-'80s. McEwan had a TV play (*Solid Geometry*) banned by the BBC in 1979 for being too sexually explicit and was an enormously up and coming writer at this point, specialising in macabre and gothic works like *The Cement Garden* and *The Comfort of Strangers*. Eyre was a force to be reckoned with at the National Theatre and both of them had worked together previously in 1980 on the BBC TV play *The Imitation Game*, which makes similar political-personal points (Eyre also did *Country* in 1981, another BBC 'political' play). But rather than the BBC picking up *The Ploughman's Lunch*, this was an early Channel 4 production and, underscoring just how serious this venture was, the credits acknowledged the input of political commentators Francis Wheen and Christopher Hitchens. In a way, this highlights why there was a degree of criticism toward Channel 4 through the '80s and '90s: they were regarded as preaching to the converted and only commissioning work - with taxpayers' money - that appealed to a select metropolitan elite. Perhaps they did in some instances, but not here, and, in any event... at least they were actually *making* stuff, unlike the rest of the UK film industry by that point.

Jonathan Pryce and Tim Curry star, and the plot has Pryce starting out as a reasonably idealistic journalist who sells out and decides to go with the flow. The action concludes at the 1982 Conservative Party Conference. Filmed during the Falklands War and screened at the point that Thatcher enjoyed a crushing electoral victory, *The Ploughman's Lunch* was a modest art-house success, which made its political point(s) well. The cast also features Charlie Dore, an actress-singer who emerged from the same Tyneside terrain as Sting, Jimmy Nail and Mark Knopfler. Signed by Island records in 1978, she had a big US hit a year later with *Pilot of the Airwaves* (No 13 US) and was briefly a name of some substance. Dominic Muldowney did the score - which remains unreleased - after his work with Bowie on *Baal*.

A few years later Channel 4 put money into *Letter to Brezhnev* ('85), which Stephen Woolley produced. A considerable figure during the nadir years of UK cinema (from which he emerged as easily the best filmmaker), Woolley also ran The Screen on the Green, Islington, and The Scala, King's Cross, both of which were essential venues for anyone interested in quality films of the past and present.

Filmed in three weeks during the 1984-5 miners' strike, this
was an adaptation of a 1983 play, staged in Liverpool, with what
was probably the most overtly political plot of the time. A Soviet
merchant ship arrives in Liverpool and two of its sailors enjoy
a run ashore. One of them has a brief, passionate fling with a
local girl, who, weighing up her options, decides that Liverpool
and the UK offer nothing but unremittingly limited prospects and
willingly travels back to rejoin him in the USSR. In other words:
Liverpool and the north in the '80s are shown as being no better
than the Soviet bloc, and in some ways worse.

Chris Bernard directed. Having begun his career at 22 in the
Science Fiction Theatre of Liverpool, appearing in Ken Campbell's
Illuminatus! with Jim Broadbent and Bill Nighy, he later worked as
a writer on the Channel 4 TV series *Brookside. Brookside*, which
ran for 21 years from 1982, also provided co-stars Margi Clarke
and Alexandra Pigg, as well as a screenplay from Frank Clarke
(Margi's brother). A case might be made today, then, for seeing
Letter to Brezhnev as a well-written feature film that arose as a side
project from a popular UK soap, and, by virtue of being compact
and to the point, made some hard-hitting observations about class
and opportunity in mid-'80s Britain. The cast here is very strong
– even Ken Campbell turns up in one of his many small roles,
as a newspaper reporter – with Peter Firth and Alfred Molina
starring. Firth had first been noted in the Italian *Daniele e Maria*
in 1973, after which came major roles in *Equus* ('77), *Tess* ('79)
and *The Aerodrome* ('83, a '40s-set dystopia not unlike *1984*). For
Molina, this was another performance that marked him out as a
significant future prospect. His career had started with a Leonard
Rossiter TV series about wrestling (*The Losers*, '78), after which he
appeared in supporting roles in *Raiders of the Lost Ark* ('81, a US
film that used much UK expertise), *Meantime* ('84) and *Number
One* ('85), before hitting the jackpot alongside Gary Oldman in
Prick Up Your Ears ('87).

The soundtrack was by Alan Gill, formerly a member of The
Teardrop Explodes, a Liverpool act who enjoyed considerable chart
success in 1980 and 1981. Gill composed the main title theme,

OUTRÉ, OUTRAGEOUS AND ALWAYS AMUSING
Divine prepares for The Alternative Miss World

FACING AN UNCERTAIN FUTURE
Young actors cowering in *Memoirs of a Survivor* (1981)

MODELLING THE NEW ANTI-STYLE STYLE
Ian Dury poses for the cameras

A KEY DOCUMENT OF THE THATCHER ERA
Burning an Illusion (1981), possibly the best film ever made
about the politicisation of a young black woman

Lewis Collins in *Who Dares Wins* (1982)

Paul Cook, Steve Jones, Paul Simonon and Ray Winstone limber up
as The Looters in *Ladies and Gentlemen, The Fabulous Stains* (1982)

Despite enormous expectations, the laconic verbal delivery of John Lydon brought him only one significant acting role – in *Order of Death* (1983)

David Bowie and Catherine Deneuve admire Bauhaus in Tony Scott's *The Hunger* (1983)

Gary Oldman and Mike Leigh avoid the wrecking ball on Haggerston's
Stonebridge Estate in Mike Leigh's *Meantime* (1984)

THE BAND WARMING UP
This Is Spinal Tap (1984), still the gold standard for mockumentaries

THE MOTION PICTURE EVENT YOU'VE BEEN WAITING FOR.

Its surface is barren.
Its true strength hidden.
Its foreboding desert conceals
the power to fold space,
to slow time, to send the mind
where the body cannot go.
It is the source of the
ultimate power.

It is the deadly battleground
where a young leader will emerge
to command an army of
six million warriors against
the tyrannical force that threatens
to enslave the universe.

It is the clash for the
greatest prize of all...

The planet called Dune.

D U N E

A world beyond your experience, beyond your imagination.

DINO DE LAURENTIIS Presents
A DAVID LYNCH Film "DUNE"

Screenplay by DAVID LYNCH Based on the novel by FRANK HERBERT Edited by ANTONY GIBBS

Mechanical Special Effects by KIT WEST Additional Visual Special Effects by ALBERT WHITLOCK Creatures Created by CARLO RAMBALDI Costume Design by BOB RINGWOOD

Production Design by ANTHONY MASTERS Director of Photography FREDDIE FRANCIS Associate Producer JOSE LOPEZ RODERO

A UNIVERSAL RELEASE © 1983 Universal City Studios, Inc. Produced by RAFFAELLA DE LAURENTIIS Directed by DAVID LYNCH DOLBY STEREO READ THE BERKLEY BOOK

COMING FOR CHRISTMAS TO SELECT THEATRES

A well made, expertly designed film with a wealth of background detail,
but also surprisingly hard to see at the time – *Dune* (1984)

YOUNG LOVE
Daniel Day-Lewis and Gordon Warnecke in the ground-breaking
My Beautiful Laundrette (1985)

THE MOST SUCCESSFUL ACTOR TO EMERGE FROM THE PUNK PERIOD
Adam Ant, aka Stuart Goddard, relaxing in *Nomads* (1985)

Gary Oldman as John Ritchie aka Sid Vicious in Alex Cox's brilliant *Sid and Nancy* (1986)

with other contributions coming from Bronski Beat (*Hit That Perfect Beat*, a No 3 UK hit), Carmel, The Fine Young Cannibals, The Redskins, A Certain Ratio, Flesh and Paul Quinn. As a time capsule of UK pop/dance music from 1985 this is incomparable. Margi Clarke also does a track, and the presence of the 1965 Sandie Shaw hit *Always Something There to Remind Me* is another nod to Shaw's resurrection around this time, via Morrissey and The Smiths. The film was a fine achievement and showed what could be done even in the least propitious circumstances.

David Puttnam produced *Defence of the Realm* ('86), which looked at today comes across as an absolutely typical '80s current affairs drama full of the angst of that time. The storyline is about a US bomber crashing at its UK base and the event being covered up. Carrying echoes of the Profumo affair (there is a subplot about the infidelity of a Government minister), *Defence of the Realm* was made after political conspiracy thrillers had enjoyed some popularity at the box office. Thus, this is a modestly budgeted UK entry, albeit a bit late, into the genre made popular by Costa Gavras, Pakula, Pollack and others in films like *State of Siege*, *The Parallax View*, *All the President's Men* and *Three Days of the Condor*.

Written by Martin Stellman (*Quadrophenia*, *Babylon*) and directed by David Drury, most of whose work was on TV, it stars Gabriel Byrne, Greta Scacchi, Denholm Elliott and Ian Bannen, with Byrne and Elliott cast as crusading journalists. When *Defence of the Realm* was in production Scacchi also appeared in the play *Airbase* with a young Mark Rylance, about drug-taking by US servicemen in the UK. This ran at the Arts Theatre, Great Newport Street, WC2, and both the play and *Defence of the Realm* reflected the anxiety that some in the UK had then, when protests at Greenham Common were an everyday event, about US activities within the country. The play caused quite a stir. Thatcher demanded a copy of the script and Mrs Whitehouse (who had presumably widened her correspondence base to an international level) apologised to President Reagan for its content.

As with *Steaming*, there is a Richard Harvey soundtrack to *Defence of the Realm*, which, like many others from this period, has yet to be formally released. The film cost £500k to make and was a modest success. Prior to this, Byrne was in the Gavras film *Hanna K* ('81) about the Arab-Israeli conflict, after which he made *Gothic* with Ken Russell. But not for the first time in his long career, Denholm Elliott steals the show. Drury later did – for TV – *Children of the North* ('91, about Ulster) and *The Secret Agent* ('92, a Conrad adaptation).

Stephen Woolley's Scala was where *Decoder* ('84) finally had its UK premiere in 1989, five years after being released in Europe. Purely via word of mouth, such was the reputation of its co-star Neil Megson, aka Genesis P-Orridge, that a crowd queued around the block to gain entry. In the late '70s Orridge and his ensemble Throbbing Gristle were a band whose notoriety matched that of The Sex Pistols, even if, strictly speaking, they were not solely 'a band' and how 'good' they were remained debatable for many. But they certainly caught the same tide, emerging in October 1976 at the ICA, a month before McLaren's protégés released their debut single. There was another connection too: Peter Christopherson, one of their multi-instrumentalists, was a photographer and commercial artist, a partner in the design studio Hipgnosis, and had done the first batch of PR shots of The Sex Pistols whilst working in McLaren and Westwood's shop.

In fact, the core of the group – Megson and his partner Christine Newby (aka Cosey Fanni Tutti) – had, like McLaren, been around since the days of deepest hippy. In 1970 both were members of COUM Transmissions, a Hull-based ensemble that did performance art with a bit of music... something quite fashionable at the time with acts like The Principal Edwards Magic Theatre and The Global Village Trucking Company, though COUM were less obviously 'musical' than either. By 1971 they were getting gigs supporting the likes of Hawkwind, had been mentioned by John Peel and were doing the occasional local radio session.

There were limits, of course, as to how far and how fast they could advance in Hull, so in 1973 they relocated to London, taking up space in a network of studios in Martello Street, London Fields, run by Bruce Lacey. (If anyone deserves crowning with the title of

UK pioneer of performance art it would be Lacey, whose credits stretch from working with Milligan and Bentine in the '50s, to The Alberts, to unforgettable film cameos in *Smashing Time* and *The Bliss of Mrs Blossom* in the '60s, to support slots with the first version of Pink Floyd.) Funded by the Arts Council from 1974, and hugely popular in Europe, they performed at the Paris Biennale. By those who considered such things, COUM Transmissions were highly regarded. A year later they hooked up with Chris Carter (a synthesiser player in the style of Brian Eno) and chose a more musical direction. After a final summer 1976 performance – as COUM – led to questions being asked about their funding in Parliament, they formally became Throbbing Gristle, a truly dreadful, but very '70s, name for a band, culled surely from the same lexicon as Spinal Tap, playing industrial noise at a blinding volume. Some of this was highly rated by connoisseurs of Krautrock and ambient music and after initial 'TG' releases appeared on an avant-garde German label, Reflection, run by Dietrich Albrecht, they started issuing their own records and rapidly produced 32 albums, of which 27 were recorded live. But notoriety was one thing. Sales were another: none charted and the group eventually folded in 1981, when Megson and Christopherson went on to Pyschic TV who were somewhat more accessible, almost psychedelic by comparison.

Gristle never made it into a commercial film, although their music was featured in Derek Jarman's 1981 short *In the Shadow of the Sun*. Along the way, Megson had opened up a communication channel to William Burroughs, a massive figure in the UK counterculture. Burroughs lived in London from 1966 to 1974 and counted Ballard and Moorcock among his literary admirers. Boasting connections to the epicentre of US bohemia (Kerouac, Ginsberg and so on), writers and musicians couldn't get enough of him. Several bands were named after his work: The Soft Machine, The Naked Lunch, Dead Fingers Talk and The Heavy Metal Kids, among others. The Pop Group – one of the key indie bands of the late '70s – had originally intended to name themselves The Wild Boys, after Burroughs' novel of that name. He also coined the phrase *Blade Runner* (a 1979 novella of his, to which the film has no connection) and Bowie copied his cut-up poetry style to write lyrics. Back in 1970 Burroughs had been at Ronan O'Rahilly's Phun City Festival, which might also have been his film debut had the Radio Caroline man got around to finishing and editing the masses of footage that was shot. Though popular, Burroughs' books were regarded as unfilmable for many years; thus *Decoder*, based on his 1971 essay *The Electronic Revolution*, turned out to be the first feature-length adaptation of his work, and as such attracted considerable attention.

Klaus Maeck, who managed the Hamburg band Abwärts, wrote and produced and the cast includes Bill Rice, an avant-garde US painter, FM Einheit (of Einstürzende Neubauten) and Vera Felscherinow (aka Christiane F.), with Megson playing 'the High Priest'. A satire, the plot is about a burger bar that incites riots against a fascist government by playing industrial noise. A lot of police repression and electronic surveillance, Stasi style, is shown throughout. Like its contemporaries *1984* and *Brazil*, *Decoder* is an Orwellian world where muzak is used to sedate people's creativity and emotions. Filmed in London, Hamburg and edgy Cold War West Berlin, it was directed by Jürgen Muschalek, a punk guitarist in Charley's Girls in 1977-8. That the film was made at all was extraordinary enough, but what really was remarkable was that a punk guitarist ended up as director: would any UK contemporary of Muscha's have landed a gig like this in the mid-'80s?

With music by Soft Cell, Blue Rondo à la Turk, Psychic TV and The The, the end product is actually quite good, with *Decoder* displaying an interesting, almost painterly, use of colour and imagery. A soundtrack LP also appeared, featuring five tracks composed by Dave Ball (of Soft Cell) with Megson/ Orridge. Compared with the solemn and worthy BFI and NFFC productions it was an entertaining work. And its appearance wasn't a pipe dream like so many UK ventures: it got made.

Megson had his devotees, but a film career never really beckoned for him, his only other appearance coming in a 2004 German gay-porn effort, *The Raspberry Reich*. Today, his former partner Christine Newby is regarded by many as the more interesting of the pair. Mixing art with music and a fearless exploration of her own sexuality (rather like a UK version of Kathy Acker), in the '70s she appeared – deliberately – in many of the UK's execrable sex films, using her experiences in these roles and photo shoots for top-shelf magazines to assemble a personal portfolio that broke probably more boundaries than anyone else's at the time. Post-Gristle, she and Chris Carter continued to make music, signing to Rough Trade for a couple of well-received albums, whilst she continued to work as a performance artist and actress, including a role in Ken Russell's *Gothic* ('86).

14

THE NEW MAINSTREAM

Given the difficulties encountered by the UK film industry in the '70s, the emergence of films that sought to portray the youth and music of the new era whilst being notably more commercial and accessible than similar productions a few years earlier was hardly surprising. For a practical example of how this worked, the career of producers Davina Belling and Clive Parsons is worthy of scrutiny. Starting with the critically acclaimed *Inserts* ('75), they followed this up with *Rosie Dixon –Night Nurse*, which made money and was one of several films based on a book by Christopher Wood, whose output ran from serious semi-autobiographical novels, via *Confessions of a Window Cleaner* to writing Bond screenplays. In 1979 they opted for *That Summer*, which with its simple plot and low-budget cast must have seemed an acceptable risk. It became the first of seven consecutive box-office hits that they produced.. Harley Cokeliss directed, having previously done the music documentary *Chicago Blues* ('70) and *Crash!* ('71), an initial sketching out of what would become JG Ballard's most (in) famous work. The cameraman is David Watkin, who, in happier times, had been engaged on much more prestigious stuff like *The Knack, How I Won the War, Catch 22* and many others.

A seaside romance comedy, *That Summer* was filmed in Torquay with a storyline about two girls (from 'the north'), who spend a summer there working in a hotel and have various dramatic, comic and amorous misadventures. Very competently made and considered by *Time Out* to be underrated, it follows, in reality, a very similar path to that trodden by a number of 'pop' entertainments made 15 years earlier, particularly *Just for Fun* and *Every Day's a Holiday*, with as many bands and singers as possible crammed on to the soundtrack. Except that in *That Summer*, unlike the early '60s films, they're heard, but not actually seen, in the film.

Because of the hiatus over *Scum*, this was the first significant exposure that cinema audiences had to Ray Winstone. Cast in the lead role, and formerly a teenage boxer from Hackney whose stage debut came in the 1975 revival of Joan Littlewood's *What a Crazy World!*, he appears alongside Tony London, Emily Moore and Julie Shipley. His performance was liked and won him a BAFTA. *That Summer* features a huge array – almost a jukebox-type selection – of music by Ian Dury and The Blockheads, Mink DeVille, Elvis Costello, The Boomtown Rats, The Zones, The Only Ones, Wreckless Eric, The Patti Smith Group, The Ramones, The Undertones, Eddie and The Hot Rods, Nick Lowe and Richard Hell and The Voidoids, all of which was released on an accompanying album by Arista. The remainder of the soundtrack was by guitarist Ray Russell, also noted for his contribution to *Rock Follies*.

As a follow-up, Belling and Parsons chose *Breaking Glass* ('80). Films about the music industry and those working within it stretch back to at least *The Glenn Miller Story* and tend towards the formulaic: a band is formed, relationships blossom and sour, the band breaks up and the industry is found to be unpleasant. *Breaking Glass* is no exception to this and is a very conventional rags to riches, back to rags and then some type of salvation drama. It was the first feature written and directed by Brian Gibson after much work for the BBC. Dodi Fayed is credited as Executive Producer (as he was on *Chariots of Fire*), this reflecting the access he provided to Middle East finance. Phil Daniels and Hazel O'Connor star. O'Connor, who had previously been in the cheap sex film *Girls Come First* ('75) and the thriller *Double Exposure* ('77), came from Coventry, like her brother Neil, a minor figure on the punk scene in EMI outfit The Flys. Fayed's money meant a strong supporting cast was possible and it was led by Jon Finch (*Macbeth, The Final Programme*) and Jonathan Pryce with Ken Campbell, Zoot Money and Gary Holton all in minor roles.

Based on her performance, you would have thought that O'Connor would have had a lengthy and significant career. Instead, things didn't really work out for her. There was a TV series, *Jangles* ('82), set in a nightclub where she was the resident act, *Car Trouble* ('85, in a supporting role) and *Fighting Back* ('86), a TV series with Derek Thompson, about a single mother struggling against the system, after which she virtually retired from the scene. At one point in *Breaking Glass* she performs as a mannequin in the style of the robotic woman in Fritz Lang's *Metropolis* – a nod towards this 1927 sci-fi masterpiece, which was being rediscovered in the '70s and '80s due to the rise in interest in modernist design and the success of German bands like Kraftwerk and Can. (A few years later a bidding war ensued to acquire the film rights, so that it could be re-edited and re-scored, with Giorgio Moroder winning out over David Bowie.)

Breaking Glass was a success in the UK (where its supporting film on general release was Julien Temple's *Biceps of Steel*, a documentary about hard rock/heavy metal outfit Samson), but not overly so elsewhere and Gibson later moved to the US where he eventually made biopics of Josephine Baker and Tina Turner.

The soundtrack LP was produced by Tony Visconti, using Bob Carter (guitar), Andy Duncan (drums), Rick Ford (bass) and Wesley Magoogan (saxophone). Carter and Duncan were simultaneously playing in the soul-funk outfit Linx and a few years later, in another demonstration of a move towards commerciality and accessibility in the arts, both would appear on *Wham Rap!*, the debut release from Wham! O'Connor wrote and sang much of the material as well as playing keyboards. A very commercial brand of mainstream pop-rock, rather than punk, the album sold heavily, reaching No 5 in the UK (with ten months in the charts) and also yielded the hit singles *Eighth Day* (No 5, August '80) and *Will You* (No 8, May '81).

For a third tilt at pop cinema Belling and Parsons went for

Party, Party ('81), a gruesomely stereotypical UK entry into the US teenage/student brat-pack genre that had been kickstarted by *National Lampoon's Animal House* ('78). About some kids organising, in the absence of their parents, a New Year's Eve party at a house in Hendon, north London that predictably gets badly out of hand, it was directed by Terry Winsor, whose later accomplishments included *Fool's Gold: The Story of the Brink's-Mat Robbery* ('92) and *Essex Boys* (2000) both thick-ear, 'based on true events' thrillers with Sean Bean.

Daniel Peacock, previously one of the mods in *Quadrophenia*, stars and also co-wrote the script with Winsor. Peacock also dabbled in music, being one of The Wild Men of Wonga, whose 1985 single *Why Don't Pretty Girls Look at Me?* turned up on the soundtrack of John Hughes' *Weird Science*. Karl Howman co-stars, having previously appeared in *That'll Be the Day*, *Stardust*, the ITV series *People Like Us* and *Get Some In!* (the latter a nostalgic comedy about National Service), as well as the somewhat grittier *Babylon*. But though competent and popular, *Party, Party* is a very limited and straight type of comic drama that aims squarely at the under-18 market and avoids complications. The plot requires little imagination and basically writes itself. It makes one yearn for the subversive undertow that either John Waters or Russ Meyer would have brought to a similar suburban situation. And, of course, it appeared six years after *Abigail's Party* cringingly explored the same terrain... so, is this the party that Abigail actually had, but we didn't see, in 1977?

The soundtrack, pieced together with assistance from A&M records by Richard Hartley of *The Rocky Horror Picture Show*, includes The Rezillos, Elvis Costello and The Attractions, Dave Edmunds, Altered Images, Bad Manners, Sting, Bananarama (doing The Sex Pistols), Madness, Modern Romance, Pauline Black (doing Bob Marley), Midge Ure (doing David Bowie) and Orchestral Manoeuvres in the Dark and concludes, as does the film, with a Chas and Dave version of *Auld Lang Syne*. With no score as such, this is just a compilation album licensed from various labels and a pointer to how many studios and production companies would cut costs in their approach to film music in the future.

More promisingly, *Times Square* ('80) visits *Midnight Cowboy* territory, but with a twist as this is a UK production by EMI and Robert Stigwood with a UK star (Tim Curry) and heaps of UK music. A fair bit of Schlesinger's 1969 classic was filmed in and around Times Square and the location, which serves again as a backdrop here, declined significantly in the years that followed. By 1980 it was strewn with sex cinemas, billboards and empty buildings and was also a dangerous place to hang out – serious crimes were a daily occurrence. Allan Moyle directed. A Canadian, his previous film *The Rubber Gun* ('78) was about a family of artists-turned-drug addicts living in a commune in Montreal and, on *Times Square*, he is well served by Jacob Brackman's script. Brackman, who wrote songs for Carly Simon, was an important figure in US independent cinema, writing the liner notes for the *Five Easy Pieces* soundtrack album ('70), doing the screenplay for *The King of Marvin Gardens* ('72) and producing *Days of Heaven* ('78). He also supplied a couple of the songs used in *Times Square*.

The plot has two depressed girls, Robin Johnson and Trini Alvarado, 16 and 13 years old respectively, running away to New York where they live on the streets and have various adventures. They adopt a punk lifestyle, form a band, meet an influential DJ (Tim Curry, with a US accent) and through him become successful/notorious. A bit too niche to be a major success, the film, nevertheless, does have its moments and is best appreciated as a fairy tale. Robin Johnson performs four songs, including one with David Johansen, former front man in The New York Dolls and a legend locally. Curry's appearance was part of a determined assault by him on the US after the underground success of *The Rocky Horror Picture Show*. This also included a recording deal with A&M and a reasonably big-selling album, *Fearless* (No 53, US '79).

A conflict arose about the direction that *Times Square* should take. Robert Stigwood wanted more music, Moyle wanted to stick to the gritty inner-urban storyline. Stigwood, replete with success from *Saturday Night Fever* and *Grease*, won, taking over the editing of the final cut and getting what he wanted: an RSO soundtrack album overseen by Blue Weaver (ex-The Amen Corner), with material by The Pretenders, Gary Numan, XTC, The Ruts and The Cure. Some might reflect that yet again this was another demonstration that the role of the UK was now to provide personnel and expertise for the US entertainments industry. Moyle's experience making the film was such that he spent a decade away from cinema, not returning until *Pump Up the Volume* ('90), another drama about a DJ. Brackman never did another screenplay, but later wrote most of the material on the satirical album *Dancing for Mental Health* (Island '83, by Will Powers aka Lynn Goldsmith, rock photographer), which produced a UK hit, *Kissing with Confidence* (No 17), with uncredited vocals by Carly Simon.

US TV company Lorimar may be best remembered for *Dallas* (a phenomenal record-breaking success between 1978 and 1991), but along the way they also produced *Helter Skelter* (a '76 drama about the Manson killings), *Americathon* ('79), *Being There* ('79) and *Cruising* ('80), after which they went for a co-production with Lyndall Hobbs, whose witty, observant short *Steppin' Out* ('79) had provided a notable set of pen portraits of various figures (Boy George, Marilyn, Steve Strange) on the London scene. The resulting film, *Urgh! A Music War* ('81), mixes live footage from the US, UK and France of no fewer than 36 different acts, all performing one song each, including Toyah Willcox, John Cooper Clarke, Orchestral Manoeuvres in the Dark, Chelsea, Echo and The Bunnymen, Splodgenessabounds, Jools Holland, XTC, Athletico Spizz 80, Steel Pulse, Gary Numan, Magazine, The Members, The Au Pairs, 999, The Gang of Four, UB40, The Police and John Otway. No great cinematic artistry is on display here, just endless scenes of bands and singers performing with neither plot nor dialogue. Most of the footage was filmed in August–September 1980 in huge stadiums, including, in the UK as well as the Lyceum and the Rainbow that the performers' styles didn't always suit. The end result was often indifferent and lacking in sound quality.

In a pre-MTV era this had some attraction, however average
the overall tone is by today's standards. Looked at now, *Urgh! A
Music War* is a valuable historical document and contains rare
footage of Klaus Nomi, a German opera singer from Berlin
who deconstructed pop/rock songs in a shrill falsetto and had a
highly stylised and completely artificial appearance, looking like a
showroom dummy. A feature of the New York counterculture, he
performed with Basquiat and Bowie and later became one of the
first celebrity casualties of AIDS.

The idea to make a film of this type came from with Jonathan
Demme, who originally wanted to do a documentary about the
emerging new-wave groups in Los Angeles. This was taken up by
IRS records, but quickly spiralled upwards and away from Demme,
who ended up playing no part at all in a project that he initiated.
Instead, Miles Copeland III, the owner of IRS, took over and
was eventually credited as creative consultant. Copeland brought
in the music acts and also attracted as producer Michael White,
noted for *Oh! Calcutta!* and *The Rocky Horror Picture Show*. Derek
Burbidge directed, taking a break from filming music videos for
acts like Gary Numan, The Police and AC/DC.

The soundtrack was released as a double LP. *Urgh! A Music War*
was, in fact, reasonably successful and remained a staple of late-
night screenings for some years, but by the early '80s rock music
in the cinema was beating a retreat before the onward march of
the music video. Perhaps they should have kept Demme on board.
After all, his concert film ventures with Talking Heads, *Stop
Making Sense* (April '84, the soundtrack album made No 24 UK)
and *True Stories* (October '86, soundtrack No 7 UK and No 28 US)
were stylish, applauded by the critics and commercial hits. Both
were a tour de force for David Byrne, the Scots-American leader
of the group, whose presence, sense of humour and energy were
very different to those of UK artists such as Lydon, Strummer and
Weller.

The first stirrings of punk had produced a number of DIY
documentaries from guerrilla filmmakers like Wolfgang Büld
and Don Letts. A few years later, somewhat larger budgets were

available for films about the emerging ska and 2-Tone acts. The first
of these came from Joe Massot, whose career, like that of James
Kenelm Clarke, had more than its fair share of oddities. After
a couple of documentaries about Fidel Castro's regime in Cuba
he arrived in 'Swinging London' for Apple's *Wonderwall* ('68), did
the two hippy dramas *Zachariah* and *Universal Soldier*, defaulted to
the bombastic Led Zeppelin concert movie *The Song Remains the
Same* ('76, from which he was removed), and ended with *Dance
Craze* ('81), funded by Chrysalis, the ultimate owner of the 2-Tone
record label. If his earlier works were noted for obscure, rambling
plots, this production of his has no storyline at all, no actors, no
script and almost no footage shot outside the recording studio or
wherever else the music is being performed. It was produced by
Gavrik Losey, like Massot a '60s survivor whose credits ran from
Modesty Blaise, via *If....* and *Villain* to *Slade in Flame*.

Between 1979 and 1982 the plethora of ska bands was looked
on with some favour as an interesting and, when they recorded
their own material, socially conscious development from punk
that was in many ways preferable to the inherent conservatism of
the mod revivalists. There must have been hopes that a number of
films that exemplified 2-Tone values would emerge, but the only
examples that appeared – other than *Dance Craze* – turned out to
be *Prostitute*, a 1980s effort from writer-director Tony Garnett, and
Knights and Emeralds ('86) from Ian Emes, both of whom hailed
from the West Midlands. In the former of these, Garnett (best
known for *Kes*, '69) produced a film about a sex worker who moves
to London to get a better chance in life. Shot in Balsall Heath,
an area with a significant amount of street prostitution, with a
largely unknown cast, one scene has an uncredited appearance
from Ali and Robin Campbell of UB40, whilst the soundtrack
includes a couple of numbers by local outfit The Gangsters, one
of which is written by Ray King. King was quite a figure in the
West Midlands scene, having in the '60s led the multiracial Ray
King Soul Band, who circa 1968 had a residency at London's
Playboy Club whilst recording for CBS subsidiary Direction. They
never reached the level of success enjoyed by The Foundations

and The Equals and King latterly assisted Jim Simpson (another West Midlands legend and once manager of Black Sabbath) in his recording chores. There were efforts made in the late '70s to bring him back to prominence as part 2-Tone, but he resisted these. For Emes, who started out doing promotional shorts for Pink Floyd, *Knights and Emeralds* was a chance to work with David Puttnam and Goldcrest. Although pretty detached from 2-Tone, the film embodies its ethos, being a white boy/black girl romance with a soundtrack featuring Princess, Maxi Priest and Slade. As it turned out, audience figures for *Prostitute* were slim and *Knights and Emeralds* seems to have been a victim of the post-*Absolute Beginners* collapse of Goldcrest and is rarely seen now.

Dance Craze started out as a documentary solely about Madness, though its scope was subsequently widened to embrace the entire 2-Tone stable of artists. The original intention behind 2-Tone was that it would be the UK's equivalent of Tamla Motown – creative, multiracial, politically aware and offering a platform to emerging musicians and singers. Massot's film, though, is very rudimentary, other than 85 minutes of various bands playing live (with a batch of '50s documentaries about teenage life in the '50s spliced in midway through as a quasi-interval). It provides little background detail or travelogue footage about the venues and towns they appear in. But it got a reasonable release and the soundtrack album made No 5 in the UK. High points are Madness performing *One Step Beyond* (No 7, November '79), The Selecter *Three Minute Hero* (No 16, March '80), The Beat *Mirror in the Bathroom* (No 4, May '80) and Bad Manners *Lip Up Fatty* (No 15, July '80).

Ska and 2-tone were heavily endorsed by Garry Bushell, then a Trotskyist journalist who wrote for *Sounds* magazine, as part of a 'working-class' mod scene that was actually very retro. Originally an adolescent political activist from Charlton, who passed through Ken Livingstone's Schools Action Union around 1970 and the SWP circa 1973, he also performed with The Gonads, playing a type of boozy skinhead agit-prop punk. He wrote a tie-in book for the film (published as a magazine and available from *Sounds*), but, by early 1982 2-Tone had passed its peak. The Specials, The

Bodysnatchers and The Selecter all split early and Jerry Dammers, the main force behind the label, had a breakdown caused by overwork whilst editing the musical footage for the film. Bushell himself gravitated to *The Sun* a few years later.

A few months later *Take It or Leave It* ('81) provided a film based entirely on the rise of Madness. Written, directed and produced by Dave Robinson, this was a 100 per cent Stiff Records venture, and as such it approaches its topic in a very different way to the much better known *The Great Rock N' Roll Swindle*. Robinson, and his approach to operating within the music industry, makes for an intriguing comparison with Malcolm McLaren, and some description of that, and how *Take It or Leave It* got made, is required.

Originally a teenage photographer in Dublin, Robinson was appointed to officially record a Rolling Stones' tour of Ireland, events that were also captured, on film, by Peter Whitehead in *Charlie is My Darling* ('66). Later he was Jimi Hendrix's road manager, a job that led to numerous US tours and similar work stewarding Eric Burdon and The Animals, The Young Rascals and Vanilla Fudge. By 1971 he was back in the UK, now a greatly diminished scene, and hooked up with Brinsley Schwarz, who arose out of the ashes of polite late '60s pop group Kippington Lodge and had a deal with United Artists, but seemed to be going nowhere. One problem for them, and many other acts of a similar type by the early '70s, was the lack of suitable venues where they could play. To counter this, Robinson made arrangements with 35 pubs around London and the home counties, where a performance space existed and gaining a music licence was feasible, thus establishing the pub-rock circuit, the forerunner of punk. By 1975, fed up with the attitude towards emerging acts by the major labels, he set up Stiff Records with Jake Riviera, manager of Dr. Feelgood, using a studio above one of his venues (the Hope and Anchor, Islington) to record many of its releases.

Thus, unlike McLaren, who preferred to extract money from existing corporations, Robinson created a chain of venues and his own record label. Stiff quickly became noted for releasing their material with neatly designed picture sleeves, many of which were done by graphic designer Barney Bubbles (aka Colin Fulcher), who started in advertising in the '60s before moving into the counterculture with his light show – hence the nickname – and album sleeves for the likes of Quintessence and Hawkwind. Within a few years Robinson was either managing or had signed to Stiff, Graham Parker, Dave Edmunds, The Damned, Motörhead, Elvis Costello, Nick Lowe, Tracey Ullman, Jona Lewie, Ian Dury and The Blockheads, Kirsty MacColl, Lene Lovich and The Pogues. In another throwback to how singers and bands had been promoted 15–20 years earlier, he sent out many of these acts on package tours, just as Hendrix (and he) had toured in late 1967 with the likes of The Move and Pink Floyd. Fond memories of these events were preserved in live albums, one of which, *Live Stiffs Live*, made No 28 in the UK LP charts in March 1978. Again, McLaren generally eschewed work of this type.

Robinson's greatest success, though, came in August 1979 when he detached Madness from 2-Tone and signed them to Stiff. A six-piece pop-ska ensemble, they brought to the scene a very London, very English, very working-class demeanour in equal parts deadpan, cheerful, chippy and self-deprecating. Between 1979 and 1986 they racked up twenty hit singles and six chart albums, writing material noted for economical and shrewd lyrics of which '....it was built in '59, in a factory on the Tyne ....' about a Morris Minor was typical. They also kickstarted the rediscovery of Michael Caine and the *Italian Job/Get Carter* era, recording a single with him (*My Name is Michael Caine*, No 11 UK '84), with a music video based on *The Ipcress File*. At the time Caine was a semi-forgotten Tory tax exile and no longer the huge figure he had been between 1965 and 1972. But people had fond memories of his laconic, cool image and the Madness collaboration was part of a reappraisal of his legacy, which in turn became – eventually – one of the building blocks in the rebirth of a specifically English pop culture from the late '80s onwards.

As for *Take It or Leave It...* It's a documentary drama/comedy about the rise of the group, with a fair amount of raw authenticity as they emerge from their working-class origins. They play themselves and even part-funded it (£20k each, against a percentage of the profits). Adequately made, and reminiscent of the type of pop biography film that was common in the '50s and '60s, it pleased their fans without making an impact on the critics. Curiously, given their success, no soundtrack album appeared, with collectors having to wait 32 years for a belated CD release. One issue it does sidestep, though, is their rowdy skinhead following. As individuals, the band were fine, but going to their gigs, certainly in their early years, could be a risky business.

This era also produced, somewhat belatedly, the first significant film coverage of a UK music festival since Glastonbury in 1971. *New Brighton Rock* ('84) was nothing like Woodstock, nor even much like the Isle of Wight. The footage in this covers an event held at what was then the largest open-air swimming pool in the world. Located in New Brighton a (very) faded nineteenth-century seaside resort near Birkenhead, and held on the eve of the miners' strike (where and when would it have been better to consider the realities of life in the UK during the '80s?), this was a Granada TV special directed by Ian Hamilton and Mary McMurray. The total production cost amounted to only £100k, a tiny amount, even by the standards of the time.

Staged over four days in May 1984, the acts on show include Eddy Grant, Frankie Goes to Hollywood, Gloria Gaynor, Helen Terry (the only one, apparently, to sing live; the others all mimed), Nick Lowe, Nik Kershaw, Spandau Ballet, The Flying Pickets and The Weather Girls. It's all quite competently done, as in a well-managed episode of *Top of the Pops*, and an effective showcase for UK pop talent at that time. But... unlike *Gimme Shelter* or *Monterey Pop* there is no sense of a connection to the world beyond the three-minute songs being belted out. This is striking given how intensely political a time this was on Merseyside and the city was, to an extent, putting on a brave, creative face after decades of neglect and urban blight, as well as the impact of extensive rioting in the early '80s. At no point does *New Brighton Rock* either observe or comment on this. In a very roundabout way, though, some sense of this is inadvertently reflected in the history of the venue itself. A classic art-deco lido dating from 1934, for many years it hosted an annual Miss New Brighton contest, the 1977 winner of which (Tracy Dodds) went out with the singer of Orchestral Manoeuvres in the Dark at one point. Alas, like many buildings of note locally, it gradually fell into serious disrepair and, after being battered by a 100mph winter storm in 1990, it was demolished soon afterwards.

Whatever shortcomings the final product may have had didn't deter the producer, Stephen Leahy, from selling the film worldwide and making a considerable profit. In August 1986 Granada and he repeated the formula with *Rock Around the Dock*, filmed at the Albert Dock, Liverpool – a happier choice of location – with Frankie Goes to Hollywood, The Damned, Cameo, Chaka Khan, Run-DMC, Feargal Sharkey, Spandau Ballet, The Style Council, UB40, Five Star and Ruby Turner. Both TV specials starred Frankie Goes to Hollywood, of whom great things were expected after they scored three consecutive No 1 hits in the UK in 1983–4. Their record label ZTT wanted them to star in a Martin Amis-scripted drama that would have them as post-apocalyptic survivors. Nicolas Roeg was lined up to direct as soon as he had finished *Castaway*, only for the group to veto the project and disintegrate a year later.

The most significant example of the move in the arts from experimental work to safe, commercial product during this period was surely played out, though, in the career of Richard Branson. Indeed, if Bowie bestrode the era musically, Richard Branson was definitely its business brain. Bearded, frowning and serious, he bobbed into view in 1967–8 running *Student* magazine, interviewing RD Laing and Mick Jagger and going on anti-Vietnam war demos with the assembled radical chic of the time. By 1969 he was running a pioneering mail-order business out of Virgin Records and Tapes in Notting Hill Gate and distributing many German bands. This duly morphed into the UK's finest and most comprehensive music arcadia, at 133–5 Oxford Street W1. Converted from the shell of a massive Lyons Corner House, in one of the historical coincidences so typical of

London, it occupied the site of the legendary Oxford Music Hall, the greatest musical entertainment venue of its time. Here, more than 50 years after Marie Lloyd, George Robey and many others had taken their final bows, Branson acted as master of ceremonies in a stupendous vinyl emporium of rock, pop, punk, soul, folk, jazz and everything else. Boasting a terrific back catalogue, if an album wasn't available at the Virgin shop on Oxford Street, it just wasn't available anywhere.

Operating out of a tiny office in Portobello Road, Branson launched Virgin Records in 1972 with Tom Newman, once of psychedelic band July. They struck it rich – forever – with their debut release, *Tubular Bells*. A continuous 55-minute long instrumental solo recording by 19-year-old guitarist Mike Oldfield, this made No 1 in the UK and No 3 in the US and had its main theme all over *The Exorcist*, the biggest film of 1973. It remained in the charts for six years and as a piece of music you couldn't avoid it in the mid-'70s: it was part of the audio-scape of the time. Better still, Oldfield wasn't a one-hit wonder. All of his follow-up albums charted and, as Virgin ploughed its immense income from him into other artists, lesser successes came from Robert Wyatt, Steve Hillage and the German outfits Tangerine Dream and Can. This was all quintessential hippy-era stuff, targeted at mainly male students (though Julie Covington was a noted female success for the label) and backed up by promotional tours of the various bands and singers on the gig circuit of student unions that were an essential outlet for much of the rock music of the time. Still decidedly countercultural and happy to cater to niche interests (German electronica, heavy dub), Virgin did not embrace either the emerging pub-rock scene or any overtly commercial pop.

Then, in early 1977 Branson sniffed the direction the wind was blowing and signed The Sex Pistols. Within a year he'd expanded effortlessly into the punk/new-wave market with The Motors, Devo, Magazine, Penetration and XTC. Later additions to the roster included The Members, The Flying Lizards, The Ruts and The Skids, together with Public Image Limited and Sid Vicious from the wreckage of McLaren's band. Arguably this was Virgin's high point in terms of artistic impact, being home to a wide range of acts that were new, interesting and cutting edge.

Post-1980, a third phase emerged as the label expanded again and Branson became increasingly mainstream: John Foxx, The Human League, Heaven 17, Japan (and spin-offs Sylvian-Sakamoto and David Sylvian), Simple Minds, Culture Club, Orchestral Manoeuvres in the Dark, China Crisis, Scritti Politti, Working Week, Kate Bush and Feargal Sharkey. Most of these were generally more commercial and accessible than the artistes Virgin had handled previously and, as intended, secured success for the label in the US market. And, increasingly, Branson now signed up those who, like him, heavily pre-dated punk... Gillan, Phil Collins, Gary Moore, Genesis, Peter Gabriel and finally, in 1986, Bowie himself. Back in 1982 Virgin bought Heaven, a capacious subterranean nightclub and music venue in the vaults and arches beneath Charing Cross Station. With hindsight, this, their record shops and the label were their 'peak', and without doubt Branson was the most outstanding example of the '60s music industry hustler to emerge and flourish in the '70s and '80s.

Instead of consolidating, though, Branson inched into film production, initially with the NASA-sponsored documentary *The Space Movie* ('80, directed by Tony Palmer and with a Mike Oldfield score) and later with *Secret Places* and *Electric Dreams* ('84). The first film solely produced by Virgin, *Electric Dreams* was shot in the US with a plot about a love triangle between a man, a woman and a PC. At that point – mid-'80s – a PC was a huge plastic box and the device shown here was one of only a few attempts to feature a computer as a character, the others being Hal in *2001* (a somewhat superior film) and Proteus IV in *Demon Seed* ('77). Unlike Kubrick, though, this film doesn't really say much about the nature of existence and the human condition. Instead, the plot has the computer outwitting a geeky architect and trying to date his girl. It's a slick rom-com, set in San Francisco and was directed by 28-year-old Steve Barron, who otherwise made many music videos from 1978 onwards for the likes of The Jam, Secret Affair, Adam and The Ants, The Human League, Heaven 17, Eddy Grant, The

Fun Boy Three, Joe Jackson, Orchestral Manoeuvres in the Dark, Simple Minds and The Skids. Barron's mum, Zelda, dabbled in this field too. She did videos for Culture Club and was similarly making her feature-film debut with another Virgin project, *Secret Places* (a retro drama set in a girls' boarding school), at the same time that her son was filming *Electric Dreams*. Presumably, both mother and son were chosen by Branson for their expertise in making short, rapidly cut promos for the label's latest music acts.

Virginia Madsen in *Electric Dreams* and was later in *Dune* and *Slam Dance*, the latter with Adam Ant. Lenny Von Dohlen played her boyfriend and Bud Cort provided the voice for Edgar (the computer). None of it is badly done... but 1984 was possibly a little early for this type of plot, as computers, mobile phones and the digital economy generally didn't really kick off for another decade. As a result, despite its topicality and direct pitch to the youth audience, the film flopped at the box office. (A similar fate befell *Digital Dreams*, a 1983 TV film about Rolling Stone Bill Wyman trying to digitalise his entire life. Written and directed by Richard O'Brien, it had a limited distribution.)

The soundtrack was entrusted to Jeff Lynne and Giorgio Moroder. On paper, this was a dream ticket. By 1984 Moroder was established as the go-to man for electronic dance music as well as a film composer whose touch had helped to define hits like *Looking for Mr Goodbar*, *Midnight Express*, *The Bitch*, *American Gigolo*, *Cat People* and *Flashdance*. For his part, Lynne had enjoyed immense success in the US with the Electric Light Orchestra (fifteen hit singles and six chart albums between 1974 and 1983) and – importantly – his band had done the music for the Olivia Newton-John fantasy *Xanadu*, which went double platinum in 1980. It's fair to conclude that Virgin would have expected their pairing to produce similar results. What emerged, though, was decidedly less than the sum of the parts. Moroder and Phil Oakey, from The Human League, did *Together in Electric Dreams*, which reached No 3 in the UK, while Culture Club went Top 30 in Italy and Spain with *Love is Love*, but greater success than this was elusive. PP Arnold did the main title theme, which passed unnoticed, as did other tracks by Heaven

17 and Helen Terry. Given the talent involved this was rather surprising. Perhaps the conclusion might be that UK musicals never really gel, even if filmed in the US, something that Branson might have noted before investing in *Absolute Beginners*.

Electric Dreams, like *Absolute Beginners*, lost a lot of money. And, despite some interesting later films like *The Raggedy Rawney* ('88), *Sex, Lies and Videotape* and *The Rachel Papers* (both '89), cinema tailed off as a Virgin endeavour when Branson invaded yet another field: general leisure and travel activities. In June 1984 Virgin Atlantic appeared (originally, and bombastically, intending to provide a direct service to the Falklands Islands with a jet leased from an Argentine airline) and from there on the simple fact was that all the good work that the record label and high-street shops did was remorselessly dragged down by the expenditure needed to keep an airline functioning. That and the decrease in vinyl sales as music went first to CDs and then online brought things to a conclusion – in 1992 Branson sold Virgin to EMI to keep his airline going and an era ended.

Away from Virgin, greater success was enjoyed by *The NeverEnding Story* ('84), which trumped *Just a Gigolo* as the most expensive West German film of all time and, when released, was the biggest budget film ever made outside the US. This was both a very serious domestic project within West Germany as well as a major European attempt at breaking into Hollywood and was based on a bestselling 1979 fantasy epic by Michael Ende, roughly a German equivalent of CS Lewis and JRR Tolkien.

Funding for such an ambitious production was secured via the involvement of three separate producers: Bernd Eichinger, who had done *Christiane F.*; Mark Damon, whose successes included *Das Boot* and *An American Werewolf in London*; and Dieter Geissler, whose lengthy CV featured *Ludwig* and *Egon Schiele: Excess and Punishment*. Wolfgang Petersen directed, having just finished *Das Boot*. Aimed squarely at the US and UK markets, it was filmed in English in Spain, Canada and Germany with a cast led by the US child stars Noah Hathaway, Barret Oliver and Tami Stronach, supported by Moses Gunn and Patricia Hayes.

The plot is almost impossible to summarise and has, like the meaning of the book, been much argued over. Its author, Ende, saw himself as a surrealist and exponent of magical realism rather than someone who wrote children's stories. At its simplest level of interpretation, the story concerns an unhappy child who gets drawn into a fantasy world from which it becomes increasingly difficult to escape. The adventures that ensue are anti-rational/anti-materialistic in sentiment and show a regret for the decline of magic and its symbolism.

The NeverEnding Story had a main theme song by Limahl, co-produced by Giorgio Moroder and Keith Forsey. It reached No 4 in the UK and No 17 in the US and, predictably, was massive across Europe. Limahl had been in the group Kajagoogoo (who arose from the ashes of synthesiser act Art Nouveau) and was pretty successful circa 1983–4 as a very straight pop act. However, the Moroder/Limahl material was not in the West German version of the film, which only features an orchestral score by Klaus Doldinger. Moroder, an Austrian-Italian, had been making records since 1964, moving into film in 1970. During this period his music could be heard in *Abigail's Party*, *The Bitch*, *American Gigolo* and *Cat People*, sung by Bowie in the latter. Forsey for his part was ex-The Spectrum, The Motherhood and Amon Düül II.

The film, which, as with adaptations of Lewis and Tolkien, only covers part of the book, was a significant international hit. It was done in a very fey pop-psychedelic style that was distinctly 'European', but actually had its origins in UK music circa 1967–8 with a distinct emphasis on whimsicality and child-like imagery (think here the big 1967 hit *Excerpt from a Teenage Opera*). Many UK special effects and production people were involved with the film and the box-office returns were good enough to lead to two sequels, released in 1990 and 1994, to diminishing returns. The box-office takings for *The NeverEnding Story* exceeded $100m solely in the US and it is interesting to consider why it outperformed *Electric Dreams* and *Absolute Beginners* to such an extent, despite all three films sharing a very safe commercial pitch.

15

CONCLUSION

This narrative ends in 1986. By then, punk, the DIY, anti-style, anti-fashion fashion on which so much had briefly been pinned was long gone. The Sex Pistols had collapsed years earlier, McLaren's replacement act Bow Wow Wow had vanished and he, too, was struggling to repeat his early solo success with *Duck Rock* ('83), hugely enjoyable but plundered wholesale, as was much of what he did, from the work of others. It was also the year that The Clash finally broke up and the year that the Pistols' John Lydon had his last great hit, *Rise*, with Public Image Limited.

What came next was very commercial indeed, and typified by the success of The Pet Shop Boys, featuring Neil Tennant of *Smash Hits* magazine. They released a stream of faultlessly produced, played and sung material that yielded forty-two hit singles and thirteen hit albums over the next three decades. This trend – towards sophisticated, well organised and accessible acts - held sway at live music venues as well and quickly took over the festival scene once that restarted. Any idea that the latter would survive, as casual ad hoc gatherings, came to an abrupt end at the 'Battle of the Beanfield' in June 1985, when a peace convoy (a ramshackle collection of vehicles driven by and containing the extended families of late-period hippies, anarchists and environmentalists) was halted, attacked and dispersed by the Wiltshire Police. Glastonbury, relaunched in 1979, became the alternative. An increasingly mainstream event, it quickly surpassed in size the show captured on film by Nic Roeg in 1971, attracting massive crowds from the mid-'90s onwards.

It took a few years for the dust to settle but eventually a new sound (or to be accurate two new sounds) emerged which would characterise the '90s and beyond in much the same way that mod and psychedelia had the '60s and punk (and its offshoots) the late '70s. Of course, this is a very broad generalisation, but by the mid-'90s the classic British guitar band and electronic dance music were both well established and comprised between them an awful lot of what was selling. Both exemplified the pick-and-mix approach pioneered by McLaren some years earlier, whereby the accumulated sounds of the preceding 30 years or more were progressively pillaged for inspiration, with an abundance of cover versions and remixes.

The guitar bands were heavily concentrated across the north of England, though with a significant presence in London as well. There had been indications for some time that live music in particular would return to this style, mainly as a reaction against the plethora of synthesiser-dominated, rather overproduced and poppy acts that dominated the charts from 1982 onwards. Siouxsie and The Banshees made an early entrance with a cover of *Dear Prudence* in 1983, following this up with their take on *This Wheel's on Fire* in 1987. At around the same time, The Damned made the charts with *Eloise* ('86) and *Alone Again Or* ('87). When The Soup Dragons, from Motherwell, hit with a version of The Rolling Stones' 1965 album track *I'm Free* ('90), it was clear that something was afoot, even if, with hindsight, it shouldn't really have come as that much of a surprise. After all, the guitar band had long been the style favoured by Paul Weller, who doggedly continued in The Style Council and then as a solo act, much as he had started in 1977 with The Jam.

Others exponents included The Fall, much loved by both John Peel and Tony Wilson, who finally came good and enjoyed a few hit records between 1987 and 1993. (Again, with a nod to the past, they broke through with a cover of the Northern Soul classic *There's a Ghost in My House* and followed this by recording a version of the 1969 Ray Davies song *Victoria* for their 1988 album

The Frenz Experiment.) Whatever the intention of their front man Mark E Smith to articulate Camus and at one point to perform in a Michael Clark ballet – captured in the 1987 film *Hail the New Puritan* – he usually came across like a character from an early '70s Alan Sillitoe novel, defiantly spitting out contrarian denunciations.

A significant factor in the emergence of the new generation of guitar bands (or 'indie rock' bands as they quickly became known) was Creation Records, formed in 1984 by Alan McGee and named after a '60s act he particularly admired: The Creation, whose output between 1966 and 1968 amounted to eight singles, depending on which country you looked at, and whose success, then, was slight. McGee even named his own group, Biff Bang Pow!, after one of their b-sides. In 1989 (a year when half a dozen or so of the new guitar bands established themselves), McGee and his label had their first massive success with Primal Scream and the guitar band juggernaut never stopped moving from that point on... The Manic Street Preachers, Blur and Suede breaking through in 1991-2, then Shed Seven, Supergrass, Pulp and Oasis (another McGee act and the only ones to be really huge in the US) by 1994. Around the time Tony Blair moved into 10 Downing Street the music scene saw the arrival of The Bluetones, Mansun, Placebo, Ocean Colour Scene, The Divine Comedy, Travis, Stereophonics and Embrace . There were many, many more.

Of course, in terms of style, sound and approach there were variations among all of these, not to mention huge rivalries as well. But the important commonality was a willingness to explore the recent musical past and rework it either directly or indirectly for contemporary ears. In terms of influences, The Beatles, as one would expect, remained widespread, with The Small Faces surprisingly important too. Nick Drake and Syd Barrett generally got nods of approval, as did Dylan, The Byrds, Iggy Pop and even Burt Bacharach. It seems that at some point after 1986 many aspiring guitarists and singers, looking askance at the production line of hits produced by Stock, Aitken and Waterman (94 in the UK Top 30 alone between 1984 and 1993), and the demise of so many of the acts prominent between 1977 and 1981, consciously began exploring simpler, more direct, earlier sounds. This desire to look again at the past was also evident in cinema, notably in *Withnail and I* ('87), a film about struggling actors at the end of the '60s that fits in with this trend. A serious UK cinematic effort to look back at the '60s, the film was hugely popular and remains today a highly regarded UK production.

Electronica, the other 'new' sound, brought together a wide range of dance music, including funk, synthesiser, Asian dance, soul, techno, rave, hip-hop and sampling. As with the 'indie rock' outfits, the origins of this can be traced back to the '60s (its key pioneer, Giorgio Moroder, had his first hit in 1968) and the success of Can, Tangerine Dream, Kraftwerk and Telex in the '70s. Its exponents were heavily centred on London and its influences, styles, connections and references were too many to mention. Part of its success and ubiquity came from new digital technology, which made flawless recording much cheaper than had been the case previously and enabled the borrowing or sampling of almost any material that came to hand. Film themes, TV themes and even easy listening were all duly raided by its protagonists, notably The Chemical Brothers, who originally ran a nightclub in Manchester called Naked Under Leather, the US title of the 1968 Marianne Faithfull film *Girl on a Motorcycle*.

By the late '80s and early '90s immense commercial success was being enjoyed by The KLF and The Orb, the former of these led by Bill Drummond and Jimmy Cauty, who had previously worked together as The Justified Ancients of Mu Mu. Named after characters in the Robert Shea and Robert Anton Wilson conspiracy trilogy *Illuminatus!* (on the theatre adaptation of which Drummond had worked with Ken Campbell), The JAM's debut release *1987 (What the Fuck is Going On?)*, intended as a withering put-down of contemporary musical mores, was a richly entertaining musical and sound collage with 50 per cent of its material swiped illegally from other sources. It was promptly banned on copyright grounds, but in 1988, as The Timelords, they hit No 1 in the UK with a reworking of the *Doctor Who* theme. Malcolm McLaren would have been proud of them.

The disappearance of the '70s milieu of protest was also reflected in cinema. The end of the notion that an oppositionist, radical (and often state-funded) counterculture might succeed commercially can be seen with the fading away of Red Wedge and the demise of its only film production, the concert movie *Turn it Up: Days like These* ('86). A record of the Artists Against Apartheid concert staged on Clapham Common in late 1985, attended by 250,000 (at least as many as went to Live Aid), it was made by Don Coutts and featured Billy Bragg and Lloyd Cole. Despite this, the film itself was hardly seen and quickly vanished from circulation, as did Red Wedge itself. Founded in 1985 out of the remnants of Rock Against Racism, and allied at one point with 2-Tone, it had attempted a 'fightback' against those seeking to end the post-1945 political settlement, principally by mobilising and politicising the young. But after Labour failed in the General Elections of 1987 and 1992, little more was heard from it.

Thus, as with music, by 1986 UK cinema was in poor shape. Its demise had, indeed, been confidently predicted for more than a decade. The official narrative (in the UK) was that apart from a few prestige venues, cinemas would vanish, everyone would watch videos in the safety of their own homes and TV would reign supreme. Given this logic, funding film production and having a well-resourced arts sector generally seemed pointless. But as with many attempts at futurology, things turned out rather differently. Instead, 1986 saw the opening of the first multiplex in the UK, in, appropriately – given its billing as 'the city of the future' – Milton Keynes; and venues of this type rapidly appeared across the country. The ability to see up to a dozen different films each week in pleasant, well-maintained surroundings, together with a switch to digital filmmaking (which, as with music, reduced production costs) gradually rebuilt the industry. Cinema admissions began climbing again and the number of films being shot in the UK increased. By 1991 admissions were back at 100m, for the first time since 1980. Since 2002 they have been at around 160–170m annually, the level they were at circa 1971-2.

Film production crept up slowly too. In 1986 just 29 UK features were made. Leaving aside co-productions with the US and similar, only seventeen of these were truly home-grown products and only nine had plots set in the present. By 2018 the UK produced or co-produced 88 films that were destined for viewing in cinemas or on Pay Per View channels like Netflix, with a further 78 listed as being shown at various film festivals before being available online. Figures like these make one realise what a sad place the UK was throughout much of the '70s and '80s and how much artistic creativity (and economic activity) went to waste then. But while the cinema of the '60s seamlessly reflected the music, fashion, design and modernist culture of its time, the emergence of the new wave of guitar bands and electronica acts did not automatically transfer into a comparable cultural renaissance in film. Instead, the biggest commercial films the UK produced after 1986 included many period dramas, harmless transatlantic rom-coms set in tourist London (*Bridget Jones, Notting Hill*), war films and Bond's never-ending adventures. It wasn't until Danny Boyle's *Trainspotting* ('96) that a contemporary, youth-oriented drama, hewn from everyday life and with a heavy music content, triumphed at the box office... the first to do so since *A Clockwork Orange* ('71), 25 years earlier.

In parallel with how music developed, and following the lead given by *Withnail and I*, many of the box-office and critical successes of the '90s were studies of the UK's recent cultural past, like *Backbeat* ('94, the Stuart Sutcliffe-era Beatles in Hamburg), *The Full Monty* ('97, deindustrialisation in Sheffield), *Billy Elliot* (2000, teenage boy escapes a mining community about to be devastated by pit closures) and *East is East* (2000, an Asian immigrant family in early '70s Yorkshire comes to terms with permissive social and sexual trends). This kind of backward-looking genre, affectionate, accurate and with good period detail, was continued with *24 Hour Party People* (2002, a brilliant biopic of the life of Tony Wilson), *Stoned* (2005, the demise of Brian Jones), *Control* (2007, Ian Curtis and Joy Division), *Nowhere Boy* (2009, John Lennon in the '50s) and *Sex and Drugs and Rock and Roll* (2010, the rise and fall of Ian Dury). Even a new film like *Lock, Stock and Two Smoking Barrels* ('99) was clearly cast from the same mould as *The Italian Job*, and its enormous commercial success duly spawned a host of similar productions. (Much of this arose from a favourable reassessment of Michael Caine which took place in the '90s, with *Alfie*, *Get Carter* and *The Italian Job* all being remade with variable success.)

This celebratory style was, in some ways, taken to its logical conclusion from 1997 by the *Austin Powers* film franchise. Written by and starring Mike Myers, these featured a central character created from elements of Simon Dee, George Lazenby, Peter Sellers and Jason King. Visually, such films were done very much in the high crime-comedy caper style of *Modesty Blaise*, albeit with slightly more outlandish plots. The end results are part *Casino Royale* and part *There's a Girl in my Soup* and work as very entertaining and brilliantly done parody. To nudge home the latter point, Michael York (*Smashing Time*, *The Guru*) co-stars. Myers was Anglo-Canadian and had appeared at the Soho Comedy Store from 1984. Circa 1993 he had originally devised the Powers character as one of the members of a faux '60s band Ming Tea (who took their name from an obscure 1965 Euro-Bond caper, *The 10th Victim*). His career trajectory thus follows that of Christopher Guest, who was Anglo-American, grounded in comedy, worked heavily in TV and devised a parody English band with accompanying characters (*Spinal Tap*) that subsequently became a monstrously successful film.

Thus by the late '90s it seemed that UK music and UK cinema had both recovered from the level to which they had dropped in the mid-'80s and this new vibrant culture – branded Cool Britannia by the media and cultural observers – was being widely celebrated. But in practical terms this phenomenon had many differences from the '60s. To start with, *Austin Powers* excepted, few of the films made from the '90s onwards had a resident band or singer in situ, or even a specially commissioned score. Instead, the jukebox-type soundtrack predominated. This trend started in the US, becoming evident around 1978 and 1979 with films like *Thank God It's Friday* and *Rock and Roll High School* (though its origin was surely with *American Graffiti*, '73). As a result, fewer film composers were required and most features by the mid-'90s had a soundtrack consisting of licensed material, much of which might be hit records that were not even necessarily date-specific to the plot of the film itself. It helped to cut costs.

Another casualty was the short or supporting feature made for cinema release. These vanished and none appears to have been made after the mid-'80s, despite some late examples like *Black Angel* ('80), which went out as the support film to *The Empire Strikes Back*, and *Wings of Death* ('85) being miniature masterpieces. What replaced them, at least in terms of work for film technicians, were thousands of rock-music videos (mainly of concerts and tours), of which a few were genuinely of interest, but most of which were of variable quality and were quickly forgotten.

Television changed as well post-'86. The '60s and '70s TV play vanished and was replaced – effectively – by long-running drama series with ensemble casts, some of which (rather like the guitar bands that emerged in the '80s) turned out to have immense longevity and are still with us 30+ years later. With a huge amount of the remaining screen time taken up by game shows, sports coverage and comedy by the end of the century, notwithstanding the launch of Channel 5 in 1997, original TV drama set in contemporary UK situations had declined to a very low level.

So, although those who celebrated Cool Britannia claimed to see in it a rebirth of the confidence of peak 'Swinging London', the similarities were in fact only skin deep. Modern music, art, design and fashion would never again, it would seem, be quite as automatically embraced as they had been in the '60s. The mere fact, though, that the UK did blossom again was reason enough for most people to celebrate. Today, even if the internet has killed off a great deal and made the business of making a living from music, art, writing and acting far harder, digitalisation and computerisation make almost anything possible, as well as visually and aurally superior to how it would have been done in the past. Anyone trying to take this narrative forward by charting a path through the huge number of films now being made, the host of cable, internet, subscription and freeview TV channels now broadcasting and the wide variety of other media platforms (some reaching huge audiences, some not) may find it very difficult to assemble a compelling narrative, or to judge what is (or isn't) a defining trend at any particular time. And, of course, money remains where there is money to be made.

ACKNOWLEDGEMENTS

The title *Looking for a New England* is drawn from the song *A New England* which appeared on the 1983 Billy Bragg album *Life's a Riot with Spy vs Spy*. The album sold well and a year later Kirsty MacColl covered the song, reaching No 7 in the UK charts with it. The tone of the lyrics, melancholy resignation throughout about life's limitations even though the person doing this is still at a very young age, is emblematic of the era this book discusses, hence my use of it for a title and my credit to both Billy and Kirsty for their unwitting contribution to this narrative.

I could not have brought this book to fruition without the design and layout skills of Elsa Mathern, together with the patience and commitment of Ion Mills and his team at Oldcastle Books. My thanks to them and to Robin Ramsay for his editorial assistance.

Many others were spoken to as this account was assembled, facts checked and often long-forgotten details dredged up. But, most importantly, a largely unsung and unheralded group of individuals needs to be recognised above all others: those who ran the network of record shops, independent cinemas, bookshops, music venues, tiny ad hoc theatres above pubs, niche fashion and clothing shops, rehearsal studios, film distribution companies, film libraries and recording studios across London and other UK cities through the difficult years of the '70s and '80s. We would all have been poorer without them and this book would not have been possible – at all – without their inadequately remunerated efforts over many years.

INDEX

INDEX

The Electronic Revolution (essay), 196
The Elephant Man, 43, 79
Elizabeth I, 62-3
Ellington, Duke, 7
Elliott, Denholm, 51, 65, 157, 189-90, 193-4
Ellis, Alton, 161
Ellis, Terry, 97
Ellison, Andy, 113
Elms, Robert, 10, 49, 82
Eloise (song), 217
Elton, Ben, 148, 150
El Topo, 64
Elvis, 42
Elwes, Cassian, 138-9
Embassy Club (venue), 146
Embrace, 218
Emerson, Keith, 21
Emes, Ian, 205-6
Emmanuelle, 12, 23
EMI, 28, 37, 46, 80, 87, 118, 122, 143, 180, 199, 202, 214
The Empire Strikes Back, 223
The End, 41
Ende, Michael, 214-15
England's Glory, 142
Eno, Brian, 44, 61, 63, 71-2, 74-5, 171, 181-2, 186, 190, 195
The Entertainer, 90
Entertaining Mr Sloane (play), 57, 138
Enter the Dragon, 42, 155
Epps, Preston, 84
The Equals, 129, 206
Equateur, 13, 23
Equus, 192
Eraserhead, 43
Erik the Viking, 85, 186
Escalation, 135
Escape from New York, 139
Escape to Athena, 74
Essential Logic, 185
Essex Boys, 201
Essex, David, 30,1
Establishment Club (venue), 140
E.T., 11
Eureka, 66
The Eurythmics, 95

Evans, Gil, 84
Evans, Victor Romero, 162-3
Evening Land, 89
Everybody Loves Sunshine, 87
Every Day's a Holiday, 199
Evil Under the Sun, 22
Evita, 54
Excalibur, 44, 146
Excerpt from a Teenage Opera (song), 215
The Exorcist, 15, 211
The Exploited, 132
Expresso Bongo, 82-3
Extremes, 33
Eyre, Richard, 190-1

F

The Fabulous Poodles, 91
The Face (magazine), 10, 82, 84
The Faces, 16, 121
Factory (record label), 130, 187-8
Faenza, Roberto, 135
Fagin, Joe, 173
Fairport Convention, 41, 94
Fairy Tales (book), 85
Faith, Adam, 36, 51
Faithfull, Marianne, 219
The Falcon and The Snowman, 80
Falklands War, 186, 190-1
The Fall, 217
The Fall and Rise of Reginald Perrin, 38
Fame, 37
Fame, Georgie, 23
The Family Arsenal (book), 24, 116
Family Life, 91, 182
Fanon, Frantz, 161
Far Far Away (song), 26
Far from the Madding Crowd, 91
Fassbinder, Rainer Werner, 76, 95, 117
Fayed, Dodi, 199
Fearless (LP), 172, 202
Feast, Michael, 159
Feel the Motion, 117

Wire, 92
Wirtz, Mark, 23
Withnail and I, 219, 221
The Wiz, 45
Wolf, Rita, 67
Wolfen, 65, 77
Wollen, Peter, 185-6
WOMAD, 16
Women Behind Bars (play), 64
Women in Rock, 130
Wonderwall, 9, 22, 205
Wood, Christopher, 198
Wood, Ronnie, 150
The Wooden Horse, 78
Woods, James, 45
Woodstock, 77, 115, 209
Woodward, Edward, 92
Woolley, Stephen, 82-3, 191, 194
The Word Came Out of LA: Son of Leaving the Twentieth Century, 187
Working Week, 212
Work is a Four Letter Word, 30, 145
World Gone Wild, 139
World in Action, 129
The World is Full of Married Men, 49-50
Woronov, Mary, 139
Wreckless Eric, 183, 199
Wyatt, Robert, 211
Wyman, Bill, 41, 213
Wyngarde, Peter, 42

X

Xanadu, 213
X, Michael, 81, 90, 154, 160
X-Ray Spex, 115, 118-9, 125, 185
XTC, 187, 203, 211

Y

Yamashta, Stomu, 70
The Year of the Sex Olympics, 90
Yellow Submarine, 21, 24, 30, 101
Yes, Minister, 38
Yesterday's Hero, 51
York, Michael, 222
You are Not Alone, 13
Young British Artists, 24
Young, Cliff de, 78
Young, Elizabeth, 126
Young, Muriel, 112
Young, Paul, 150
Young Frankenstein, 60
The Young Ones, 148
The Young Rascals, 207
You're Gonna Wake Up One Morning and Know What Side of The Bed You've Been Lying On! (T Shirt), 111
You Think You're a Man (song), 65
Yu, Jimmy Wang, 155-6

Z

Zabriskie Point, 27
Zachariah, 96, 151, 205
Zardoz, 32, 52, 145
Z Cars, 100
A Zed & Two Noughts, 108
Zee and Co, 48, 50, 157
Zetterling, Mai, 121-2
Ziggy Stardust (song), 78
Ziggy Stardust and the Spiders from Mars (LP), 81
ZigZag (magazine), 10, 110
Zina, 92
The Zones, 199

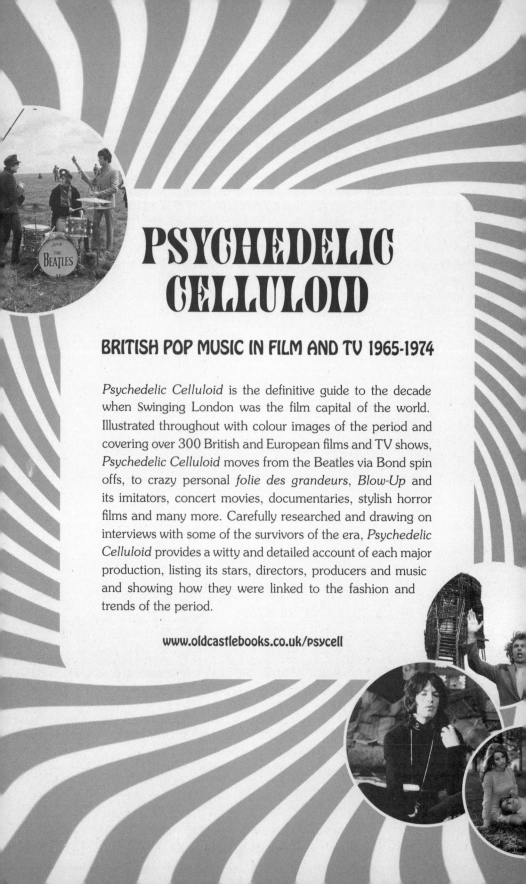

PSYCHEDELIC CELLULOID

BRITISH POP MUSIC IN FILM AND TV 1965-1974

Psychedelic Celluloid is the definitive guide to the decade when Swinging London was the film capital of the world. Illustrated throughout with colour images of the period and covering over 300 British and European films and TV shows, *Psychedelic Celluloid* moves from the Beatles via Bond spin offs, to crazy personal *folie des grandeurs*, *Blow-Up* and its imitators, concert movies, documentaries, stylish horror films and many more. Carefully researched and drawing on interviews with some of the survivors of the era, *Psychedelic Celluloid* provides a witty and detailed account of each major production, listing its stars, directors, producers and music and showing how they were linked to the fashion and trends of the period.

www.oldcastlebooks.co.uk/psycell